MALORIE BLACKMAN

Noughts & Crosses

OXFORD
UNIVERSITY PRESS

OXFORD

UNIVERSITY PRESS

Great Clarendon Street, Oxford OX2 6DP

Published in association with Random House

Oxford University Press is a department of the University of Oxford.
It furthers the University's objective of excellence in research, scholarship,
and education by publishing worldwide in

Oxford   New York

Auckland   Cape Town   Dar es Salaam   Hong Kong   Karachi
Kuala Lumpur   Madrid   Melbourne   Mexico City   Nairobi
New Delhi   Shanghai   Taipei   Toronto

With offices in

Argentina   Austria   Brazil   Chile   Czech Republic   France   Greece
Guatemala   Hungary   Italy   Japan   Poland   Portugal   Singapore
South Korea   Switzerland   Thailand   Turkey   Ukraine   Vietnam

Oxford is a registered trade mark of Oxford University Press
in the UK and in certain other countries

The song lyrics quoted on page 7 are by Bruce Hornsby and the Range:
The Way It Is
Words and Music by Bruce Hornsby
© 1994 Basically Zappo Music, USA
Warner/Chappell Music Ltd, London W6 8BS
Reprinted by permission of International Music Publications Ltd

The moral rights of the author have been asserted

Database right Oxford University Press (maker)

First published by Random House Children's Books,
a division of The Random House Group Limited

This educational edition first published in 2008

British Library Cataloguing in Publication Data available

ISBN 978-0-19-832861-2

3 5 7 9 10 8 6 4

Printed by Printplus, China

This book is dedicated with love to my husband, Neil,
And to our daughter, Elizabeth

'That's just the way it is.
Some things will never change.
That's just the way it is.
But don't you believe them.'

BRUCE HORNSBY AND THE RANGE

'Honestly, Mrs Hadley,' said Meggie McGregor, wiping her eyes. 'That sense of humour of yours will be the death of me yet!'

Jasmine Hadley allowed herself a rare giggle. 'The things I tell you, Meggie. It's lucky we're such good friends!'

Meggie's smile wavered only slightly. She looked out across the vast lawn at Callum and Sephy. Her son and her employer's daughter. They were good friends playing together. *Real* good friends. No barriers. No boundaries. Not yet anyway. It was a typical early summer's day, light and bright and, in the Hadley household anyway, not a cloud in their sky.

'Excuse me, Mrs Hadley.' Sarah Pike, Mrs Hadley's secretary, approached from the house. She had shoulder-length straw-coloured hair and timid green eyes which appeared permanently startled. 'I'm sorry to disturb you but your husband has just arrived. He's in the study.'

'Kamal is here?' Mrs Hadley was astounded. 'Thank you, Sarah.' She turned to Meggie. 'His fourth visit home in as many months! We're honoured!'

Meggie smiled sympathetically, making sure to keep

her mouth well and truly shut. No way was she going to get in the middle of another inevitable squabble between Kamal Hadley and his wife. Mrs Hadley stood up and made her way into the house.

'So, Sarah, how is Mr Hadley?' Meggie lowered her voice to ask. 'Is he in a good mood, d'you think?'

Sarah shook her head. 'He looks about ready to blow a fuse.'

'Why?'

'No idea.'

Meggie digested this news in silence.

'I'd better get back to work,' Sarah sighed.

'Would you like something to drink?' Meggie pointed to the jug of ginger beer on the patio table.

'No, thanks. I don't want to get into trouble . . .' With obvious trepidation, Sarah went back into the house.

What was she afraid of? Meggie sighed. No matter how hard she tried, Sarah insisted on keeping her distance. Meggie turned back to watch the children. Life was so simple for them. Their biggest worry was what they'd get for their birthdays. Their biggest grumble was the time they had to go to bed. Maybe things would be different for them . . . Better. Maggie forced herself to believe that things would be better for the children, otherwise what was the point of it all?

On those rare occasions when she had a moment to herself, she couldn't help but play 'what if' games. Not the big 'what if's that her husband sometimes liked to indulge in, like, 'What if a virus wiped out every single Cross and not a single nought?' or 'What if there was a revolution and all the Crosses were overthrown? Killed.

Wiped off the face of the planet.' No, Meggie McGregor didn't believe in wasting her time on big, global fantasies. Her dreams were more specific, more unattainable than that. Her dreams were all around one subject. What if Callum and Sephy . . .? What if Sephy and Callum . . .?

Meggie felt a peculiar, burning sensation on the back of her neck. She turned to find Mr Hadley standing on the patio, watching her with the strangest expression on his face.

'Is everything all right, Mr Hadley?'

'No. But I'll survive,' Mr Hadley moved forward to the patio table to stand over Meggie. 'You were deep in thought there. Penny for them?'

Flustered by his presence, Meggie began, 'I was just thinking about my son and your daughter. Wouldn't it be nice if . . ?' Appalled, she bit back the rest of the sentence, but it was too late.

'What would be nice?' Mr Hadley prompted, silkily.

'If they could . . . could always stay as they are now.' At Mr Hadley's raised eyebrows, Meggie rushed on. 'At this age, I mean. They're so wonderful at this age – children, I mean. So . . . so . . .'

'Yes, indeed.'

Pause.

Kamal Hadley sat down. Mrs Hadley emerged from the kitchen to lean against the door frame. She had a strange, wary expression on her face. Meggie felt nervous. She started to get to her feet.

'I understand you had a wonderful time yesterday.' Mr Hadley smiled at Meggie.

'A . . . a wonderful time?'

'Yesterday evening?' Mr Hadley prompted.

'Yes. It was quite quiet really . . .' Meggie replied, confused. She looked from Mr to Mrs Hadley and back again. Mrs Hadley was watching her intently. What was going on? The temperature in the garden had dropped by several degrees and despite his smiles, Mr Hadley was obviously furious at something − or someone. Meggie swallowed hard. Had she done something wrong? She didn't think so, but God only knew that being around Crosses was like walking on eggshells.

'So what did you do?' Mr Hadley prompted.

'P-pardon?'

'Last night?' Mr Hadley's smile was very friendly. Too friendly.

'I . . . we stayed home and watched telly,' Meggie said slowly.

'It's nice to have a relaxing evening at home with your own family,' Mr Hadley agreed.

Meggie nodded. What did he expect her to say to that? *What was going on?* Mr Hadley stood up, his smile now a thing of the past. He walked over to his wife. They both stood just watching each other as the seconds ticked by. Mrs Hadley began to straighten up. Without warning, Mr Hadley slapped his wife full across the face. The force of the blow sent Mrs Hadley's head snapping backwards to strike against the door frame.

Meggie was on her feet in a second, her horrified gasp audible, her hand out in silent protest. Kamal Hadley gave his wife a look of such contempt and loathing that Mrs Hadley flinched back from it. Without a word passing between them, Mr Hadley went back into the house.

Meggie was at Mrs Hadley's side in an instant.

'Are you OK?' Meggie's hand went out to examine the side of Mrs Hadley's face.

Mrs Hadley knocked her hand away. With a puzzled frown, Meggie tried again. The same thing happened.

'Leave me alone,' Mrs Hadley hissed at her. 'When I needed your help, you didn't give it.'

'I . . . what . . ?' And only then did Meggie realize what she'd done. Mrs Hadley had obviously used Meggie as an alibi for the previous night and Meggie had been too slow to pick up on what Kamal Hadley had really been asking her.

Meggie's hand dropped back to her side. 'I think I should get back to work . . .'

'Yes, I think that would be best.' Mrs Hadley's look was venomous before she turned and walked back into the house.

Meggie turned around. Callum and Sephy were still playing at the other end of the vast garden, oblivious to everything that had just happened. She stood and watched them, trying to capture for herself some small part of their pure joy in each other. She needed something good to hold on to. But even the distant sound of their laughter couldn't dampen down the deep sense of foreboding creeping through her. What would happen now?

That night, Meggie sat at the table sewing patches over the patches in Jude's school trousers.

'Meggie, I'm sure you're worrying about nothing,' Ryan, her husband sighed.

'Ryan, you didn't see the look on her face. I did.'

Meggie bit off the thread and picked up another patch. Jude's school trousers were more patch than original material.

The phone started to ring. Meggie picked it up before the first ring had even died away.

'Hello?'

'Meggie McGregor?'

'That's right.' Meggie's sewing fell unheeded to her feet.

'It's Sarah Pike here . . .'

Meggie couldn't help but notice the apology already in her voice. 'How are you, Sarah?'

'Fine, er . . . OK. Look, I've got some bad news . . .'

Meggie nodded slowly. 'I'm listening.'

Sarah gave an embarrassed cough before she continued. 'Mrs Hadley has asked me to inform you that . . . that your services at the Hadley household will no longer be required. She will pay you four weeks' wages in lieu of proper notice, plus give you a good reference.'

Meggie's blood turned to ice water in her veins. Whatever else she'd been expecting, it wasn't this. Heaven only knew it wasn't this.

'She's . . . she's really sacking me?'

'I'm sorry.'

'I see.'

'I'm really sorry,' Sarah's voice dropped to a whisper. 'Between you and me, I think it's grossly unfair.'

From one nought to another . . .

'It's OK, Sarah. It's not your fault.' Meggie replied.

She looked across at Ryan. His expression grew harder and tighter by degrees. Let him get upset. Let him be angry. All she could feel was . . . nothing. A nothing that went way beyond the numbness enveloping every part of her body.

'Sorry, Meggie,' Sarah said again.

'That's OK. Thanks for letting me know. Bye, Sarah.'

'Bye.'

Meggie put down the phone. The clock on the TV counted out the silent moments that passed. 'That's the end of Jude's education,' she sighed at last.

'But we promised him we'd pay for him to carry on at school,' Ryan said, aghast.

'Pay with what?' Meggie rounded on her husband. 'The leaves off the trees? The hairs off our legs? What?'

'We'll find a way . . .'

'How? We're barely managing to survive as it was. What will we do without my wages coming in? Jude will have to forget about school. He'll have to go out to work.'

'You'll get another job,' Ryan tried.

'Not with another Cross family I won't. D'you really think Mrs Hadley will stand idly by whilst I get another job with one of her friends?'

There was dawning horror on Ryan's face as he realized what his wife meant.

'Yes, exactly,' Meggie sighed.

She stood up and moved to sit next to her husband on the old sofa in front of the fire. Ryan put his arm around her. They sat in silence for a long, long time.

'Ryan, we're in trouble,' Meggie said at last.

'I know,' Ryan replied.

Meggie jumped to her feet, her expression hard and

determined. 'I'm going to see her.'

'What're you talking about?' Ryan frowned.

'I've worked for that woman for fourteen years, ever since she was pregnant with her daughter Minerva. Seeing me is the very least she can do.'

'I don't think that's a good idea . . .' Ryan's frown deepened.

'Ryan, I need to get my job back. And if I have to beg, then so be it,' Meggie insisted, pulling on her coat. Her expression was now so hard, it might've been carved in granite.

'No, Meggie . . .'

'I don't like it any more than you do, but we have no choice.' Meggie didn't wait for any further argument. She headed out of the door.

Ryan watched his wife leave the house. No good would come of this. He could feel it.

Two hours later, Meggie was back.

And that was the night that Lynette disappeared . . .

THREE YEARS LATER . . .

Callum And Sephy

one. Sephy

I wriggled my toes, enjoying the feel of the warm sand trickling like fine baby powder between them. Digging my feet even deeper into the dry, yellow-white sand, I tilted back my head. It was such a beautiful August afternoon. Nothing bad could ever happen on a day like today. And what made it even better was the fact that I could share it – something rare and special in itself, as I knew only too well. I turned to the boy next to me, my face about to split wide open from the smile on my face.

'Can I kiss you?'

My smile faded. I stared at my best friend. 'Pardon?'

'Can I kiss you?'

'What on earth for?'

'Just to see what it's like,' Callum replied.

Yeuk! I mean, *yeuk*!! I wrinkled up my nose – I couldn't help it. Kissing! Why on earth would Callum want to do anything so . . . so feeble?

'Do you really want to?' I asked.

Callum shrugged. 'Yeah, I do.'

'Oh, all right then.' I wrinkled up my nose again at the prospect. 'But make it fast!'

Callum turned to kneel beside me. I turned my head up towards his, watching with growing curiosity to see what he'd do next. I tilted my head to the left. So did he. I tilted my head to the right. Callum did the same. He was moving his head like he was my reflection or something. I put my hands on Callum's face to keep it still and dead centre.

'D'you want me to tilt my head to the left or the right?' I asked, impatiently.

'Er . . . which way do girls usually tilt their heads when they're being kissed?' asked Callum.

'Does it matter? Besides, how should I know?' I frowned. 'Have I ever kissed a boy before?'

'Tilt your head to the left then.'

'My left or your left?'

'Er . . . your left.'

I did as asked. 'Hurry up, before I get a crick in my neck.'

Callum licked his lips before his face moved slowly closer towards mine.

'Oh no you don't,' I drew back. 'Wipe your lips first.'

'Why?'

'You just licked them.'

'Oh! OK!' Callum wiped his mouth with the back of his hand.

I moved forward to resume my original position. Keeping my lips tight together, I wondered what I should do with them. Purse them so that they stuck out slightly? Or should I smile to make them seem wider and more appealing? I'd only ever practised kissing with my pillow. This was a lot different – and seemed just as silly!

'Hurry up!' I urged.

I kept my eyes wide open as I watched Callum's face

move down towards mine. Callum's grey eyes were open too. I was going cross-eyed trying to keep my focus on his face. And then his lips were touching mine. How funny! I'd expected Callum's lips to be hard and dry and scaly like a lizard's skin. But they weren't. They were soft. Callum closed his eyes. After a moment, I did the same. Our lips were still touching. Callum's mouth opened, making mine open at the same time. Callum's breath mingled with mine and felt warm and sweet. And then without warning his tongue was touching mine.

'Yeuk!' I drew back immediately and stuck my tongue out, wiping it with my hand. 'What did you do that for?'

'It wasn't that bad, was it?'

'I don't want your tongue on mine.' I shook my head.

'Why not?'

' 'Cause . . .' I shuddered at the thought of it, '. . . our spit will mix up.'

'So? It's meant to.'

I considered this.

'Well?'

'OK! OK!' I frowned, adding. 'The things I do for you! Let's try it again.'

Callum smiled at me, the familiar twinkle in his eyes. That's the thing about Callum – he looks at me a certain way and I'm never quite sure if he's laughing at me. Before I could change my mind, Callum's lips were already on mine – and just as soft and gentle as before. His tongue flicked into my mouth again. After a brief moment of thinking *ugh*! I found that it wasn't too bad. In fact it was actually quite nice in a gross-to-think-about-but-OK-to-do sort of way. I closed my eyes and began to return Callum's kiss. His tongue licked over mine. It was warm and wet but it didn't make me want to heave. And then my tongue did the same to him. I began to feel a little strange. My heart was beginning to thump in a peculiar, hiccupy way that made me feel like I was racing down a roller-coaster, roaring out of control. Someone was tying knots with my insides. I pulled away.

'That's enough.'

'Sorry.' Callum sat back.

'Why're you apologizing?' I frowned. 'Didn't you like it?'

Callum shrugged. 'It was OK.'

I was annoyed. I didn't know why, but I couldn't help it. 'Have you kissed any other girls besides me?'

'No.'

'Any Cross girls?'

'No.'

'Any nought girls?'

'No means no.' Callum huffed with exasperation.

'So why did you want to kiss me?'

'We're friends, aren't we?' Callum shrugged.

I relaxed into a smile. 'Of course we are.'

'And if you can't kiss your friends then who can you kiss?' Callum smiled.

I turned back to the sea. It shone like a shattered mirror, each fragment reflecting and dazzling. It never ceased to amaze me just how beautiful the sand and the sea and the gentle breeze on my face could be. My family's private beach was my favourite place in the whole world. Kilometres of coastline that was all ours, with just a couple of signs declaring that it was private property and some old wooden fencing at each end, through which Callum and I had made a gap. And I was here with my favourite person. I turned to look at Callum. He was looking at me, the strangest expression on his face.

'What's the matter?'

'Nothing.'

'What're you thinking?' I asked.

'About you and me.'

'What about us?'

Callum turned to look out over the sea. 'Sometimes I wish there was just you and me and no-one else in the whole world.'

'We'd drive each other crazy, wouldn't we?' I teased.

At first I thought that Callum wasn't going to answer.

'Sephy, d'you ever dream of just . . . escaping? Hopping on the first boat or plane you come across and just letting it take you away.' There was no mistaking the wistfully wishful note in Callum's voice. 'I do . . .'

'Where would you go?'

'That's just the point,' Callum said with sudden bitterness. 'This place is like the whole world and the whole world is like this place. So where could I go?'

'This place isn't so bad, is it?' I asked, gently.

'Depends on your point of view,' Callum replied. 'You're on the inside, Sephy. I'm not.'

I couldn't think of an answer to that, so I didn't reply. We both sat in silence for a while longer.

'Wherever you went, I'd go with you,' I decided. 'Though you'd soon get bored with me.'

Callum sighed. A long, heartfelt sigh which immediately

made me feel like I'd failed some test I hadn't even known I was taking.

'We'd better get on with it,' he said at last. 'What's the lesson for today, teacher?'

Disappointment raced through me. But then, what did I expect? '*Sephy, I could never be bored of you, with you, around you. You're exciting, scintillating, overwhelming company!*' Yeah, right! Dream on, Sephy!!

'So what're we doing today?' Callum's voice was tinged with impatience.

'OK! OK!' I said, exasperated. Honestly! The sun was too warm and the sea was too blue to do any schoolwork. 'Callum you've already passed the entrance exam. Why do we still have to do this?'

'I don't want to give any of the teachers an excuse to kick me out.'

'You haven't even started school yet and already you're talking about being kicked out?' I was puzzled. Why was he so cynical about my school? 'You've got nothing to worry about. You're in now. The school accepted you.'

'Being in and being accepted are two different things.' Callum shrugged. 'Besides, I want to learn as much as I can so I don't look like a complete dunce.'

I sat up suddenly. 'I've just had a thought. Maybe you'll be in my class. Oh, I do hope so,' I said eagerly. 'Wouldn't that be great?'

'You think so?'

I tried – and failed, I think – to keep the hurt out of my voice. 'Don't you?'

Callum looked at me and smiled. 'You shouldn't answer a question with a question,' he teased.

'Why not?' I forced myself to smile back.

Taking me by surprise, Callum pushed me over onto the sand. Indignant, I scrambled up to kneel in front of him.

'D'you mind?' I huffed.

'No. Not at all.' Callum smirked.

We looked at each other and burst out laughing. I stopped laughing first.

'Callum, wouldn't . . . wouldn't you like to be in my class . . ?'

Callum couldn't meet my eyes. 'It's a bit . . . humiliating for us noughts to be stuck in the baby class.'

'What d'you mean? I'm not a baby.' I jumped to my feet, scowling down at him.

'Jeez, Sephy, I'm fifteen, for heaven's sake! In six months' time I'll be sixteen and they're still sticking me in with twelve- and thirteen-year-olds. How would you like to be in a class with kids at least a year younger than you?' Callum asked.

'I . . . well . . .' I sat back down.

'Exactly!'

'I'm fourteen in three weeks,' I said, unwilling to let it drop.

'That's not the point, and you know it.'

'But the school explained why. You're all at least a year behind and . . .'

'And whose fault is that?' Callum said with erupting bitterness. 'Until a few years ago we were only allowed to be educated up to the age of fourteen – and in noughts-only schools at that, which don't have a quarter of the money or resources that your schools have.'

I had no answer.

'Sorry. I didn't mean to bite your head off.'

'You didn't.' I said. 'Are any of your friends from your old school going to join you at Heathcrofts?'

'No. None of them got in,' Callum replied. 'I wouldn't've got in either if you hadn't helped me.'

He made it sound like an accusation. I wanted to say sorry and I had no idea why.

Callum sighed. 'Come on, we'd better get to work . . .'

'OK.' I turned and dug into my bag for my school books. 'What d'you want to do first? Maths or History?'

'Maths. I like Maths.'

'Yeuk!' I shook my head. How could anyone in their right mind like Maths?! Languages were my favourite subjects, followed by Human Biology and Sociology and Chemistry. Maths fought with Physics for the subject I liked the least. 'Right then. Maths it is.' I wrinkled my nose. 'I'll tell you what I've been revising over the last week and then you can explain it to me!'

Callum laughed. 'You should get into Maths. It's the universal language.'

'Says who?'

'Says anyone with any sense. Look at how many different languages are spoken on our planet. The only thing that doesn't change, no matter what the language, is Maths. And it's probably the same on other planets too.'

'Pardon?'

'That's probably how we'll talk to aliens from other planets when they get here or when we get to them. We'll use Maths.'

I stared at Callum. Sometimes when I talked to him, the seventeen months between us seemed to stretch to seventy years. 'Are . . . are you winding me up?'

Callum's smile was no answer.

'Stop it! You're giving me a headache.' I frowned. 'Can we just get on with the Maths in my book and forget about chatting with aliens for a while?'

'OK,' Callum said at last. 'But Sephy, you should think above and beyond just us. You should free your mind and think about other cultures and other planets and oh, I don't know, just think about the future.'

'I've got plenty of time to think about the future when I'm tons older and don't have much future left, thank you very much. And my mind is quite free enough.'

'Is it?' Callum asked slowly. 'There's more to life than just us noughts and you Crosses.'

My stomach jerked. Callum's words hurt. Why did they hurt? 'Don't say that . . .'

'Don't say what?'

'*Us* noughts and *you* Crosses.' I shook my head. 'It makes it sound like . . . like you're in one place and I'm in another, with a huge, great wall between us.'

Callum looked out across the sea. 'Maybe we are in different places . . .'

'No, we aren't. Not if we don't want to be, we aren't.' I willed Callum to look at me.

'I wish it was that simple.'

'It is.'

'Maybe from where you're sitting.' At last Callum turned towards me, but his expression stemmed the words I was about to say. And then, just like that, his expression cleared and his easy smile was back. 'You're very young, Sephy.'

'I'm only a year and a bit younger than you, so don't start talking down to me.' I fumed. 'I get enough of that at home.'

'OK! OK! Sorry!' Callum raised his hand in a placatory manner. 'Now then, how about some Maths?'

Still annoyed, I opened my school study book. Callum shuffled closer until his arm and mine were touching. His skin was warm, almost hot – or was it mine? It was hard to tell. I handed him the book and watched as the pages on polygons instantly caught and held his attention.

Callum was the one person in the world I could tell anything and everything to without having to think twice about it. So why did I now feel so . . . out of step? Like he was leaving me behind? He suddenly seemed so much older, not just in years but in the things he knew and had experienced. His eyes were a lot older than fifteen. My eyes were different – they reflected my exact age, less than one month away from my fourteenth birthday. Not a day less and certainly not a day more. I didn't want things to change between us – ever. But at that moment I felt as if I might as well stand on the beach and command the sea never to move again.

'How does this bit work?' Callum asked, pointing to an interior angle of a regular octagon.

I shook my head, telling myself not to be so silly. Nothing would ever come between me and Callum. I wouldn't let it. Neither would Callum. He needed our friendship just as much as I did.

Needed . . . That was a strange way to put it. Why had

I thought of it that way? As a friendship both of us needed? That didn't make any sense at all. I had friends at school. And a huge, extended family with cousins and aunts and uncles, and plenty of great whatevers and great-great whatevers to send Christmas and birthday cards to. But it wasn't the same as Callum and me. Callum glanced up impatiently. I smiled at him. After a brief puzzled look, he smiled back.

'It works like this,' I began and we both looked down at the book as I began to explain.

'We'd better be getting back – before your mum has every police officer in the country searching for you,' Callum said at last.

'Suppose so.' I picked up my sandals and rose to my feet. Than I had a brilliant idea. 'Why don't we go back to yours? I haven't been to your house in ages and I could always phone up Mother once I'm there and . . .'

'Better not,' Callum said, shaking his head. He'd started shaking his head the moment the suggestion had left my mouth. He picked up my bag and slung it over his shoulder.

I frowned at Callum. 'We used to be in and out of each other's houses all the time . . .'

'Used to be. Let's leave it for a while – OK?'

'How come I never go to your house any more? Aren't I welcome?'

' 'Course you are. But the beach is better,' Callum shrugged and set off.

'Is it because of Lynette? 'Cause if it is, I really don't mind about your sister being . . . being . . .' My voice trailed off at Callum's furious expression.

'Being what?' Callum prompted, fiercely.

'Nothing,' I shrugged. 'Sorry.'

'This has nothing to do with Lynette,' Callum snapped.

I immediately shut up. I seemed to have an acute case of foot-in-mouth disease today. We walked back in silence. Up the stone steps, worn to satin smoothness by the procession of centuries of feet and along the cliff side, heading further and further inland, away from the sea. I looked across the open grassland towards the house which dominated the view for kilometres around. My parents' country house. Seven bedrooms and five reception rooms for four people. What a waste. Four people in such a vast house – four lonely peas rolling about in a can. We were still some distance from it but it rose like an all-seeing giant above us. I pretended I didn't see Callum flinch at the sight of it. Is it any wonder I preferred the laughter of his house to the dignified silence of my own? We walked on for wordless minutes until Callum's steps slowed and stopped altogether.

'What's wrong?' I asked.

'It's just . . .' Callum turned to face me. 'It doesn't matter. Give me a hug?'

Why was Callum in such a touchy-feely mood this afternoon? After a moment's hesitation, I decided not to ask. Callum looked different. What I'd thought of as a permanent teasing sparkle in his eyes when he looked at me was gone without a trace. His eyes were storm-grey and just as troubled. He ran his fingers over his short-cut, chestnut brown hair in a gesture that seemed almost nervous. I opened my arms and stepped towards Callum.

I wrapped my arms around him, my head on his shoulder. He was holding me, squeezing me too tightly but I didn't say a word. I held my breath so it wouldn't hurt so much. Just when I thought I'd have to gasp or protest, Callum suddenly let me go.

'I can't go any further,' Callum said.

'Just up to the rose garden.'

'Not today.' Callum shook his head. 'I have to go.' He handed back my bag.

'I am going to see you tomorrow after school, aren't I? In our usual place?'

Callum shrugged. He was already walking away.

'Callum, wait! What's the ma . . ?'

But Callum was running now – faster and faster. I watched my best friend tear away from me, his hands over his ears. What was going on? I carried on walking up to the house, my head bent as I tried to figure it out.

'PERSEPHONE! INSIDE! NOW!'

My head snapped up at the sound of my mother's voice. Mother came hurtling down the steps, her expression dour and fierce – as always. She'd obviously not had as many glasses of wine today as she normally did, otherwise she wouldn't be in such a bad mood. I turned back to where Callum had been, but he was already out of sight – which was just as well. Mother grabbed my arm with bony fingers that bit like pincers.

'I have been calling you for the last half an hour.'

'You should've called louder then. I was down on the beach.'

'Don't be cheeky. I told you not to wander off today.' Mother started dragging me up the stairs behind her.

'Ouch!' I banged my shin against one of the stone steps where I'd been too slow to pick up my feet. I tried to bend to rub my bruised skin but Mother was still dragging me.

'Let go. Stop pulling me. I'm not luggage.' I pulled my arm out of Mother's grasp.

'Get in the house now.'

'Where's the fire?' I glared at Mother as I rubbed my arm.

'You're not to leave the house for the rest of the day.' Mother entered the house. I had no choice but to follow.

'Why not?'

' 'Cause I said so.'

'What's the . . ?'

'And stop asking so many questions.'

I scowled at Mother but she was oblivious – as always. To her, my dirty looks were water off a duck's feathers. The warm, wonderful afternoon was excluded from our house with the closing of the front door. Mother was one of those 'refined' women who could make the quiet closing of a door as forceful as a slam. Every time Mother looked at me, I could feel her wishing that I was more ladylike, like my scabby big sister, Minerva. I called her Minnie for short when I wanted to annoy her, because she hated it so much. I called her Minnie all the time. She loved our house as much as I hated it. She called it 'grand'. To me it was like a bad museum – all cold floors and marble pillars and carved stonework which glossy magazines loved to photograph but which no-one with half a gram of sense would ever want to live in.

Thank God for Callum. I hugged the knowledge of

how I'd spent my day to myself with a secret smile. Callum had kissed me. Wow!

Callum had actually *kissed* me!

Wowee! *Zowee!*

My smile slowly faded as a unbidden thought crept into my head. There was just one thing that stopped my day from being entirely perfect. If only Callum and I didn't have to sneak and creep around.

If only Callum wasn't a nought.

two. Callum

'I live in a palace with golden walls and silver turrets and marble floors . . .' I opened my eyes and looked at my house. My heart sank. I closed my eyes again. 'I live in a mansion with mullion windows and leaded light casements and a swimming pool and stables in the acres and acres of grounds.' I opened one eye. It still hadn't worked. 'I live in a three up, two down house with a lock on the front door and a little garden where we grow veggies.' I opened both eyes. It never worked. I hesitated outside my house – if you could call it that. Every time I came back from Sephy's, I flinched at the sight of the shack that was meant to be my home. Why couldn't my family live in a house like Sephy's? Why didn't any nought I knew of live in a house like Sephy's? Looking at our rundown hovel, I could feel the usual burning, churning sensation begin to rise up inside me. My stomach tightened, my eyes began to narrow . . . So I forced myself to look away. Forced myself to look around at the oak and beech and chestnut trees that lined our street, lifting their branches up to the sky. I watched a solitary cloud slowdance above me, watched a swallow dart and soar without a care in the world.

'Come on . . . you can do this . . . do this . . . do this . . .' I closed my eyes and took a deep breath. Steeling myself, I pushed open the front door and walked inside.

'Where've you been, Callum? I was worried sick.'

Mum launched in before I'd even closed the door behind me. There was no hall or passageway with rooms leading off it like in Sephy's house. As soon as you opened our front door, there was our living room with its fifth-hand threadbare nylon carpet and its seventh-hand cloth sofa. The only thing in the room that was worth a damn was the oaken table. Years before, Dad had cut it and shaped it and carved the dragon's leaf pattern into it, put it together and polished it himself. A lot of love and work had gone into that table. Sephy's mother had once tried to buy it but Mum and Dad wouldn't part with it.

'Well? I'm waiting, Callum. Where were you?' Mum repeated.

I sat down at my place around the table and looked away from Mum. Dad wasn't bothered about me – or anything else, for that matter. He was totally focused on his food. Jude, my seventeen-year-old brother, grinned knowingly at me. He's a really irritating toad. I looked away from him as well.

'He was with his dagger friend.' Jude smirked.

I scowled at him. 'What dagger friend? If you don't know what you're talking about you should shut your mouth.' *Don't you call my best friend that . . . Say that again and I'll knock you flat . . .*

Jude could see what I was thinking because his smirk broadened. 'What should I call her then? Your dagger what?'

He never called them Crosses. They were always *daggers*.

'Why don't you go and get stuffed?!'

'Callum, son, don't talk to your brother like . . .' Dad didn't get any further.

'Callum, were you with *her* again?' Mum's eyes took on a fierce, bitter gleam.

'No, Mum. I went for a walk, that's all.'

'That had better be all.' Mum banged down the dinner pan. Pasta sloshed over the sides and onto the table. Seconds later, Jude had whipped up the overspill and it was in his mouth!

Astounded seconds ticked past as everyone at the table stared at Jude. He even had Lynette's attention – and that was saying something. Not much brought my sister out of her mysterious world.

'How come the only time you move faster than greased lightning is when food is involved?' Mum said, her lips twitching somewhere between disgust and amusement.

'It's called incentive, Mum,' Jude grinned.

Amusement won. Mum started to laugh. 'I'll give you incentive, my lad!'

And for once I was grateful to Jude for drawing attention away from what I'd been doing all afternoon. I glanced around the table. Already Lynette was turning away, her head bowed as always, her attention on her lap – as always.

'Hi, Lynny . . .' I spoke softly to my big sister. She looked up and gave me the briefest of smiles before returning her gaze to her lap.

My sister looks like me – the same brown hair, eyes the same shade of grey. Jude's got black hair and brown eyes and looks like Mum. Lynny and I don't look like Mum or Dad particularly. Maybe that's part of the reason why we've always been close. Closer than Jude and I. She was the one who looked after me when Mum had to work and couldn't take me with her. But now she can't even look after herself. She's a bit simple. She looks her age, twenty, but her mind is outside time. She's away with the fairies as my grandma used to say. She wasn't always that way. Three years ago something happened which changed her. An accident. And just like that the sister I knew was gone. Now she doesn't go out, doesn't talk much, doesn't think much as far as I can tell. She just *is*. She stays lost in the middle of her own world somewhere. We can't get in and she doesn't come out. Not often anyway, and certainly not for any length of time. But her mind takes her to somewhere kind, I think, to judge by the peaceful, serene look on her face most of the time. Sometimes I wondered if it was worth losing your marbles to find that kind of peace. Sometimes I envied her.

'So where have you been all this time?' Mum resumed her previous conversation.

And I'd thought I'd got away with it. I should've guessed that Mum wouldn't let the matter rest. Once she gets a bee in her knickers . . .

'Just walking, I told you.'

'Hhmmm . . .' Mum's eyes narrowed but she turned around and headed back to the cooker for the mince. I breathed an outward sigh of relief. Mum was obviously tired because for once she'd chosen to believe me.

Lynette gave me one of her secret smiles. She turned to spoon pasta onto her plate as Mum returned with the pan of mince.

'Ready for school tomorrow, Callum?' Dad said warmly, seemingly oblivious to the instant tension rising up around the table like razor wire.

'Ready as I'll ever be, Dad,' I muttered, pouring myself a glass of milk from the dinner jug so that I wouldn't have to look at anyone.

'It'll be tough, son, but at least it's a start. My son is going to Heathcroft High School. Imagine that!' Dad took a deep breath, his chest actually puffing up with pride as he smiled at me.

'I still think he's making a big mistake . . .' Mum sniffed.

'Well, I don't.' Dad's smile vanished as he turned to Mum.

'He doesn't need to go to their schools. We noughts should have our own schools with the same opportunities that the Crosses enjoy,' Mum retorted. 'We don't need to mix with them.'

'What's wrong with mixing?' I asked, surprised.

'It doesn't work,' Mum replied at once. 'As long as the schools are run by Crosses, we'll always be treated as second-class, second-best nothings. We should look after and educate our own, not wait for the Crosses to do it for us.'

'You never used to believe that,' said Dad.

'I'm not as naïve as I used to be – if that's what you mean,' Mum replied.

I opened my mouth to speak but the words wouldn't come. They were just a jumble in my head. If a Cross had said that to me, I'd be accusing them of all sorts. It seemed to me we'd practised segregation for centuries now and that hadn't worked either. What would satisfy all the noughts and the Crosses who felt the same as Mum? Separate countries? Separate planets? How far away was far enough? What was it about the differences in others that scared some people so much?

'Meggie, if our boy is going to get anywhere in this life, he has to go to their schools and learn to play the game by their rules. He just has to be better at it, that's all.'

'That's all?'

'Don't you want something more for your son than we ever had?' Dad asked, annoyed.

'How can you ask me that? If you think . . .'

'I'm sure everything will be fine, Mum. Don't worry,' I interrupted.

Mum clamped her lips together, her expression thunderous. She stood up and went over to the fridge. I could tell from the way she took out the water bottle and slammed the fridge door shut that she wasn't happy. My going to school was the only thing I'd ever heard my parents argue about. Mum twisted the top off the bottle and tipped it so that it was directly over the yellow painted pottery jug she'd made a few weeks back. Water gushed out, rising up in the jug to slosh over the sides and down onto the work surface, but she didn't alter the angle of the bottle.

'You'll soon think you're too good for us.' Jude punched me on the arm for good measure. 'Just don't go getting too big for your boots!'

'Of course he won't. And you'll be on your best behaviour at Heathcroft, won't you?' Dad beamed. 'You'll be representing all of us noughts at the school.'

Why did I have to represent all noughts? Why couldn't I just represent myself?

'You must show them they're wrong about us. Show them we're just as good as they are,' Dad continued.

'He doesn't need to go to their stuck-up school to show them that.' Mum came back to the table, slamming the water jug down on the plastic tablecloth.

Milk and water, water and milk – that was all we ever had with our dinner. Unless we were extra short of money, in which case it was just water. I lifted my glass of milk to my mouth and closed my eyes. I could almost smell the orange juice Sephy's family nearly always had at their dinner table. Chardonnay for her mother and a claret for her dad and a choice of fizzy water, fruit juice – usually orange – and/or fizzy ginger beer for Sephy and her sister, Minerva. No bottled tap water for them. I remembered years ago when Sephy had snuck me my first taste of orange juice. It was icy-cold and oh, so sweet and I held each sip in my mouth until it became warm because I was so loath to swallow. I wanted the orange juice to last – but of course it hadn't. Sephy snuck me orange juice as often as she could after that. She couldn't understand why I loved it so much. I think she still can't.

I took a sip of my drink. My juice had too obviously passed through a cow first! I guess I didn't have enough imagination to turn milk into orange juice.

'He'll soon be as stuck-up as them.' Jude prodded me in the same place where he'd just punched me, turning his finger this way and that to make sure that it really hurt.

I put down my glass and glared at Jude.

'Come on then . . .' Jude whispered for my ears only.

I carefully placed my hands on my lap, my fingers interlocked.

'What's the matter? Am I embarrassing you?' Jude teased maliciously.

Beneath the table, my fingertips were beginning to go numb, I was pressing them together so hard. Ever since I'd passed the exam and got into Heathcroft, Jude had become totally unbearable. He spent every waking moment trying to goad me into hitting out at him. So far I'd managed to resist the intense temptation – but only just. I had sense enough to know that if Jude and I got into a fight, he'd wipe the floor with me. I hated it here so much. Oh, to get away. Far away. Even if I couldn't get up and physically leave the table, I had to get out of here before . . . before I exploded.

Sephy . . . Sephy and the beach . . . and Maths . . . and our kiss. I smiled as I remembered her insisting that I wipe my mouth before our first kiss. She did make me laugh.

That's right, Callum. Just drift away. Out of the house . . . back to the beach . . . back to Sephy . . .

She did make me laugh . . .

'You're not listening to a single word, are you?' Mum's rasp cut through my reverie.

'I was listening,' I denied.

'What did I just say then?'

'My new uniform is over my chair and I'm to get up extra early and have a wash before putting them on. My writing books are in the school bag under my bed,' I repeated.

'You heard me. That doesn't mean you were listening!' Mum replied.

I smiled. 'What's the difference?'

'My reaction!' Mum said at once. Smiling reluctantly, she sat down. The atmosphere wasn't perfect, but at least it was better than it had threatened to be less than five minutes ago.

'A son of mine at Heathcroft School.' Dad shook his head, his spoon poised before his lips. 'Imagine that!'

'Shut up and eat your food, fool!' Mum snapped.

Dad looked at her and burst out laughing. Everyone else joined in — except Lynette.

I spooned pasta and mince into my mouth, smiling as I chewed. To tell the truth, I was looking forward to school tomorrow. I was actually going to secondary school. I could make something of myself, do something with my life. Once I had a proper education behind me, no-one could turn around and say, 'You're not smart enough or good enough'. No-one. I was on my way UP! And with a proper education behind me, nothing could stand between Sephy and me. Nothing.

three. Sephy

I moved the cursor over to SHUT DOWN and clicked, yawning as I waited for my PC to switch off. It seemed to be taking for ever tonight. At last, there was a clunk and the screen went black. I pressed the button to switch off my monitor and switched off the loudspeakers. Now for a quick drink and then bed. First day of school tomorrow. I groaned at the thought. School! I'd see all my friends again and we'd have the usual conversations, about the places we'd visited, the films we'd seen, the parties we'd posed at – and before long it would be like we'd never been away from school at all. The same old faces, the same old teachers, the same old, same old! But that wasn't strictly true, was it? At least tomorrow would be a bit different from the start of every other new term. Four noughts, including Callum, were starting at my school. Maybe he'd even be in my class. And if he wasn't we were bound to share some lessons together. *My best friend was going to attend my very own school.* That one thought alone was enough to make me grin like a silly idiot!

'Please God, let Callum be in my class,' I whispered.

I walked out of my room and headed along the landing. Callum in my class . . . That would be so great! I was looking forward to showing him the playing fields and the swimming pool, the gym and the music rooms, the dining hall and the science labs. And I'd introduce him to all my friends. Once they got to know him, they'd think he was as great as I did. It was going to be wonderful.

I crept down the stairs. As thirsty as I was, I didn't relish the prospect of running into Mother. She was so miserable. I couldn't understand it. I could still remember when Mother had been all smiles and hugs and jokes – but that was long ago and far away now. About three years ago. Since then, there had been a complete change. Her sense of humour had grown old and died before the rest of her and these days her lips were turned down in a frown that was permanently carved into her skin.

I shook my head. If that's what growing old was about then I never wanted to grow old. At least Dad was still fun – when he was around, which wasn't often. Every adult I met for the first time loved to tell me how great my dad was – how he was so smart, so funny, so handsome, how he was destined to go all the way to the top. I'd've liked to discover those things about my dad for myself. A man with oily hands and a sweaty smell who came to Mother and Dad's last dinner party had spent his entire time with me talking about how Dad would be Prime Minister one day and how I must be so proud of him. I mean, that man could've won a gold medal at the International Games for being the most boring person in the world. Why on earth would I care about Dad becoming the Prime Minister? I saw little enough of him as it was. If he became Prime Minister I'd have to watch the telly just to remember what he looked like.

'Those bleeding heart liberals in the Pangaean Economic Community make sick! They said we in this country had to open our schools to noughts, so we did. They said we had to open our doors to recruiting noughts into our police and armed forces, so we did. And they're still not satisfied. And as for the Liberation Militia, I thought letting a few blankers into our schools would spike their guns . . .'

I froze on the bottom step at the sound of Dad's bitterly angry voice.

'It wasn't enough. Now the Liberation Militia have had one of their demands met, they don't see why they can't have a few more. And then it'll be a few more after that.' Another voice − Dad had a guest.

'Over my cold and rotting body! I knew granting even one of the Pangaean EC's demands was a mistake. God spare us from liberals and blankers!'

I winced at the venom in Dad's voice. And I'd never heard him refer to noughts as blankers before. *Blankers* . . . What a horrible word! A nasty word. My friend Callum wasn't a blanker. He wasn't . . .

'The Liberation Militia are growing impatient with the rate of change in this country. They want . . .'

'And just who are "they"?' Dad demanded. 'Who's the head of the Liberation Militia?'

'I don't know, sir. It's been a slow business working my way up the ranks and the Liberation Militia are very careful. Each military group is divided into different cells or units, with multiple drop-off points if they want to communicate with others in the Militia. It's very hard to find out who's in charge.'

'I don't want excuses. Just do it. That's what I'm paying you for. I'm not going to lose my place in the government because of some terrorist rabble-rousers.'

'They call themselves Freedom Fighters,' Dad's guest stated.

'I don't care if they call themselves descendants of the angel Shaka, they're scum and I want them wiped out. All of them.'

Silence.

'I'll keep working on it.'

Dad's derisive snort was the only reply the other man got.

'Sir, about these meetings . . . they're becoming more and more dangerous. We should find a safer way to communicate.'

'I still want these face-to-face meetings at least once a month.'

'But it's not safe,' the man with Dad protested. 'I'm putting my life on the line every time . . .'

'I don't want to hear it. You can e-mail me or phone as often as you like but I want to see you at least once a month. Is that understood?' Dad snapped.

At first I thought the other man wasn't going to answer. But at last he said, 'Yes, sir.'

I tiptoed closer to the drawing room. Who was Dad talking to? I could only hear their voices.

'Blankers going to my daughter's school . . .' I could almost hear Dad shaking his head. 'If my plan doesn't work, it'll take a miracle to get re-elected next year. I'll be crucified.'

'There are only three or four going to Heathcroft, aren't there?' the other man asked.

'That's three or four more than I thought would pass

the entrance exam,' Dad said with disgust. 'If I'd thought any of them stood a chance of passing the test, I would never have amended the education bill in the first place.'

Every word was like a poison dart. An icy shiver shot through me and it was like my heart was being ripped apart. I was so . . . so *hurt*. Dad . . . My dad . . .

'Less than two dozen noughts are going to Cross schools nationwide. That's not so many, surely?' the other man pointed out.

'When I want your point of view, I'll buy it,' Dad dismissed.

Did he even know that Callum was one of the noughts going to my school? Did he even care? I doubted it. I took another tentative step forward. I glanced across the hall. Dad's reflection was clearly visible in the long hall mirror opposite the drawing room. I could only see the back of Dad's guest reflected in the mirror as he had his back to the door, but I was more than a little stunned to see it was a nought. He had blond hair, tied back in a pony-tail and he was wearing a stained sheepskin coat and big brown boots with a silver-coloured chain above the heel of each one. I couldn't remember the last time I'd seen a nought in our house, except in the kitchen, or cleaning. Why was he here? Who was he? It didn't make any sense. Nothing they were saying made any sense.

I took another step forward, my eyes still focused on the mirror across from the drawing room – which was my mistake. I tripped over the telephone cord making the phone drag slightly across the table. It wasn't much of a noise. But it was enough. Dad looked around and saw me via the hall mirror just as I could see him. His guest turned around.

'Sephy, go to bed – NOW.'

Dad didn't even wait for me to leave before he slammed the drawing-room door shut. I'd barely gathered my scattered wits when the door opened again and Dad marched out alone, slamming the door shut behind him.

'What did you see?' he demanded as he strode over to me.

'P-pardon?'

'What did you see?' Dad grasped my shoulders. A drop of spit came out of his mouth and landed on my cheek but I didn't wipe it away.

'N-nothing.'

'What did you hear?'

'Nothing, Dad. I just came down for a drink. I'm thirsty.'

Dad's eyes blazed with rage as he scowled at me. He looked like he wanted to hit me.

'I didn't see or hear anything. Honest.'

Long moments passed before Dad's grip on my shoulders slowly slackened off. His contorted face relaxed.

'C-can I get my drink now?'

'Go on then. Just hurry up.'

I walked off towards the kitchen even though I wasn't thirsty any more. My heart was slamming against my ribs and my blood was roaring in my ears. I knew without turning around that Dad was still watching me. Once I reached the kitchen, I poured myself a glass of water and headed back up to my bedroom. I was out of Dad's sight in the kitchen but I still went at a 'normal' pace, as if somehow he could see me through the walls. I left the kitchen and started to head upstairs, my glass of water in my hand.

'Princess, wait . . .' Dad called me back.

I turned my head.

'I'm sorry I bit your head off.' Dad forced a smile as he came up the stairs behind me. 'I've been a bit . . . edgy all day.'

'That's OK,' I whispered.

'You're still my princess, aren't you?' asked Dad, hugging me.

I nodded, trying to get past the lump in my throat. Trying not to spill my water.

'Off you go to bed then.'

I carried on walking up the stairs, my pace carefully careless. And Dad stood in the hall, watching my every move.

four. Callum

I tipped everything out of my school bag and onto my bottom bunk-bed – for the umpteenth time. Ruler, pencil-case, pens, pencils, exercise book, calculator. I went through the list Heathcroft High had sent to my mum and dad. I had everything they'd specified and yet it still felt as if there was something missing, as if it wasn't enough. I took the corner of my bed sheet and rubbed it over the calculator again. No amount of polishing would ever make this dinosaur calculator look brand new. I rubbed my hand over my tired eyes.

'Don't be so ungrateful. At least you've got a calculator.' *Just keep telling yourself that, Callum . . .*

Slowly, carefully, I started packing all my school stuff back into my bag.

I'm lucky . . I'm lucky . . . I'm lucky . . . I'm going to school . . .

I played that one thought over and over again in my head, scared to let it go in case of what might happen. Someone knocked at my door. It was either Mum or Lynette. Jude didn't knock, he just barged straight in and Dad never came into our room. If he wanted to talk to me, he always called me out on to the landing. I hoped it was Lynette.

Mum popped her head around the door. 'Can I come in?'

I shrugged, placing my calculator on top of the other stuff in my bag. Mum came into the room, carefully shutting the door behind her. I could guess what was about to come next. She sat on my bed, picked up my school bag and immediately emptied everything out. Very carefully, Mum started packing all my stuff back. Moments passed before she spoke. 'I just wanted to say that whatever happens tomorrow, well done for getting into Heathcroft High.'

That I hadn't expected. I stared at her.

'What d'you mean, whatever happens tomorrow?'

'Nothing.' Mum's smile wobbled before disappearing altogether. 'It's just that . . . that I want you to be happy.'

'I am happy.' I frowned.

'I don't want to see you . . . upset. I don't want you to get hurt.'

What on earth was she talking about? 'Mum, I'm only going to school. I'm not going into the army!'

Mum's attempt at a smile was back. 'I know. But I think you and your father are underestimating how much of a . . . challenge it's going to be. I don't want to see you upset. Besides which . . . well, we've heard some rumours . . .'

'What kind of rumours?'

'Some of the Crosses aren't happy about noughts going to their schools. We've heard rumours that some of them are determined to cause trouble. So, no matter what happens, don't let yourself be provoked into lashing out. Don't give them a reason to kick you out.'

'Is that what you've been worrying about?'

Mum didn't reply.

'Don't worry,' I told her. 'I've got into Heathcroft now and nothing, not even dynamite, is going to get me out again.'

'Good for you.' Mum stroked my cheek. I brushed her hand away. I mean, *please!*

'Too old for that?' Mum teased.

'Much too old,' I replied.

'Too old for a kiss goodnight?'

I was just about to give Mum my honest opinion when the look on her face halted the words on my lips. I realized that the kiss wasn't for my benefit, it was for hers.

'Go on then. If you must,' I grumbled, offering her my cheek.

Silence. I turned to see why the dreaded kiss hadn't been delivered but the moment I looked at Mum she burst out laughing.

'What's so funny?' I frowned.

'You are, my darling.' Mum put me in a bear hug and kissed my cheek like she was trying to burrow her lips into it. Jeez!

'Make sure you set your alarm so you've got plenty of time for a wash before school.' Mum stood up and headed for the door.

'I'm not going to bed yet, Mum. I'm coming downstairs for a while to watch telly.'

'Just for a little while. You've got school tomorrow.' Mum wagged her finger. Her hand dropped to her side and she smiled. '*You've got school tomorrow* . . . I like the sound of that!'

'So do I!'

Mum headed downstairs with me following close behind her. Halfway down the stairs, Mum stopped so abruptly that I almost collided with her.

'Cal?'

'Yes, Mum?'

'You . . . you mustn't think I'm not proud of you, 'cause I am.'

'I know, Mum,' I said.

Mum carried on walking downstairs. I thought about what she'd just said. The funny thing was, until she said it, I didn't think she was proud of me. In fact, part of me still suspected that Mum would've rather I'd failed the Heathcroft High entrance exam. But I hadn't. I'd passed. And no-one could take that away from me. *I'd passed.*

We walked into the downstairs room. Lynette and Dad sat on the sofa. Jude sat at the dinner table poring over what looked like a map – not that I was particularly interested. Mum sat down next to Dad and I sat next to Lynette. It was a squash but a cosy squash.

I looked at my sister. 'You OK?'

Lynette nodded. Then a slow-burning frown spread out over her face. And *that* look was back in her eyes. My heart plunged down to my shoes and bounced back up again.

Please, Lynette. Not tonight . . . not now . . .

'Lynny, d'you remember my seventh birthday?' I began desperately. 'You took me to see my first film at the cinema. There was just you and me and you got annoyed with me because I wouldn't take my eyes off the screen, not for a second. D'you remember you told me that I could blink because the screen wasn't about to vanish. Lynny . . ?'

'Why am I here?' My sister's troubled grey eyes narrowed. 'I shouldn't be here. I'm not one of you. I'm a Cross.'

My stomach lurched, like I was in a lift which had suddenly plunged down at least fifty storeys in about five seconds flat. Every time I convinced myself that Lynette was getting better, she'd get that look on her face . . . She'd stare at us like we were all strangers and she'd insist she was one of them.

'What're you talking about. You're a nought,' Jude said with scorn. 'Look at your skin. You're as white as the rest of us. Whiter.'

'No, I'm not.'

'Jude, that's enough,' said Dad.

'No, it's not. I'm fed up with this. Keeping Lynette in this house so she won't embarrass us by telling everyone she's a Cross. She's barking mad, that's what she is. And Callum's just as bad. He thinks he's better than us and as good as the Crosses, even if he doesn't say it.'

'You don't know what you're talking about,' I hissed.

'No? I've seen you looking up at this house when you've come back from your dagger friend. I've seen you hating it and hating us and hating yourself because you weren't born one of them,' Jude spewed out. 'I'm the only one of the three of us who knows what he is and accepts it.'

'Now listen here, you brainless . . .'

Jude sprang out of his chair, but only a couple of seconds before I did.

'Come on then, if you reckon you're hard enough,' Jude challenged.

I stepped forward but Dad got between the two of us before I could do little more than clench my fists.

'See?' Lynette's small, puzzled voice rang out as clear as a bell. 'I don't behave like that. I can't be a nought. I just can't.'

All the fight went out of me. Slowly, I sat back down again.

'Listen, Lynette . . .' Mum began.

'Look at my skin,' Lynette spoke as if Mum hadn't. 'Such a beautiful colour. So dark and rich and wonderful. I'm so lucky. I'm a Cross – closer to God . . .' Lynette looked around at all of us and smiled. A broad, beaming, genuinely happy smile that lit every line and crease of her face and squeezed my heart.

'Stupid cow,' Jude muttered.

'That's enough!' Dad shouted at him.

Jude sat, a sullen, brooding look on his face. Lynette looked down at her hands stroking one over the other. I looked too. All I could see were pale white hands, blue veins clearly visible through the almost translucent skin. She looked up at me and smiled. I smiled back. Forced it really, but at least I tried.

'Don't you think I'm beautiful, Callum?' Lynette whispered.

'Yes,' I replied truthfully. 'Very.'

five. Sephy

I looked out of the car window, watching the trees and fields and sky melt and merge into each other in a passing blur. The first day of term. I sat up straighter, a smile of pure happiness creeping across my face. Callum . . . He alone made the first day of term new and exciting and different.

'OK back there, Miss Sephy?'

'Fine thanks, Harry.' I directed my smile at our nought driver. He was watching me via the driver's interior mirror.

'Nervous?'

I laughed. 'Are you kidding?'

'I guess not,' Harry replied ruefully.

'Harry, could you drop me . . ?'

'Off around the corner from school.' Harry finished for me.

'If that's OK.'

'Well, it'll have to be – won't it?' Harry shook his head. 'If your mother finds out . . .'

'She won't.'

'I still don't see . . .'

I sighed. During term-time, Harry and I had this conversation at least three times a week.

'Harry, you know how I get teased if my friends see you driving me. I get all kinds of comments about having feet which are too precious to touch the pavement or I get asked when I'm going to have my wings fitted and all sorts. I'm not in the mood to be teased – not on my first day back.'

'I know but . . .'

'Please?'

'Oh, all right then.'

'Thanks, Harry.'

'If I get into trouble . . .'

'You won't. I promise,' I smiled.

Harry turned into Cherry Wood Grove, a couple of streets away from Heathcroft, my school. I hopped out, dragging my school bag off the white leather seat.

'See you later.'

'Yes, Miss Sephy.'

I waited until Harry had driven off and was out of sight before taking a step. He'd caught me out like that before

– pretending to drive off and then doubling back when my back was turned. As I ambled along, I heard a strange, rumbling sound – like someone playing a radio really loudly, but far enough away so that I couldn't make out exactly what was being said. As I approached the corner, shouts like an angry wave rolled up towards me. But even that couldn't prepare me for what was about to happen next. I turned the corner and . . .

And.

At the far end of the road, there was a huge crowd outside my school. And they were shouting and chanting. I froze for a moment, then started to walk towards them. Then I started to run. What on earth was going on? It didn't take me long to find out.

'NO BLANKERS IN OUR SCHOOL. NO BLANKERS IN OUR SCHOOL.'

The slogan was shouted out over and over again. Callum and three other noughts were surrounded by police officers who were trying to push their way through the crowd to get to the school entrance. More police stood in an arm-linked line trying to push the crowd of Crosses back into two orderly groups. I ran faster, but the closer I got, the less I could see. I pushed and elbowed my way through the crowd.

'Callum! CALLUM!'

'NO BLANKERS IN OUR SCHOOL . . .'

The police officers were still trying to push through the crowds of adults and Heathcroft pupils who in turn were determined not to let them pass.

'BLANKERS OUT . . .'

I forced my way up the steps to the school entrance

ahead of the crowd and the police, watching as the police battled to hold back the crowd, watching as Callum and the others looked neither to the right nor the left but straight ahead without even blinking.

'NO BLANKERS IN OUR SCHOOL . . .'

I spotted Julianna and Adam and Ezra in the crowd, all of whom were my good friends. But worst of all I saw my own sister Minnie in the crowd. And she was shouting just as hard as all the others.

'NO BLANKERS IN OUR SCHOOL . . .'

There was a roaring in my head which matched the roaring all around me. I was in the middle of chaos. Callum and the other noughts tried to make their way up the steps to the school entrance. The crowd surged forward at that, the palpable wave of their anger hitting me almost like a punch. Suddenly a cry went up. Callum's head dipped down, followed by the heads of the police officers.

'One of them is hurt!'

Callum . . . it wasn't Callum, was it?

'A blanker's hurt.'

The news spread through the crowd like a virulent disease.

'HOORAY!' Spontaneous cheers filled the air. The police lines trying to hold the crowds back were knocked to the ground as the crowd rushed forward like air into a vacuum. I was on the very top step looking down at it all. And I've never felt such fist-clenching, teeth-gritting fury. A policewoman stepped to one side and I saw Callum squatting down by a nought girl who looked like she was in a bad way. Blood trickled from her forehead and her eyes were closed.

Mr Corsa, the headmaster, emerged from behind me. He stared at the crowd – the *mob* before him – looking shocked and ashen.

'Mr Corsa, we have to help that girl,' I pointed. 'She's hurt.'

Mr Corsa didn't move, even when I repeated what I'd just said. I was caught up in a hurricane, with all the noise and madness whirling round me until my head was about to explode.

'Stop it! Just stop it!'

Nothing.

'STOP IT! YOU'RE ALL BEHAVING LIKE ANIMALS!' I shouted so hard my throat immediately began to hurt. 'WORSE THAN ANIMALS – LIKE BLANKERS!'

The sounds of the crowd slowly died away. 'Just look at you,' I continued. 'Stop it.' I glanced down at Callum. He was staring at me, the strangest expression on his face.

Callum, don't look at me like that. I didn't mean you. I'd never mean you. It was just for the others, to get them to stop, to get them to help. I didn't mean you . . .

six. Callum

She didn't say that. She couldn't have. Not Sephy. I'm going to wake up in a moment. Wake up from this chaos, this nightmare. Wake up and laugh – or bawl – at the tricks my mind's playing. She didn't say that . . .

But she did . . .

I'm not a blanker. I may be a nought but I'm worth more than nothing. I'm not a blanker. A waste of time and space. A zero. I'm not a blanker. I'M NOT A BLANKER.

Sephy . . .

seven. Sephy

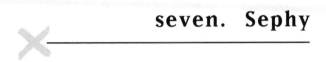

The waves lapped up onto the beach. It was a lovely autumn evening, a beautiful end to a lousy day. I couldn't remember when I'd felt so miserable, so wretched. Callum was sitting right next to me but he might as well have been sitting on the moon.

'Aren't you going to say anything?' At first I thought he wasn't going to answer.

'What would you like me to say?'

'I said I'm sorry,' I tried again.

'I know.'

I watched Callum's profile – unreadable and implacable. And it was my fault. I understood that much, even if I didn't quite understand what I'd done.

'It's just a word, Callum.'

'Just a word . . .' Callum repeated slowly.

'Sticks and stones, Callum. It's one word, that's all,' I pleaded.

'Sephy, if you'd slapped me or punched me or even stabbed me, sooner or later it would've stopped hurting. Sooner or later. But I'll never forget what you called me, Sephy. Never. Not if I live to be five hundred.'

I wiped my cheeks but the tears still came. 'I didn't mean it. I didn't mean you. I was . . . I was trying to help.'

Callum looked at me then and the expression on his face made my tears flow faster. 'Sephy . . .'

'Please. I'm so sorry.' I dreaded to hear what he was going to say next.

'Sephy, maybe we shouldn't see so much of each other any more . . .'

'Callum, no. I said I was sorry.'

'And that makes everything all right, does it?'

'No, it doesn't. Not even close. But don't do this. You're my best friend. I don't know what I'd do without you.'

Callum turned away. I held my breath.

'You must promise me something,' he said softly.

'Anything.'

'You must promise me that you'll never *ever* use that word again.'

Why couldn't he understand that I hadn't been talking about *him*? It was just a word. A word Dad had used. But it was a word that had hurt my best friend. A word that was now hurting me so very, very much. I hadn't fully realized just how powerful words could be before this. Whoever came up with the saying 'sticks and stones may break my bones but words will never hurt me' was talking out of his or her armpit.

'Promise me,' Callum insisted.

'I promise.'

We both turned to look out across the sea then. I knew I should go home. I was so late for dinner it was almost breakfast-time. Mother would go ballistic. But I wasn't going to leave first. I didn't want to get up. So I didn't. I shivered, even though the evening wasn't cold.

Callum took off his jacket and put it around my shoulders. It smelt of soap, and chips – and him. I hugged it tighter around me.

'What about you?' I asked.

'What about me?' he replied.

'Aren't you going to get cold?'

'I'll survive.'

I moved in closer and put my head on his shoulder. His body stiffened and for a moment I thought he was going to move away, but then he relaxed and though he didn't hug me the way he usually did, he didn't shrug me off either. One word . . . one word had caused all this trouble between us. If I lived to be five million, I would never, ever say that horrible word again. Ever. The sun was beginning to set now, burning the sky pink and orange. We sat and watched in silence.

'I've been thinking it over and . . . well, we can still be together outside school but I don't think you should talk to me when we're in school,' Callum said.

I was more than stunned. 'Why on earth not?'

'I don't want you to lose any of your friends because of me. I know how much they mean to you.'

'You're my friend too.'

'Not when we're both at school I'm not,' Callum told me.

'But that's just silly.'

'Is it?'

My mouth opened and closed like a drowning fish, but what could I say? Callum stood up.

'I have to go home now. You coming?'

I shook my head.

'Your mum will hit the roof and then the nearest orbiting satellite!'

'It's Monday. She's visiting friends,' I told him.

'What about your dad?'

'You know he's never home during the week. He's at our town house.'

'And Minerva?'

'I don't know. Probably with her boyfriend. Don't worry about me, Callum. I'll stay here for a little while longer.'

'Not for too long, OK?'

'OK.' I handed back his jacket.

Almost reluctantly, he took it. Then he walked away. I watched, willing him to turn around, to turn back. But he didn't. It was as if I was outside myself, watching the two of us. More and more I was beginning to feel like a spectator in my own life. I had to make a choice. I had to decide what kind of friend Callum was going to be to me. But what surprised – and upset me – was that I even had to think about it.

eight. Callum

'D'you know what time it is?' Mum ranted the moment I set foot through the door. She and I rarely had any other conversation.

'Sorry,' I mumbled.

'Your dinner's in the oven – dried out and not fit for eating by now.'

'It'll be fine, Mum.'

'So where have you been until ten o'clock at night?' Dad surprised me by asking. He didn't usually nag me about coming home late. That was Mum's department.

'Well?' he prompted when I didn't answer.

What did he want me to say? '*Well, I said goodbye to Sephy at the beach almost two hours ago, but then I hid in the shadows and followed her home to make sure she got back OK. Then it took me over an hour to walk home.*' Yeah, right! That little snippet of truth would go down like a lead balloon.

'I was just out walking. I had a lot to think about.' And that part at least was the truth.

'Are you OK, son?' Dad asked. 'I went down to Heathcroft as soon as I heard what was going on, but the police wouldn't let me in.'

'Why not?'

'I had no official business on the premises – unquote.'

Dad couldn't mask the bitterness in his voice.

'Those rotten, stinking . . .'

'Jude, not at the dinner table please,' Mum admonished.

Glancing at Jude, I saw he had enough anger in him for everyone else around. He was scowling at me like I was the one who'd had Dad kept off the school premises.

'So how was school? How were your lessons, son?' Dad asked quietly.

The honest answer or the acceptable one?

'I was OK, Dad,' I fibbed. 'Once we got into school it was all right.'

Except that the teachers had totally ignored us, and the Crosses had used any excuse to bump into us and knock our books on the floor, and even the noughts serving in the food hall had made sure they served everyone else in the queue before us. 'It was fine.'

'You're in there now, Callum. Don't let any dagger swine drive you out – you understand?'

'I understand.'

'Excuse me.' Mum rounded on Dad. 'But when I say I don't want swearing at the dinner table, that applies to everyone – including you.'

'Sorry, love,' Dad said ruefully, winking conspiratorially at us into the bargain.

'You were on the telly,' Jude told me. 'So was your "friend". The whole world heard what she said . . .'

'She didn't mean it like that.' The words slipped out before I could stop them. Big mistake.

'She didn't mean it?' Jude scoffed. 'Have you lost your mind? How can you not mean to say something like that?

She meant it all right.'

'That family are all the same.' Mum sniffed. 'I see Miss Sephy is growing up to be just like her mother.'

I had to bite my lip at that. I knew better than to argue.

'You're better off out of that house,' Dad told Mum vehemently.

'You don't have to tell me twice,' Mum agreed at once. 'I miss the money but I wouldn't go back for all the stars in space. Anyone who can put up with that stuck-up cow Mrs Hadley is a better person than me.'

'You were friends once . . .' I reminded her, spooning some totally dried out mashed potato into my mouth.

'Friends? We were never friends,' Mum snorted. 'She patronised me and I put up with it 'cause I needed a job – that's all.'

That wasn't how I remembered it. A few years ago and a lifetime away, Mum and Mrs Hadley had been really close. Mum was Minerva's, then Sephy's, nanny and a general mother's helper from the time Minerva was born. In fact, I was closer to Sephy than I'd ever been to anyone, even my own sister Lynette who was my best friend in this house. I remembered when I was a toddler and Sephy was just a baby – I'd helped to bathe her and change her nappy. And when she got older, we played hide-and-seek and catch and tag in the Hadley grounds, whilst Mum and sometimes Mrs Hadley watched us and chatted and laughed. I still don't know what happened to change all that. One week Mrs Hadley and Mum were like best friends and the next week, Mum and I were no longer welcome anywhere near the Hadley house. That was over three years ago now.

I still sometimes wondered how Mrs Hadley expected Sephy and I to go from being so close to not seeing each other at all? Sephy told her it was impossible. I told my mum the same thing. Neither of them listened. But it didn't matter. Sephy and I still saw each other at least every other day and we'd never stop. We'd promised each other. The most sacred of promises − an oath sealed with our blood. We just couldn't tell anyone about it, that's all. We had our own world, our own secret place on the beach where no-one went and where no-one would ever find us − not if they didn't know where to look. It was a small space, tiny really, but it was *ours*.

'Shush, everyone. The news is on,' Dad admonished.

I held my breath.

What happened at Heathcroft wasn't the first item of news at least. The first item was about the Liberation Militia.

'Today Kamal Hadley, Home Office Minister, declared that there would be no hiding place, no safe haven for those noughts misguided enough to join the Liberation Militia.' The newscaster's face disappeared to be replaced by that of Sephy's dad outside the Houses of Parliament. His face seemed to fill the whole screen.

'Isn't it true, Mr Hadley, that your government's decision to allow selected noughts in our schools was as a direct result of pressure from the Liberation Militia?'

'Not at all,' Sephy's dad immediately denied. 'This government does not allow itself to be blackmailed by an illegal terrorist group. We acted on a P.E.C. directive that this government had been on the verge of implementing anyway.'

My dad snorted at that.

'Our decision to allow the crème-de-la-crème of nought youth to join our educational institutions makes sound social and economic sense. In a civilized society, equality of education for those noughts with sufficient aptitude . . .'

I tuned out at that. Sephy's dad hadn't changed since the last time I'd spoken to him which was yonks ago now. He never used one word where twenty patronizing ones would do. I didn't like him much. Correction! Pompous twit! I didn't like him at all. I didn't like any of Sephy's family. They were all the same. Minerva was a snob. Her mum was a bitch and her dad was a git. They all looked at us noughts through their nostrils.

'The Liberation Militia are misguided terrorists and we will leave no stone unturned in our efforts to bring them to justice . . .' Sephy's dad was still at it. I was about to mentally switch off again, but then Jude did something that brought me out of my daydream.

'Long live the Liberation Militia!' My brother punched the air, his fingers locked in a fist so tight that I reckoned it would surely hurt to straighten them again.

'Too right, son.' Dad and Jude exchanged a knowing look, before they both turned back to the telly. I frowned at them, then turned to look at Mum. She immediately glanced away. I looked back at Jude and Dad. There was something going on. Something to do with the Liberation Militia and my brother and my dad. I didn't mind that. What I did mind was that I was being excluded.

'There have been unconfirmed reports that the car bomb found outside the International Trade Centre last month was the work of the Liberation Militia,' the news-caster continued. 'What attempts are being made to find those responsible?'

'I can tell you that our highest priority is to find those responsible and bring them to swift and irrevocable justice. Political terrorism which results in the death or serious injury of even one Cross always has been and always will be a capital crime. Those found guilty will suffer the death sentence, no two ways about it . . .'

Blah! Blah! Blah! Sephy's dad droned on for at least another minute, not letting the newscaster get a word in edgeways, sideways or any other ways. I tuned out again, waiting for him to finish, hoping he wouldn't.

nine. Sephy

'Sephy, your dad's on the telly.' Mother opened my bed-room door to tell me.

I mean, big deal! Mother still thought I was five, bouncing up and down with excitement at the sight of my daddy on the TV.

'Sephy!'

'Yes, Mother. I'm watching.' I pressed my TV remote control to switch it on. Anything for a quiet life! I got the right channel first time. How lucky!

'. . . is misguided to say the least.' Dad didn't look too

pleased. 'Minister Pelango is very young and doesn't realize that the rate of change in our society needs to be slow and steady . . .'

'Any slower and we'd be going backwards,' Minister Pelango interjected.

Dad didn't looked too pleased at that either, though it made me smile.

'We call ourselves civilized, yet noughts have more rights in other P.E.C. countries than they do here,' Pelango continued.

'And in plenty of other countries they have a lot less,' Dad snapped back.

'And that makes the way we treat them right, does it?'

'If our ruling party politics don't gel with Mr Pelango's beliefs, then maybe he should do the honourable thing and resign his seat on the government,' Dad said silkily.

'No chance!' came the immediate reply. 'Too many people in this government live in the past. It's my duty to drag them into the present or none of us – noughts or Crosses – will have a decent future.'

Mum left my room. The click of my bedroom door closing was immediately followed by the press of another TV channel button. I didn't care which one. Any other channel would do. I'd grown up with politics, politics, politics being rammed down my throat. I wasn't interested in being caught up in it in any manner, shape or form. Why couldn't Mother understand that?

ten. Callum

When at last Kamal Hadley had stopped dribbling on, Heathcroft School appeared on the telly. Of course, they didn't bother showing the fact that the police officers who were meant to be guarding us were letting the crowd get to us to poke and pinch and punch. Somehow the camera was never in the right place to show that the whole back of my jacket was awash with Cross spit. Surprise! Surprise! There wasn't even a hint of any of that.

'The noughts admitted to Heathcroft High School met with some hostility today . . .' the news reporter began.

Some hostility? This reporter's middle name was obviously 'Euphy', short for Euphemism!

'Police officers were drafted in to keep the peace as it was feared that nought extremists might try to take advantage of the volatile situation . . .' the newscaster continued.

Jude started muttering under his breath and to be honest, I didn't blame him. Even I was disgusted at that and I had a much longer fuse than my brother. Lynette took hold of my hand. She smiled at me and I could feel the anger seeping out of my body. Only Lynette and Sephy could do that – make all the rage that sometimes threatened to blow up inside me just fade to nothing. But sometimes . . . sometimes I got so angry that I scared even myself.

The image on the screen cut from Shania falling over to Sephy shouting at the crowd. The TV camera zoomed in for a close-up. The newscaster announced as a voiceover, 'Persephone Hadley, daughter of Kamal Hadley, had a hand in stopping the fracas . . .'

'I'm going up to my room. I've got homework.' I leapt to my feet.

I was too late. Those words spilt out of the telly before I could leave. I knew what to expect, what she was going to say, and it still made me wince. I left the room before anyone could say a word to me, but I knew my entire family was watching me leave. Closing the door quietly behind me, I leaned against it and took a deep breath.

Sephy . . .

'They are all the same,' I heard Jude scoff. 'Crosses and noughts will never live in peace, let alone be friends and Callum's just fooling himself if he thinks that Cross girl cares one clipped toenail about him. When push comes to shove she'll dump him so fast his body will turn pear-shaped!'

'You and I may know that, but he doesn't,' Dad surprised me by saying.

'Well, the sooner he learns it, the better,' Mum sighed.

'And are you going to be the one that tells him?' Dad asked. ' 'Cause I'm not.'

'There's not one of those Crosses that can be trusted,' Jude declared.

No-one disagreed.

'Someone should tell Callum the truth. Otherwise he's

going to get hurt,' Jude continued.

'Are you volunteering?' asked Dad.

'I will, if I have to,' replied Jude.

'No! No, I'll do it,' Mum said. 'I'll do it.'

'When?'

'When I get round to it. Now back off, both of you,' Mum snapped.

I couldn't listen to any more. I went upstairs, my shoulders slumped, my head hanging down. For the first time ever, I wondered if maybe my family was right and I was wrong.

eleven. Sephy

It was time for History. I hate History. It's a total waste of time. There was only one good thing about it. Callum was down to take History as well. My friend Claire tried to sit next to me.

'Er . . . Claire, could you sit somewhere else today. I'm saving this seat for someone.'

'Who?'

'Someone.'

Claire gave me a scathing look. 'Be like that then.' And she flounced off without a backwards glance. I sighed and watched the door eagerly. Callum and the other noughts were the last ones to come in. Others barged past them and Callum let them get away with it. I wouldn't have.

I smiled at Callum and indicated the seat next to me. Callum looked at me, then looked away and sat next to another nought. Others in the class looked from me to him and back again. My face burned with humiliation. How could he show me up like that? How could he? I know what he'd said the previous evening, but I wanted to show him I didn't care who knew we were friends. It didn't bother me one little bit. So why would Callum turn his back on me like that?

Mr Jason entered the room and launched into the lesson before he'd even shut the door. And within the space of two minutes it was clear he was in a foul mood – even worse than usual. Nobody could do anything right, especially the noughts.

'Who can tell me one of the significant events of the year 146 BC?' Mr Jason asked tersely.

146 BC! I mean, who cared?!! I decided to wind down and sleep with my eyes open until the lesson was over. Callum bent down to get something out of his bag. From my position I couldn't see what. CRACK! Mr Jason smacked a big heavy History textbook down on Callum's desk.

'What's the matter, boy?' Mr Jason asked. 'Too poor to even pay attention?'

Callum didn't answer. Some in the class tittered. A few didn't. Mr Jason was being a real pig and when he walked past me, I glared at him to let him know exactly what I thought about the way he was carrying on. That put his back up as well. I got told off twice in less than thirty minutes. But I didn't care. Mr Jason wasn't important. I had other things on my mind – like how to prove to Callum that I really didn't care if people knew he was my friend. In fact, I was proud of it. But how to do it . . ? And then it came to me! Eureka! The perfect solution. If only this lesson would hurry up and finish. All I could think about was lunch-time. I was desperate to be one of the first to get to the food hall. When at last the buzzer sounded, I was the first out of my chair. Trying to be the first out of the room, I barged past my teacher.

'Er, d'you mind?'

'Sorry, sir,' I tried to carry on moving past him. Big mistake!

'As you're in such a tearing hurry you can wait until last to leave the classroom.'

'But, sir . . .'

Mr Jason raised a warning hand. 'Any arguments and you'll be lucky to get lunch at all.'

I shut up. Mr Jason was a real, ill-tempered, ill-mannered slug. And he had to toil hard to work his way up to that. So I waited whilst everyone else grinned smugly at me as they strolled past. I was late getting to the food hall when today of all days I wanted to be one of the first. Callum and the other noughts already had their food and were sitting down by the time I walked through the food-hall doors. All the noughts were sitting at a table by themselves, just like yesterday.

I lined up in the food queue. I wasn't going to do anything out of the ordinary, so why was my heart bumping in such a strange way? I collected my chicken and mushroom pie with the usual over-boiled trimmings, my jam tart with over-sweet custard and my carton of milk and, taking a deep breath, I headed for Callum's table. Callum and the other noughts glanced up as I approached their table, only to look away again almost immediately.

'D'you mind if I join you?'

They all looked so shocked, it wasn't even funny. The other noughts continued to look stunned, but Callum's expression turned. I sat down before he could say no and before I could bottle out.

'What d'you think you're doing?' he snapped.

'Eating my lunch,' I replied before cutting into my pie. I tried to smile at the other three noughts but they instantly returned to eating their food.

'Hi. I'm Sephy Hadley.' I thrust my hand under the nose of the nought girl I was sitting next to. She had a dark brown plaster on her forehead which stuck out on her pale white skin like a throbbing thumb. 'Welcome to Heathcroft.'

She looked at my hand like it was about to bite her. Wiping her own hand on her tunic, she then took mine and shook it slowly.

'I'm Shania,' she said softly.

'That's a pretty name. What does it mean?' I asked.

Shania shrugged. 'It doesn't mean anything.'

'My mother told me my name means "serene night",' I laughed. 'But Callum will tell you I'm anything but serene!'

Shania smiled at me. It was tentative and brief but at least it was genuine − whilst it lasted.

'How's your head?' I asked, pointing at the plaster.

'It's OK. It'll take more than a stone step to dent my head.'

I smiled. 'That plaster's a bit noticeable.'

'They don't sell pink plasters. Only dark brown ones.' Shania shrugged.

My eyes widened at that. I'd never really thought about it before, but she was right. I'd never seen any pink plasters. Plasters were the colour of us Crosses, not the noughts.

'Sephy, just what d'you think you're doing?' Mrs Bawden, the deputy headmistress, appeared from nowhere to scowl down at me.

'Pardon?'

'What're you doing?'

'I'm eating my lunch.' I frowned.

'Don't be facetious.'

'I'm not. I'm eating my lunch.'

'Get back to your own table – at once.' Mrs Bawden looked like she was about to erupt kittens.

I looked around. I was now the centre of attention – the very last thing I'd wanted.

'B-but I'm sitting h-here,' I stammered.

'Get back to your own table – NOW!'

What table? I didn't have my own table. And then it dawned on me exactly what Mrs Bawden meant. She wasn't talking about me getting back to my own table. She was talking about me getting back to my own kind. I glanced around. Callum and the others weren't looking at me. Everyone else was. They weren't.

'I'm sitting with my friend, Callum,' I whispered. I could hardly hear my own voice so I have no idea how Mrs Bawden heard me – but she did. She grabbed my arm and pulled me out of my chair. I was still holding on to my tray, and everything on it went flying.

'Persephone Hadley, you will come with me.' Mrs Bawden yanked me away from the table and dragged me across the food hall. I tried to twist away from her, but she had a grip like a python on steroids. I turned my head this way and that. Wasn't anyone going to do anything? Not from the look at it. I twisted sharply to look at Callum. He was watching but the moment I caught his eye, he looked away. I stopped struggling after that. I straightened up and followed Mrs Bawden to the headmaster's office.

Callum had turned away from me. I didn't care about the rest, but I cared about that. He'd turned away ... Well, I was slow getting the message, but I'd finally got it. God knows, I'd finally got it.

twelve. Callum

I had to get out of there. I left my lunch half-eaten and walked out of the food hall without saying a word to any of the others.

I had to get out of there.

I walked out of the food hall and out of the building and out of the school, my steps growing ever faster and more frantic − until by the time I was out of the school gates, I was running. Running until my back ached and my feet hurt and my heart was ready to burst and still I kept running. I ran all the way out of the town and down to the beach. I collapsed onto the cool sand, my body bathed in sweat. I lay on my stomach and punched the sand. And again, and again. Until I was pounding it with both fists. Until my knuckles were red raw and bleeding.

And I wished more than anything else in the world that the sand beneath my fists was Sephy's face.

thirteen. Sephy

I spotted our Mercedes in its usual place, just outside the main school building. As I approached it, a strange man got out and opened one of the back doors for me. He had mousy-brown hair which lay flat and lank against his head, and ice-light, ghost-like blue eyes.

'Who are you?'

'Karl, your new driver.'

'Where's Harry?' I asked, climbing into the car.

'He decided to move on.'

'Without telling me?'

Karl shrugged and slammed the door shut. I watched him sit behind the wheel and start the car, a frown digging deep into my face.

'Where did he move on to?'

'I don't know, Miss.'

'Why did he want to leave?'

'I don't know that either.'

'Where does Harry live?'

'Why, Miss Sephy?'

'I'd like to send him a Good Luck card.'

'If you give it to me, Miss, I'll make sure he gets it.'

Karl's eyes and mine met in the internal driver's mirror. 'OK,' I said at last. What else could I say?

Harry wouldn't go away and leave me, not without saying goodbye first. I knew he wouldn't – just as surely as I knew my own name. Something horrible then occurred to me.

'You . . . you r-really are my new driver, aren't you?'

'Of course, Miss Sephy. Your mother employed me this morning. I can show you my ID card if you'd like.' Karl's smile flitted fleetingly across his face.

'No, that's OK,' I said. I sat back in my seat and clipped up my seat-belt.

We drove off. I saw some others, pointing to me and whispering or laughing or both as our car went past. My sitting at the noughts table had spread around the school like a bad dose of the flu. And I knew I hadn't heard the end of it. Mr Corsa threatened that he was going to send a letter home to my mum and e-mail my dad. No doubt a protest to the Queen was in the offing too. And I wouldn't have minded any of that if Callum hadn't turned his back on me. But he had. And I was never going to forget it. He had looked away from me like . . . like he didn't know me. Like I was nothing. Maybe Mother was right, after all. Maybe Crosses and noughts could never be friends. Maybe there was too much difference between us.

Did I really believe that?

I didn't know what I believed any more.

fourteen. Callum

I don't know how long I sat there, watching the sun burn into the sky as it set, watching the night grow steadily more secretive. Why had my life suddenly become so complicated? For the last year all I could think about, or even dream about, was going to school. Sephy's school. I was so busy concentrating on getting into Heathcroft that I hadn't given much thought to what I'd do when I actually got there. I hadn't really thought about what it would be like to be so . . . unwanted. And what was the point anyway? It wasn't as if I'd get a decent job after it. No Cross would ever employ me for more than the most mundane, menial job, so why bother? But I wanted to learn. A yawning hole deep inside me was begging to be filled up with words and thoughts and ideas and facts and fictions. But if I did that, what would I do with the rest of my life? What would I be? How could I ever be truly happy knowing that I could do so much more, *be* so much more, than I would ever be allowed?

I was trying so hard to understand how and why things were the way they were. The Crosses were meant to be closer to God. The Good Book said so. The son of God was dark-skinned like them, had eyes like them, had hair like them. The Good Book said so. But the Good Book said a lot of things. Like 'love thy neighbour', and 'do unto others as you would have them do unto you'. If nothing else, wasn't the whole message of the Good Book to live and let live? So how could the Crosses call themselves 'God's chosen' and still treat us the way they did? OK, we weren't their slaves any more, but Dad said the name had changed but nothing else. Dad didn't believe in the Good Book. Neither did Mum. They said it'd been written and translated by Crosses, so it was bound to be biased in their favour. But the truth was the truth, wasn't it? Noughts . . . Even the word was negative. Nothing. Nil. Zero. Nonentities. It wasn't a name we'd chosen for ourselves. It was a name we'd been given. But why?

'I DON'T UNDERSTAND . . .' The words erupted from me in an angry rush, heading for the sky and beyond.

I sat there for I don't know how long, furious thoughts darting around my head like bluebottles, my head aching, my chest hurting. Until I suddenly snapped out of it with a jolt. Someone was watching me. I turned sharply and a shock like static electricity zapped through my body. Sephy was further up the beach, standing perfectly still as the wind whipped around her, making her jacket and skirt billow out. We were about seven metres apart – or seven million light years, depending on how you looked at it. Then Sephy turned around and started to walk away.

'Sephy, wait.' I jumped to my feet and sprinted after her.

She carried on walking.

'Sephy, please. Wait.' I caught up with her and pulled her around to face me. She pulled away from my grasp like I was contaminated.

'Yes?'

'Don't be like that?' I pleaded.

'Like what?'

I glared at her. 'Aren't you going to stay?'

'I don't think so.'

'Why not?'

At first, I thought she wasn't going to answer.

'I don't stay where I'm not wanted.' Sephy turned around again. I ran to stand in front of her.

'I did it for your own good.'

A strange expression flitted across her face. 'Did you? Was it my good or your own you were thinking about?'

'Maybe a bit of both,' I admitted.

'Maybe a lot of one and none of the other,' Sephy contradicted.

'I'm sorry – OK?'

'So am I. I'll see you, Callum.' Sephy tried to walk around me again, but I moved directly into her path. Fear tore at my insides. If she left now, that would be the end. Funny how a few hours ago, that'd been exactly what I was wishing for.

'Sephy, wait!'

'For what?'

'H–how about if you and I go up to Celebration Wood this Saturday? We could have a picnic.'

Sephy's eyes lit up although she tried her best to hide it. I breathed an inward sigh of relief although I was careful not to show it.

'Celebration Wood . . ?'

'Yeah. Just you and me.'

'Are you sure you won't be ashamed to be seen with me?' Sephy asked.

'Don't be ridiculous.'

Sephy regarded me. 'What time shall I meet you?' she said at last.

'How about ten-thirty at the train station? I'll meet you on the platform.'

'OK.' Sephy turned away.

'Where're you going?' I asked.

'Home.'

'Why don't you stay a while?'

'I don't want to disturb you.'

'Sephy, get off it,' I snapped.

'Get off what? You're a snob, Callum. And I never realized it until today,' Sephy snapped back, just as angry. 'I thought you were better than that, above all that nonsense. But you're just like anyone else. "Crosses and noughts shouldn't be seen together. Crosses and noughts shouldn't be friends. Crosses and noughts shouldn't even live on the same planet together".'

'That's rubbish!' I fumed. 'I don't believe any of that, you know I don't.'

'Do I?' Sephy tilted her head to one side as she continued to scrutinize me. 'Well, if you're not a snob, you're a hypocrite, which is even worse. I'm OK to talk to as long as no-one can see us, as long as no-one knows.'

'Don't talk to me like that . . .'

'Why? Does the truth hurt?' asked Sephy. 'Which one is it, Callum? Are you a snob or a hypocrite?'

'Get lost, Sephy.'

'With pleasure.'

And this time, when Sephy walked away I didn't try to stop her. I just watched her leave.

fifteen. Sephy

There's a proverb which says, 'Be careful what you wish for, because you might get it!' I never really knew what that meant – until now. All those months helping Callum with his work so he'd pass the Heathcroft entrance exam. All those nights wishing on every blazing star that Callum would pass so we could go to the same school together, be in the same class together even. And now it'd all come true.

And it was horrible. Everything was going wrong.

I sighed, then sighed again. I couldn't hide in this toilet cubicle for ever. And who was I hiding from anyway? I was hiding from all those people who'd been pointing and whispering as I walked past them in the school corridor – but mainly from Callum. After what had happened the previous evening, I was afraid to face him. I was so afraid he wouldn't be my friend any more. So if I didn't see him, I could pretend that nothing between us had changed. But I couldn't sit on the toilet lid for ever. The bell rang for the end of break-time. I stood up and took a deep breath.

'OK . . . Here goes . . .' I muttered to myself.

I drew back the bolt and opened the cubicle door. I was just stepping out of the cubicle when it happened. Lola, Joanne and Dionne from Mrs Watson's class in the year above mine, pushed me back into the cubicle and crowded in after me.

'We want to have a word with you,' Lola began.

'And it has to be in here, does it?' I asked.

Joanne shoved me so hard, I had to put out my hand to stop myself from toppling over.

'We heard about what you did yesterday . . .' Joanne said.

'I did a lot of things yesterday.' My heart began to thump in my chest, but I wasn't about to give these three the satisfaction of knowing I was scared.

'In the food hall,' Joanne continued. 'You sat on the blankers table.'

'What's it to you?' I asked.

Lola slapped my face. Shocked, my hand flew to my stinging cheek. It wasn't that she'd slapped me particularly hard, it was just that no-one had ever hit me before. Not even Minerva, my sister.

'I don't care if your dad is God Almighty himself,' Lola told me. 'Stick to your own kind. If you sit with the blankers again, everyone in this school will treat you like one of them.'

'You need to wake up and check which side you're on,' added Joanne.

'Why d'you want to be around them anyway?' Dionne piped up. 'They smell funny and they eat peculiar foods and everyone knows that none of them are keen to make friends with soap and water.'

'What a load of rubbish!' The words tumbled out of my mouth before I could stop them. 'Callum has a wash every day and he doesn't smell. None of them do.'

Dionne, Jo and Lola all looked at each other.

Lola pushed me down so I ended up sitting down on the toilet lid looking up at them.

Any second now the door will open and someone will come in . . . Callum will come in and stop them. He'll pull them off me and sort them out. Any second now . . .

I tried to get to my feet but Lola pushed me down again and kept her hand on my shoulder, her fingers biting into my skin.

'We're only going to say this once,' Lola told me icily. 'Choose who your friends are very carefully. If you don't stay away from those blankers, you'll find you don't have a single friend left in this school.'

'Why d'you hate them so much?' I asked, bewildered. 'I bet none of you has even spoken to a nought before.'

'Of course we have,' Joanne piped up. 'I've spoken to blankers lots of times – when they serve us in shops and restaurants . . .'

'And there are some working in our own food hall . . .'

'Yeah, that's right. And besides we don't need to speak to them. We see them on the news practically every other day. Everyone knows they all belong to the Liberation Militia and all they do is cause trouble and commit crimes and stuff like that . . .'

I stared at them, astounded. They can't really be serious, I thought. But they could obviously read what I was thinking all over my face.

'The news doesn't lie,' Lola told me huffily.

'The news lies all the time. They tell us what they think we want to hear,' I said. Callum had told me that and at the time I didn't fully understand what he meant. But I did now.

'Who told you that?' Joanne's eyes narrowed. 'Your dad?'

'I bet it was one of her blanker friends,' Lola said with scorn. 'They're blank by name and blank by nature.'

'What d'you mean?' I asked.

'Blank, white faces with not a hint of colour in them. Blank minds which can't hold a single original thought. Blank, blank, blank,' Lola recited. 'That's why they serve us and not the other way around.'

'You ought to sell that horse manure worldwide. It's quality stuff. You'd make a fortune!' I sprung up. 'Noughts are people, just like us. You're the ones who are stupid and ignorant and . . .'

Lola gave me another slap around my face for that, but this time I was ready for it. Win or lose they weren't going to get away with it. I made a fist, drew it back and punched Lola in the stomach. She doubled over with an 'Oof!' I struck out with my elbows and my fists and my feet all at the same time, trying to make as many of my blows count before they could react. I had the element of surprise on my side, but not for long. Joanne and Lola each grabbed a flailing arm whilst Dionne straightened up to glare down at me. Dionne was the best fighter in her year and everyone knew it. But if she was expecting me to beg or cry, she'd have a long wait. She gave me a slow smile of satisfaction.

'Blanker-lover . . . You've had this coming for a long time,' she said softly.

And then she let me have it.

THE TURNING

sixteen. Callum

'Callum, wait.'

It was the end of another lousy school day where the most obvious lesson I'd learnt was how much the Crosses despised and resented us. I tried to tell myself that only a few Crosses had bashed into me; it wasn't all of them by any means, but that didn't help much. I mean, it wasn't exactly as if any of the other Crosses had tried to stop it either.

'Callum, hold on. WAIT!'

I turned and watched Shania race towards me, her school bag slapping up and down against her side.

'What's the matter?'

'Have you heard?' Shania puffed.

'Heard what?'

'About Sephy?'

'What about Sephy?'

'She's been beaten up,' Shania said with relish. 'She was found crying in the girls' toilets, the ones next to the library.'

My heart stopped. I swear it did. Just for a second, but it did stop. I stared at Shania. I couldn't have said a word then if my life had depended on it.

'Serve her right!' Shania said with glee. 'Coming over

to our table and acting like the big "I am".'

'She didn't. It wasn't like that.' Was that really my voice, so hollow and cold?

'Of course it was. She wanted to lord it over us, a little kid like that sitting at our table. Well, we didn't have to teach her a thing or two; her own kind did it for us.'

I shook my head. 'What're you talking about?'

'Just 'cause her dad's in the government, that Sephy Hadley thought she'd play Lady Magnanimous and sit with us. I bet she went and scrubbed her hand after I shook it.' Shania sniffed.

'W-where is she now?'

'They sent for her mum but no-one knew where she was so the chauffeur came to pick her up instead. Her mum was probably having her nails . . .'

I didn't bother to listen to any more. I walked away whilst Shania was in mid-sentence.

'Hey, Callum. Wait for me. D'you fancy an ice-cream at the . . ?'

I started to run until my legs were moving so quickly, my feet scarcely touched the ground. I ran and ran and I didn't stop until I was at the Hadley's. I pressed on the bell and kept my finger on it for the fifteen or twenty seconds it took for someone to open the front door.

'Yes?' Sarah Pike, Mrs Hadley's secretary, opened the door and glared at me with angry suspicion.

'I want to see Sephy – please.'

'I'm afraid the doctor said she's not to be disturbed.' Sarah tried to shut the door in my face. I stuck my foot in the door.

'I want to see Sephy. Is she all right?'

'She's badly bruised and very upset. The doctor has advised that she be kept at home for the rest of the week.'

'What happened? Why . . ?' I didn't get any further.

'Who is it, Sarah?' At the sound of Mrs Hadley's voice, Sarah almost broke my foot in her haste to shut the door. I pushed back and Sarah had to spring back to stop the door from walloping the side of her head. Mrs Hadley stopped on the stairs when she saw me. She recognized me at once.

'You're the McGregor boy, aren't you?'

'That's right, Mrs Hadley.' She didn't have to say that. She knew who I was all right.

'What can I do for you?' Her voice dripped with frost.

'I just heard what happened. I'd like to see Sephy, please.'

'Don't you think you've done enough.' At my blank expression, Mrs Hadley went on, 'I believe my daughter was beaten up for sitting at your lunch table yesterday. You must be so proud of yourself.'

I shook my head. The words wouldn't come. I tried to think of something, anything to say – but what?

'And as I understand it, you turned your back on her and told her to go away,' said Mrs Hadley. 'Is that right?'

Mrs Hadley didn't understand. No-one understood. Not even Sephy. 'Should I have let her sit at our table for longer then? I knew this was going to happen. That's why I didn't want her sitting with us. That's the only reason.'

'So you say.' Mrs Hadley turned around and started to go back up the stairs.

'If I'd welcomed her on to our table with open arms,

you'd have been the first to condemn her and me as well,' I shouted after her.

'Sarah, see this . . . boy out. And make sure he doesn't set foot in my house again.' Mrs Hadley issued her orders without even turning around. She just carried on walking up the stairs in her ladylike, unhurried fashion.

'Please let me see Sephy,' I begged her.

'You're going to have to go now,' Sarah told me apologetically.

'Please . . .'

'I'm sorry.' Sarah gently but firmly kicked my foot back and shut the door.

I rubbed a weary hand over my face which was dripping with perspiration. No-one understood. No-one.

Least of all – me.

seventeen. Sephy

There was absolutely nothing on the telly. What a choice! Silly cartoons, a brainless quiz game, the news or a war film. With a sigh I plumped for the news. I looked at the screen without really watching it. The newsreader finished the story of a banker who'd been sent to prison for fraud and was now talking about three nought robbers who'd smashed in the front of an exclusive jewellery store and made off on motorbikes with gems and jewellery and watches worth close to a million. Why was it that when noughts committed criminal acts, the fact that they were noughts was always pointed out? The banker was a Cross. The newsreader didn't even mention it.

'Who did it?'

I turned to face my sister, Minnie.

'Who was it, Sephy?' she repeated. 'Who beat you up? 'Cause whoever it was, I'll kill them.'

I shook my head, switching off the telly before turning away. *Go away, Minnie*, I thought.

Her outrage was comforting, if more than a little surprising. But all I wanted was to be left alone. There were about three eyelashes over each eye that didn't hurt. The rest of my body ached like blazes. And the last thing I wanted to do was open my sore, bruised lips to speak.

'How many of them were there?'

I held up three fingers.

'Would you recognize them if you saw them again?'

I shrugged.

'Would you?'

'I don't know. Maybe. Go away.' I was talking like my mouth was full of stones – and sharp, jagged ones at that.

'No-one thumps my sister and gets away with it. No-one.'

'Well, they did, and they have.'

'I'll find out who did this and when I do – they'll be really, *really* sorry.' And the look in my sister's eyes told me that she was serious. Deadly serious. For the first time since the three pigs had started laying into me, I felt almost good. Minnie had never been on my side like this before. It was almost – but not quite – worth it if it meant Minnie and I would grow closer . . .

'No-one touches a Hadley. No-one,' Minnie stormed. 'If they think they can get to you with no comeback, then it won't be long before someone tries it on with me. I won't have that.'

My tentative bubble of well-being was well and truly burst.

'Go away, Minnie. Now!' I shouted, the words slurred and blurred as they left my mouth. But even if the words were practically incomprehensible, the look on my face obviously wasn't. Minnie stood up and slammed out of my bedroom without another word.

I closed my eyes, trying to find something to focus on besides the bruises all over my body. Callum . . . Even thinking of him didn't bring me the comfort it usually did. No-one cared. Not about *me* – not about who I really was and what I thought and felt inside. What was it about me that made everyone turn away? Even my best friend had turned his back on me. I knew I was feeling well and truly sorry for myself, but I couldn't help it. I had no-one now. I had nothing.

Ruddy noughts . . . This was all their fault. If it hadn't been for them . . . And as for Lola and the others. I was going to get them, if it was the very last thing I did. I was going to get them – and good. I opened my eyes and stared out into nothing but hate. Minnie and I had a lot more in common than I'd ever imagined. And I wasn't sorry either.

eighteen. Callum

Maths! This was something I could do! Something in this world I could make sense of. Mrs Paxton had already taken me to one side and told me that I would probably be moving to the top Maths stream for my own year after the Crossmas holidays. Mrs Paxton was one of the few Cross teachers who didn't treat me like poo she wanted to scrape off her shoes. And she'd offered me extra lunchtime or early-morning tuition if I wanted it. I was on the last question of my sheet on simultaneous equations when a strange ripple swept through the classroom. I looked up.

Sephy.

My heart bounced about like it was pinging on elastic. Sephy was back. A whole five days without seeing her. A whole five days with no word from her. She looked OK. Maybe one cheek was a little puffy but otherwise just the same as before. Except for her eyes. She looked everywhere but directly at me.

'Welcome back, Persephone,' smiled Mrs Paxton.

'Thank you.' Sephy's smile was fleeting.

'Take a seat.' Already Mrs Paxton was turning back to the whiteboard.

Sephy looked around, as did everyone else. The only free seat was next to me. Sephy looked at me, then immediately looked away again. Her gaze swept around the room. I bent my head. Another ripple spread round the room. Mrs Paxton turned around.

'Is something wrong, Persephone?'

'There's nowhere for me to sit, Mrs Paxton,' Sephy said quietly.

'There's a seat next to Callum. Er . . . that's quite enough noise from the rest of you. Get on with your work,' Mrs Paxton called out against the rising tide of voices.

'But Mrs Bawden said I wasn't to sit with any of the noughts . . .'

'Mrs Bawden meant at lunch-time,' Mrs Paxton declared. 'There's only one spare seat left in the class and unless you'd rather sit on the floor, I suggest you use it.'

Dragging her feet, Sephy came and sat down next to me, drawing her chair away as she did so. And she didn't look at me once. Inside, my guts were melting.

'OK, who's finished the first equation?' Mrs Paxton said.

A few hands went up. Mine stayed down. I wanted to look at Sephy but I didn't dare.

Clasp my hands together. Bow my head. Close my eyes.

I know . . . I know noughts aren't really supposed to believe in you or pray to you because you're really the God of the Crosses, but please, please don't let anything or anyone come between me and Sephy. I'm begging you. Please. If you're up there.

nineteen. Sephy

Jeez! Time crawled like it was dragging a blue whale behind it. That sounded like something Callum would say. I smiled, but it died almost immediately. Something Callum would say – when he used to talk to me. When he used to be my friend. Mrs Paxton was blathering on about simultaneous equations like they were the best thing since computers were invented. And every word was flying zip-zap straight over my head! When was the bell going to sound? Come on . . . Come on . . . At last!

I didn't even take time to gather up my books. I just swept the whole lot into my school bag.

'Sephy, wait.'

I hovered in between sitting and standing, looking like a hen trying to hatch an egg. Slowly, I sat back down.

'How are you? Are you OK now?'

'Yes, thank you.' I still couldn't look at him. I went to stand up again. Callum's hand on my forearm stopped me. He immediately removed it. He couldn't even bear to touch me.

'I'm glad,' he whispered.

'Are you?' I turned to him. 'You could've fooled me.'

'What does that mean?'

My hands itched to knock the bewildered look off his

face. Just who did Callum think he was fooling? I glanced around the room. Others were listening intently even though they were trying to pretend they weren't. I lowered my voice so only Callum would hear what I was going to say. And I was determined it'd be the last thing I ever said to him.

'Don't pretend you were worried about me,' I told him. 'You didn't come to see me once. You didn't even send me a Get Well Soon card.'

Callum's face cleared. He leaned forward, also aware of our audience. 'I came to see you every day. Every single day,' he whispered. 'Your mum gave orders that I wasn't to be let in. I stood outside your gates every afternoon after school. Ask your mum . . . no, ask her secretary Sarah if you don't believe me.'

Silence.

'You came to see me?'

'Every day?'

'Really?'

'Ask Sarah . . .'

I didn't need to ask Sarah.

'Sephy, wild horses couldn't have kept me away.'

We regarded each other, our expressions equally sombre.

'I have to go now.' I stood up. We were attracting way too much attention. Callum stood up too.

'Look, meet me in our special place after dinner tonight. We can't talk here.'

I turned to walk away.

'Sephy, if you're not there, I'll understand,' Callum whispered.

twenty. Callum

She wasn't going to show. Why should she after every-thing she'd been through? After I'd let her down? Be truthful. What I did in the food hall wasn't for Sephy's own good or even my own. It was because I was scared. Scared of standing out, scared of being invisible. Scared of seeming too big, scared of being too small. Scared of being with Sephy, scared of being away from her. No jokes, no prevarications, no sarcasm, no lies. Just scared scared scared.

God only knew how tired I was of being afraid all the time. When was it going to stop?

'Hello, Callum.'

Sephy's voice behind me had me whipping around to face her.

'Hi. Hello. How are you?'

'Fine.' She turned to look out over the sea. 'Isn't it a lovely evening?'

'Is it? I hadn't noticed.' My gaze followed hers. She was right. It was beautiful. The sky was on fire and the waves broke relentlessly silver and white on the rocky beach. But I turned away from it. I had other things on my mind.

'Persephone, you have to believe me. I did come to visit you, I swear ...'

'I know you did.' Sephy smiled at me.

I frowned. 'You spoke to Sarah?'

'Didn't have to.' Sephy shrugged.

'I don't understand. Why didn't you talk to Sarah?'

'Because I believed you.'

I looked at Sephy carefully then and realized that the old Sephy, *my* Sephy, was back. Relief whirled through me on angel's wings. Such relief that my body actually shook with it.

'Besides, it sounds like just the sort of thing my mother would do,' Sephy sniffed.

I wanted to ask her what and where and how, but I couldn't. I didn't want to push my luck. We stood for a while, just being. But the need to explain by way of apology gnawed away at me, eating a bigger hole in my insides with each passing moment.

'I'm sorry I missed our trip to Celebration Park last Saturday,' Sephy sighed. 'I was looking forward to that.'

'Never mind. We've been there before and we'll go again.' I shrugged.

Pause.

'Sephy, do you remember the last time we went to Celebration Park?'

Sephy frowned. 'When we had our summer picnic?'

I nodded.

'Yeah, of course I remember. What about it?'

'What d'you remember?' I asked.

Sephy shrugged. 'We travelled up by train. We went to the park, found a secluded spot, had our picnic, played silly games, came home – the end of a lovely day.'

'Is that how you remember it?'

'Of course. Why?'

I studied Sephy, wondering if she was telling the truth. Or was it simply a case of the truth as she saw it, where her vision wasn't and never would be the same as mine. A lovely day . . . Was that really all she remembered? How strange. My memory of the day was slightly different . . .

THE PICNIC

twenty-one. Sephy

We had a wonderful day together, the day we went to Celebration Park. I'd lied and told Mother that I was spending the day with Helena's family. I knew Mother wouldn't check. Helena's family were almost as rich as us and in my mother's mind that meant that I couldn't be lying. I mean, why would I lie about spending the day with one of the richest but most boring girls in my class? In my class? In the northern hemisphere more like. Helena's family were 'like us' – as Mother was fond of saying. I could spend as much time with her as I liked.

So I'd lied. And met Callum at the train station instead. The park was wonderful. The whole day was just brilliant.

Except for the train journey . . .

twenty-two. Callum

I hadn't been sure if Sephy was going to show. But then I was never sure – and she *always* did turn up. And every time she did show, I'd tell myself, 'See! You should have more faith in her.' And then I'd answer myself, 'Next time. Next time I will.'

But next time always found me wondering if this would be the day that Sephy wouldn't be able to make it. Unfair as it was, I wondered each time if today was the day that Sephy was going to let me down.

'Penny for them.' Sephy's voice sounded in my ears at the exact same time as her bony, pointy fingers prodded me in my kidneys, making me jump.

'Jeez, Sephy. I do wish you wouldn't do that.'

'You love it!' Sephy's grin was huge as she walked around me.

'No, I don't actually.'

'I see you're in one of your sunshine moods.'

I took a deep breath and smiled. It wasn't me, it was my doubts snapping at her. And she was here now. She was here.

twenty-three. Sephy

One of these days, Callum's going to forget himself and actually look pleased to see me.

I just won't hold my breath whilst I'm waiting, that's all.

'There's your ticket.' I handed it over to Callum. I'd raided my bank account to get enough to buy two first-class tickets. I could've asked Mother for the money, or Sarah, but then they would've wanted to know exactly why I wanted it. No, this was much better. It made the day 'ours' somehow, because the money was mine and nothing to do with my mother or anyone else. I smiled. 'This day is going to be perfect.'

I could feel it in my water.

twenty-four. Callum

The train journey from hell, that's what it was. A journey which ruined the rest of the day as far as I was concerned. We were on our way to Celebration Park. There were only three more stops to go – when they got on. Police officers on a routine inspection. Two of them, boredom plastered over their faces.

'ID passes please. ID passes please.'

Sephy looked surprised. I wasn't. We both dug out our ID cards as they made their way up the first-class train carriage. I watched the cursory glances they gave the ID passes of all the Crosses in the carriage. I was the only nought. Would they stop and ask me lots of questions? Huh! Is pig poo smelly?

An officer of trim build and sporting a pencil-thin moustache stood right in front of me. He looked at me then took my ID pass without a word.

'Name?' he snapped out.

What's the matter? Can't you read?

'Callum McGregor.'

'Age?'

'Fifteen.'

Can't read numbers either, huh? That's too bad.

'Where are you going?'

None of your business.

'Celebration Park.'

'Why?'

To cut my toenails.

'Picnic.'

'Where d'you live?'

On the moon.

'Meadowview.' Meadowview by euphemistic name only. Rubbishshackview would've been more appropriate. The officer looked from my ID card to my face and back again. My thumbprint was on the card. Was he going to break out a magnifying glass and ask me to hold out my right hand so he could compare the imprint on the card to my print? It wouldn't've surprised me.

'You're a long way from home, boy.'

I bit down on the inside of my bottom lip, not trusting myself to speak. Both officious officials stood in front of me now. There was barely enough room to get a paper-clip between their legs and my knees. I sighed.

Ladies and gentlemen, for your delectation and delight, another performance of 'You're a nought and don't you ever forget it, blanker boy.'

'Let me see your ticket.'

I handed it over.

'Where did you get the money to buy this kind of ticket?'

I looked up at them, but didn't speak. What was there to say? They had the scent of blood in their nostrils and I didn't stand a chance, no matter what I said or did. So why bother?

'I asked you a question,' Moustaches reminded me.

As if I'd forgotten.

'Did you buy this ticket?' Moustache's accomplice asked.

The truth or prevarication? What was Sephy thinking? I couldn't see her. The no-brain brothers were in the way. If only I could see her face.

'I asked you a question, boy. Did you buy this ticket?'

'No, I didn't,' I replied.

'Come with us, please.'

Time to get my posterior pummelled. Time to get my derrière dealt with. Time to get my bum bounced right off the train.

How dare a nought sit in first class? It's outrageous. It's a scandal. It's disgusting. Disinfect that seat at once.

'Officer, he's with me. I bought the tickets.' Sephy was on her feet. 'Is there a problem?'

'And you are?'

'Persephone Hadley. My dad's the Home Office Minister, Kamal Hadley. Callum is my friend,' Sephy said firmly.

'He is?'

'Yes, he is.' Sephy's voice had a steely tone to it that I'd never heard before. Not from her anyway.

'I see,' said Moustaches.

'I can give you my father's private phone number. I'm sure he'll sort all this out in a moment. Or you'll be able to talk to Juno Ayelette, his personal secretary.'

Careful, Sephy. I'm tripping over all those names you're dropping.

'So is there a problem, Officer?' repeated Sephy.

Sniff! Sniff! Was I imagining things or was there the definite hint of a threat in the air? And I wasn't the only one to smell it. Moustaches handed back my ID pass.

'Would you like to see my ID as well?' Sephy held out her pass.

'That won't be necessary, Miss Hadley.' Moustaches almost bowed.

'I really don't mind.' Sephy thrust it under Moustaches' nose.

'That won't be necessary,' Moustaches repeated, looking straight at Sephy. He didn't even glance at her ID card.

Sephy sat back down again. 'Well, if you're sure.'

She turned to look out of the window. Moustaches was effectively dismissed. Sephy's mother would've been proud. Moustaches glared at me like it was my fault. He'd been humiliated, and by a child no less, and he wanted to take it out on someone. Sephy was off-limits, and now, so was I. He was burning to re-establish his authority but he couldn't. Not with us anyway. Moustaches and his colleague moved off down the carriage. Sephy turned to me and winked.

'You OK?' she asked.

'Fine,' I lied. 'Wasn't that fun?'

'Not so as you'd notice.' Sephy's gaze returned to the passing scenery. 'But I'm not going to let them or anyone else ruin my day. Celebration Park, here we come!'

I turned to look out of the window. I didn't want to look at Sephy. Not yet. I didn't want to blame her for the way the police treated me and every other nought I knew. I didn't want to hold her responsible for the way security guards and store detectives followed me around every time I entered a department store. And I'd stopped going into bookshops and toy shops and gift shops when I realized that no matter where I went in them, all eyes were upon me. After all, it was one of those well-known Cross-initiated facts that we noughts didn't pay for anything when there was the chance of stealing it instead. I didn't want to resent Sephy for the way my education was automatically assumed to be less important than hers. I didn't want to hate her because she was a Cross and different to me. So I carried on looking out of the window, pushing the knot of loathing deeper inside me. Deeper and deeper. The way I always did.

No, I didn't want to look at Sephy. Not yet. *Not yet.*

BREAKDOWN

twenty-five. Sephy

'You're thinking about those police officers on the train, aren't you?' I asked.

Callum didn't even bother to deny it. But then why should he? In his shoes, they would've annoyed me as well.

Annoyed . . . Come on, Sephy, be honest. You were a lot more than just 'annoyed'. And they weren't even picking on you.

'Why did you want me to remember our trip to Celebration Park?' I asked.

Callum shrugged, then smiled. 'Because it was a good day. A day we had all to ourselves once we got to the park.'

That wasn't true. He'd wanted to say something about our train journey to Celebration Park and my mother not letting him in to see me. Somehow, he felt one was connected with the other. I'm not completely stupid. I'm not as naïve as I used to be either. I'm finally growing up. I wanted Callum to tell me what he was really thinking, what he was really feeling, but part of me was afraid, I admit it. So I nodded noncommittally instead. It didn't matter what I said to Callum or anyone else; my main memory of that day was of the police officers and how they'd treated Callum and how I'd burned with resentment for him and how I'd been ashamed of them. And myself. I'd felt ashamed of myself a lot recently, and, if I'm honest, part of me resented Callum for it. I didn't want to feel guilty for just being, but that's how he was beginning to make me feel.

Suddenly all I had were questions. How come in all the early black-and-white films, the nought men were always ignorant drunkards or womanisers or both? And the women were always near-brainless servants? Noughts used to be our slaves but slavery was abolished a long time ago. Why were noughts never in the news unless it was bad news? Why couldn't I stop looking at each stranger I passed and wondering about their lives?

I'd started watching people – noughts and Crosses. Their faces, their body language, the way they spoke to their 'own' kind. The way they spoke to others who weren't the same. And there were so many differences, they swamped the similarities. Noughts relaxed around each other in a way they rarely did around Crosses. And Crosses were constantly on their guard when near noughts. Bags got clutched tighter, footsteps quickened, voices grew brisker and brusquer. All our lives criss-crossing but never really touching. A world full of strangers living with all that *fear*. Nothing was a given any more. Not my life. Not theirs. Nothing.

I can't remember when our lives had become so complicated. A few years ago . . . or maybe even a few months ago, life had been so easy. But the ache in my chest told me like words couldn't that those days were over.

'It *was* a good day, wasn't it?' Callum smiled.

It took me a second to catch up. 'Yes, it was.'

The truth, but not the whole truth and nothing but.

Say it, Callum. Whatever it is, say it. I can take it. At least, I'll try . . .

But he didn't. The silence dragged between us and the moment passed.

'It'll be winter soon,' I sighed.

Winter always made it harder for me to leave the house and meet Callum. Mother accepted my many trips to the beach because as far as she was concerned, I was a dreamer and the beach was where I did my dreaming. Unlike the town house, our country place had minimum security so I could pretty much come and go as I pleased – within reason. And going down to the beach in winter was beyond reason as far as Mother was concerned. To be honest, walking down to the beach in the dark wasn't my most favourite thing. Dusk and the air heavy with silence and long shadows made me . . . nervous.

'Who pummelled you?'

'Pardon?'

'Who beat you up?' Callum repeated.

'Everyone's asking me that,' I sighed. 'Can't we just let it rest?'

'You don't want them to get away with it, do you?'

''Course not. But there's not a lot I can do about it. Sure, I was going to tell the headmaster about them and get them expelled or put drawing-pins in their shoes or jump out at them when they were each alone. I was going to do all those things, but they're not worth it. It happened and now it's over, and I just want to forget about it.'

'Tell me who did it and then you can,' Callum said.

I frowned. 'You're not going to do anything stupid, are you?'

''Course not. I'd just like to know who did this to you.'

'Lola, Joanne and Dionne in Mrs Watson's class.' I said at last. 'But it's over now. OK?'

'OK.'

'Callum . . .'

'I was just curious. Besides, what could I do? They're Crosses and I'm a lowly nought.' Callum tugged on his forelock before bowing low.

'Stop it . . .'

'Stop what?'

'Callum, it's me. Sephy. I'm not your enemy.'

'I never said . . .'

I took Callum's face in my hands. 'Look at me, Callum.'

Only when I felt his whole body relax did I remove my hands from his face.

'Sorry,' he said at last.

'So am I,' I told him. 'So am I.'

twenty-six. Callum

When I got home, the house was in uproar – and for once
it had nothing to do with me. Lynette was having one of
her 'turns' and Jude was letting it wind him up, as usual.
When I stepped through the front door and heard him
shouting at her, I thought, 'Same old, same old!'

But I was wrong.

For the first time ever, Lynette was shouting back at
him. My sister and Jude were squaring up to each other,
with Dad in the middle of them, desperately trying to
keep them apart. And Jude's lip was bleeding . . .

'You're nothing but a git, and a vulgar git at that,'
Lynette screamed at the top of her lungs.

'At least I don't delude myself,' Jude shot back at her.

'And what's that supposed to mean?' asked Lynette.

'Jude, don't. Lynette, please.' Dad wasn't getting very
far.

I looked around for Mum, knowing as I did so that she
must be out. There was no way she'd have let things get
this far. Dad was there, being his usual feeble self.

'Dad, what's going on?' I asked, pulling on his arm.

Dad turned to shrug me off and that was all the space
Jude needed. He lashed out at Lynette. She hit him
straight back. Seconds later, Dad was between them,

again pushing them apart. I hadn't seen Lynette and Jude fight since before my sister's mind had shut down.

'Look at you! You think you're too good to even breathe the same air as us,' Jude hissed. 'Well, I've got news for you, sis. When the daggers look at you, they see someone who's just as white as me, for all your airs and graces.'

Daggers again. Every other sentence out of his mouth these days seemed to be 'ruddy daggers this' and 'ruddy daggers that'.

'I'm not like you. I'm ... I'm different. I'm brown. Look at my dark skin. Look ...'

Pushing past Dad, Jude grabbed Lynette's hands and pulled her to the cracked wall-mirror behind the sofa. He pulled her back against him, his cheek against her cheek. Lynette instantly tried to pull away but Jude wouldn't let her.

'See that!' Jude roared. 'You're the same as me. As white as me. Who d'you think you are? I'm sick and tired of being looked down on by you. You're the most pathetic person I know. If you hate what you are, do something about it. Just die or something! And if there is a God, you'll come back as one of those ruddy daggers you love so much, and then I can stop feeling guilty about hating you.'

Jude pushed Lynette away from him. She stumbled and fell, arms outstretched against the mirror.

'Dad, do something,' I shouted at him.

'Jude, that's enough. More than enough,' said Dad.

'It's not even close.' Jude turned on him, nostrils flaring. 'It's time she heard the truth from someone and who else is going to tell her? You? The spineless wonder? Mum won't say a word because Lynette is her favourite and the only person Callum cares about is his dagger friend Persephone. So who else is going to show Lynette how it really is?'

'And who are you to show anyone how it really is?' I challenged. 'You're always so sure you're right, aren't you? You make me sick. Lynette isn't the only one here who can't stand you.'

Jude stared at me. Without warning he let out a howl like an animal in pain and charged at me. I had time to do little more than take a step back before Jude's head smashed into my stomach and he knocked me to the ground, knocking all the wind out of me. Dazed, I wondered why his fists weren't laying into me until I realized that crashing to the ground had knocked the wind out of him as well. I pushed him up and backwards, drawing up my legs at the same time to knee him in the back. He groaned but didn't get off me. He drew back his fist. I crossed my arms in front of me, getting in his way so he couldn't hit my face.

The next thing I knew, Jude was being pulled off me.

'What the hell is the matter with you?' Dad shouted at Jude, his face almost puce with anger.

I leapt to my feet ready to do battle. Jude tried to turn back to me but Dad wasn't having it.

'Don't turn your back on me when I'm talking to you,' Dad raged.

'Oh, get lost, Dad.' Jude was already turning away from him.

Dad did something that stunned both of us. He spun Jude around and slapped him across the face. Mum was handy with a slipper whenever we gave her cheek but Dad had never so much as raised his voice to any of us before, let alone hit us.

'Don't you ever, *ever* talk to me like that again as long as you live.' Dad's voice was quiet and all the more menacing for it. 'I'm too old and I've had to contend with too much crap in my life to put up with disrespect in my own house. You have no idea what your sister's been through, so how dare you judge her?'

'W-what's she been through?' Jude sniffed, rubbing his face. It was like he was no longer seventeen years old but seven.

'Three years ago, Lynette and her boyfriend were attacked. By our own. Three or four nought men.' Dad's voice rasped with contempt. 'D'you remember when your mum lost her job so you had to leave school, and around the same time, Lynette was away from home for a while?'

'You said she'd gone to stay with Aunt Amanda.' The horrified words crept out of my mouth. 'You said Aunt Amanda was ill and Lynny had volunteered to look after her.'

'Your mum and I said what we had to say. Those men almost beat Lynette's boy to death and they beat Lynette so badly she was in hospital for over two weeks. She begged us not to tell you what had really happened.'

'I didn't know . . .' Jude breathed.

'And d'you know why Lynette was attacked?' Dad carried on as if Jude hadn't spoken. 'Because her boyfriend was a Cross. Your sister was beaten and l-left for dead because she was dating a Cross. And she didn't even tell us. She was afraid of what we'd all say. So is it any wonder that she can't bear to think of herself as one of us any more? Is it any wonder she can't even leave this house any more? Her mind hasn't been right since 'cause she's still hurting. So leave her alone. D'you hear me? D'YOU HEAR ME?'

Jude nodded. I nodded, even though Dad wasn't talking directly to me. I turned to look at Lynette. My sister, Lynette.

'Dad, she's bleeding.' I pointed.

Dad was by her side in a second. Lynette's palms were bleeding where she'd banged them into the cracked mirror. Lynette was staring down at the crimson patches on her hands as if she'd never seen her own blood before. She looked up to stare at her reflection in the mirror, as if she'd never seen her face before either.

'Where's Jed, Daddy?' Lynette whispered.

'Jed?' Dad looked stricken. 'Honey, Jed went away a long, long time ago. Let me clean up your hands.'

Lynette pulled her hands out of Dad's grasp. She turned them this way and that, before she slowly raised her head to look at Dad. That faraway, peaceful expression she always wore was dead and gone.

'Where am I?'

'At home.' Dad's smile was as fake as plastic. 'You're safe now. I'm here. I'll look after you.'

'Where's Jed?' Lynette looked around the room.

'Listen, honey, Jed and his family moved away a long time ago. They've gone. He's gone . . .'

'Not a long time ago . . . Yesterday . . . Last week . . .' Lynette's voice was barely above a whisper.

'Darling, it was years ago,' Dad persisted.

'I'm . . . I'm seventeen?'

'No, love. You're twenty. Twenty last April.' Dad swallowed hard. 'Come on, let me . . .'

'I thought I was seventeen. Eighteen . . .' Lynette buried her face in her hands, smearing her cheeks with blood. 'I don't know what I thought.'

'Lynette, please . . .'

'Lynette, I didn't know.' Jude stretched out his hand towards Lynette. She slapped it away.

'Keep your hands away from me,' she said with vehemence.

Jude's hand fell to his side. 'My nought hands, you mean?'

Silence. Lynette looked down at her hands again.

'Your hands are the same as mine. The same as *theirs*.' And Lynette turned and ran up to her room before any of us could say another word.

Dad and Jude regarded each other and, never before had I seen either of them look so . . . lost. Looking at them made my eyes begin to sting and water but I stared and didn't blink, waiting for the feeling to, if not die, then at least lessen to the extent where I wouldn't make a complete fool of myself. I turned so Dad and Jude wouldn't see my expression and caught sight of myself in the mirror.

My face was the reflection of Dad and Jude. My expression was theirs. My thoughts and feelings and hates and fears were all theirs, just as theirs were mine, and though I like to think I'm quick and on the ball, I hadn't even realized. Until now.

twenty-seven. Sephy

I stood in the doorway, watching Mother sip at her glass of white wine. I realized with a start that I had to think back a long way to remember seeing her without a glass of Chardonnay in her hand.

'Mother, can I have a party for my fourteenth birthday?'

Mother looked up from her magazine. That's all she ever did, read and drink, spend time in the gym or the pool and drink, shop and drink. And the only things she ever read were those glossy magazines with impossibly beautiful women on the cover and inside. Women with polished mahogany skin who looked like they'd never had a pimple in their lives – nor a decent meal either come to that. Women with teeth which shone like fresh snow in sunshine.

Something else struck me. I'd never seen a nought in any of my mother's magazines. Not one. No white or pink faces anywhere. In fact, there'd actually been something on the news at the beginning of the year when the first nought model was featured in one of the high fashion magazines. I couldn't see what all the fuss was about at the time. To be honest, I still couldn't.

'A party, eh?' Mother's voice brought me back to the

here and now. 'I don't see why not.'

And that was it! I was so surprised, I couldn't speak. I'd expected far more of an argument!

'After all, your teenage years don't last very long. You should make sure you enjoy every moment of them,' Mother smiled.

I wondered how many glasses of wine it had taken to bring on this good mood. And even though I knew I was being uncharitable, I still resented the glass in her hand for making Mother happy where my sister Minnie and I couldn't.

'Where would you like to have it?' Mother continued.

'Couldn't we have it here, in our house?'

'I suppose so.' Mother shrugged. 'We could take on some extra help for the day to help out. D'you want an entertainer or a magician?'

'Mother, I'll be fourteen.'

Mother raised her eyebrows. 'So?'

'So I'll have an entertainer!' I smiled.

Mother smiled back. One of our rare moments of connection.

'So how many guests d'you think you'll have?' asked Mother.

'Everyone in my class. And some of my cousins. And my other friends from ballet school and riding. About forty odd, I suppose.'

'Fine. Run along and talk to Sarah. Get her to sort it out.' Mother's nose was already back in her magazine.

I might've guessed Mother wouldn't want to get her hands dirty. And with a personal secretary and chauffeur and maids and servants, why should she? But I would've loved it if she'd been interested enough to even ask me what I wanted as a birthday present. Oh, I got birthday and Crossmas presents from Mother and Dad. It's just that they never bought them. They never even chose them. Mother's secretary Sarah had very good taste. But each one of her selected presents sat at the back of my wardrobe or at the back of a drawer or under my bed, unused. And no-one ever asked me if I liked my presents. No-one ever even asked why they never saw them again after the day they were given. The presents didn't matter. Maybe because I didn't either. Only one person cared if I lived or died. He'd done so much for me in the past and now it was my turn to do something for him.

I had a little surprise for Mother and everyone else. A surprise that would ensure that my birthday party was talked about and remembered for ages to come. I hugged my secret to me. I would get into awful trouble but I didn't care. I really didn't. I'd had enough of this attitude of 'live and let live – but not in my neighbourhood'. It wasn't that I thought I was better than everyone else or anything, but someone had to start somewhere, show them all what hypocrites they were.

So why not now?

And why not me?

twenty-eight. Callum

'Ryan, this isn't the way to change things. Alex Luther, for instance . . .'

'Alex Luther, my left buttock!'

'Ryan, language!' Mum told him off.

'Meggie, get real!' Dad said impatiently. 'Alex Luther is barely living, just about breathing proof that trying to change the way it is by using peaceful methods doesn't work. That blanker has been in prison more times than any eight prison governors I know.'

'Don't call him that,' Mum said furiously. 'It's bad enough when ignorant Crosses call us blankers without us calling ourselves by the same name.'

'We name it, we claim it,' said Dad.

'Nonsense! We use it, Crosses think they can too. Besides, that's not my point. Alex Luther is a great man . . .'

'I'm not saying he isn't, but the General is making more of an impact than Alex Luther.'

'And if my granny had wheels she'd be a wagon!' Mum snorted.

'What's your point? The General is . . .'

'A warmonger!' Mum's tone made it very clear what she thought of the General, the anonymous head of the

Liberation Militia. 'Killing and maiming always make more of an impression than peaceful protests and sit-ins and passive resistance, but that doesn't make it right.'

'The General . . .'

'I don't want to hear one more word about the General. You talk about him as if he were God's brother or something.'

'As head of the L.M., he's the next best thing . . .' Dad replied.

In response, Mum used a series of words I'd never heard her say before. I left her and Dad arguing about the General versus Alex Luther and crept down the stairs. Weren't the two of them ever going to sleep? I'd already been waiting half an hour for them to give up and shut up. How many times had they had the same argument? No-one ever won. It just made them mad at each other. What was the point?

I glanced up at the clock in our living room. Two-thirty in the morning. Earlier, Sephy had left her usual message that she wanted to talk to me urgently. We had a secret signal. She'd phone three times, each time letting the phone ring twice before calling off. That way she didn't have to talk to anyone or let my mum and dad or Jude know that she was phoning. Of course the phone ringing then stopping drove Mum and Dad nuts but the trick was not to do it too often. If I needed to get hold of her urgently, I did the same thing, although it was more tricky phoning during the day because one of Sephy's house servants usually picked it up pretty quickly. Once I heard the signal, I knew Sephy would phone me between two-thirty and three in the morning – whenever it was safe for her to sneak out of her room and use one of the phones in her house. When I phoned her with our signal, we'd usually meet in her rose garden around the same time of night. So here I was, hovering over our one and only phone like a vulture, waiting for the first brrrr to sound so that I could pick it up before it disturbed everyone else in the house.

Quarter to three came and went, as did three o'clock. At five past three I decided that Sephy was obviously not going to call me. Maybe it'd just been too difficult to get to a phone. I was heading up the stairs when the first trill sounded. I've never moved so fast. But even then a full brrrrr rang out before I could pick up the receiver.

'Callum?'

'Shush!' I whispered. I anxiously looked up the darkened stairs, listening intently for the sound of a bedroom door opening. Moments passed. Nothing.

'Sephy?'

'Sorry I'm late, but Mum came down ten minutes ago and she's only just gone back upstairs.'

'That's OK.'

Sephy's voice barely made it to a whisper, the same as mine. I was standing in our living room talking to my best friend in the pitch dark. It made it feel adventurous and illicit somehow.

'Callum . . .'

'I'm glad you phoned.' I got in first. 'What lessons do we have tomorrow?'

'Double Maths, then History. English, P.E., I.T. and Music in the afternoon. Where's your timetable?'

'I left it at school,' I replied softly. And then something

Sephy had said sunk in. 'Oh no, not History!'

'What's wrong with History?'

'Mr Jason,' I said grimly. 'He's going to use the lesson to stick it to me the way he always does.'

'What're you talking about?'

'If you don't know then I can't tell you,' I said.

Silence stretched between us.

'You still there, Sephy?'

'Yes, I'm still here,' Sephy replied.

'So why did you want to talk to me?' I asked. 'What was so urgent?'

'What're you doing on the twenty-seventh of September, that's two weeks on Saturday?'

I frowned into the darkness. 'Nothing as far as I know. Why?'

'D'you want to meet up for my birthday?'

'Sure. But your birthday's on the twenty-third, isn't it?'

'Yeah, but I'm having a birthday party at the house on the twenty-seventh. You can come round.'

I'd obviously misheard her. 'Round to your house?'

'That's right.'

'I see.'

'See what?'

'You want me to come round to your house?'

'That's what I said, isn't it?'

'I see.'

'Stop saying that.'

What else did she want me to say? Why was she inviting me to her house when her mum would take one look at me and have me carried from the building? What was the point? What was she up to?

'You're sure you want me to come over?' I asked.

'I'm positive. Will you?'

'Does your mum know you're inviting me?' At first I thought Sephy wasn't going to answer.

'No,' she said at last.

'But you are going to tell her?'

' 'Course.'

'Before or after I turn up at your party?'

'Don't be so ruddy smart!' Sephy snapped, which more than answered my question. 'So are you coming?'

'If you want me to,' I said slowly.

'I do. I'll give you all the details after school tomorrow. OK?'

'OK.'

'Bye, Callum.'

I put down the phone, getting it right first time now that my eyes were accustomed to the dark. Sephy wanted me at her birthday party, knowing it would cause nothing but trouble.

What was she up to? There was only one reason I could think of, but if I was right, it would mean that Sephy didn't think of me the way I thought of her. If I was right, it would prove that to Sephy I was a nought first and everything else came afterwards.

twenty-nine. Sephy

I couldn't get to sleep. I turned to the left, then turned to the right, I lay on my stomach, then lay on my back. I'd've stood on my head if it would've done any good. I just couldn't get to sleep. What had seemed like a good idea at the time was now growing fungus all over it and beginning to smell. I wanted Callum at my birthday party. Hell, if things were different, he'd be the first on my invite list.

But things weren't different.

I lay on my stomach and punched my pillow. Why was nothing ever simple?

thirty. Callum

'The purpose of today's history lesson is to show you all how famous scientists, inventors, arts and media celebrities and other people of note are all people, just like you and me.'

'But we already know that, sir,' Sade said. 'I mean, what else would they be?'

I'd been wondering that myself.

'When we think of great explorers or inventors or actors or anything else, it's sometimes very easy to think of them as "out there" – somewhere above and beyond us. I want all of you to realize that they're just like you and me, that we too can aspire to greatness. Anyone in this room can be a scientist or an astronaut or anything they want to be if they work hard and are determined.' Mr Jason looked directly at me when he said that, the familiar look of contempt on his face. What was it about me that rubbed him up the wrong way? Was it just my colour he despised so much? I couldn't help being white, any more than he could help being black. I mean, he wasn't even that black anyway. He was more beige than brown, and a very light beige at that, so he had nothing to gloat about. I smiled secretly to myself as I remembered the saying Dad was always spouting: '*If you're black, that's where it's at. If you're brown, stick around. If you're white, say goodnight.*'

When you got right down to it, Mr Jason had less cause to look down on me than Mrs Paxton who was dark, dark brown, but she was totally different. She treated me like a real person. She didn't see me as just a colour – first, last and always. I liked her. She was like an oasis in this scorching hot desert.

'Now then, can anyone tell me who invented automatic traffic signals which led to the traffic lights we use today, and he also invented a type of gas mask used by soldiers during World War One?'

Everyone sat silent. Slowly, I put my hand up. Mr Jason saw my hand but looked around for someone else to ask. Everyone else's hands stayed down.

'Yes, Callum?' Mr Jason asked reluctantly.

'Garrett Morgan, sir.'

'Correct. What about this one, class? Who pioneered blood banks?'

Once again, no hands went up – except mine.

'Yes, Callum?' Mr Jason's voice was now tinged with sarcasm.

'Dr Charles Drew,' I replied.

'And I suppose you also know who was the first person to perform open heart surgery?'

'Dr Daniel Hale Williams.'

'The first man to reach the North Pole?'

'Matthew Henson.'

All eyes were upon me now. Mr Jason gave me one of the filthiest looks I've every had in my life.

'The saying "The Real McCoy" is named after?'

'Elijah J. McCoy,' I replied.

Mr Jason drew himself up to his full height. 'Why don't I just sit down and you can teach this lesson?'

What did he want from me? He was asking questions that I knew the answers to. Was I supposed to just sit there and pretend to be ignorant?

'Can anyone tell me what all these scientists and pioneers really had in common?' Mr Jason asked.

A few more hands went up at that. Mr Jason wasn't the only one who was relieved – not that I was going to answer any more questions anyway.

'Yes, Harriet?' said Mr Jason.

'They're all men?' Harriet replied.

'Our examples are, but there have been plenty of women pioneers and scientists and achievers as well,' Mr Jason smiled. 'So can anyone tell me what else all the people mentioned have in common?'

There were a couple more guesses after that – like, 'They're all dead,' 'They all won the Nobel prize', 'They all made a lot of money from what they did' – but none of them were right. And it was so obvious. At last, I couldn't stand it any longer. My hand crept up.

'Ah! I wondered if we were going to hear from you again.' Mr Jason directed more of a smirk than a smile in my direction. 'So what's the answer then, Callum?'

'They were all Crosses,' I replied.

Mr Jason's smirk grew so wide I'm surprised he didn't swallow his ears. 'Correct! Well done!' He started moving round the class. My face burned pink then scarlet as every eye in the class turned on me.

'Throughout history, from the time our ancestors in Cafrique sailed to other lands and acquired knowledge of gunpowder, writing, weapon-making, the arts and so on, we have been the dominant race on Earth. We have been the explorers, the ones to move entire backward civilizations onwards . . .'

I couldn't let him get away with that. My hand shot up again.

'Yes, Callum?'

'Sir, I read somewhere that noughts have made a significant contribution to the way we live today too . . .'

'Oh yes? Like how?' Mr Jason folded his arms across his chest as he waited for my answer.

'Well, for example, Matthew Henson was *joint* first to the North Pole. Robert E. Peary was with him.'

'Robert who?'

'Robert Peary. He was co-discoverer of the geographic North Pole.'

'How come I've never heard of him then?' Mr Jason challenged.

'Because all the history books are written by Crosses and you never write about anyone else except your own. Noughts have done lots of significant things, but I bet no-one in this class knows . . .'

'That's quite enough.' Mr Jason cut me off in mid-tirade.

'But, sir . . .'

'How dare you spread these pathetic lies about nought scientists and inventors?' Mr Jason's hands were clenched at his side now and he glared at me furiously.

'They're not lies,' I protested.

'Who's been filling your head with all this nonsense?'

'It's not nonsense. My dad told me.'

'And where did your dad get it from?'

'I . . . I . . .' My voice trailed away.

'Exactly!' said Mr Jason. 'Now go and stand outside the headmaster's room. And don't come back into this room until you've got all that nonsense out of your head and you're ready to accept my teaching.'

I grabbed my bag and jumped to my feet, knocking my chair over in the process. I turned and glared at Sephy. Her gaze dropped away from mine almost at once. Not bothering to pick up my chair, I slammed out of the room. I knew that little act of defiance would probably get me in even more trouble. But as I marched down the corridor towards Mr Costa's room, I was so livid I was shaking. It wasn't nonsense. It wasn't lies. It was the truth. Centuries ago, Crosses had moved across northern and eastern Pangaea from the south, acquiring along the way the know-how to make the guns and weapons that made everyone else bow down to them. But that didn't mean that what they did was right. We noughts had been their slaves for so long, and even though slavery had been formally abolished over half a century ago, I didn't see that we were much better off. We were only just beginning to be let into their schools. The number of noughts in positions of authority in the country could be counted on the fingers of one hand – without including the thumb! It wasn't right. *It wasn't fair.*

And though I knew that nowhere was it written that life was meant to be fair, it still made my blood bubble to think about it. Why should I feel grateful to any of them just because they'd let me into one of their precious schools? What was the point? Maybe Mum and Jude were right. Maybe this was a complete waste of my time?

My steps slowed as I approached the school secretary's room. Was I meant to stand in the corridor or go into the secretary's office and wait outside the headmaster's door. After dithering about for a few moments, I decided that Mr Jason probably wanted me to stand where I could get into the maximum amount of trouble. That meant standing right outside Mr Costa's door. I peered in through the glass in the secretary's door. She wasn't there. That was something at any rate. I went in, carefully shutting the door behind me. I reckoned I'd slammed enough doors that morning. I'd taken two steps into the office when quiet but angry voices floated out past Mr Costa's slightly ajar door to meet me.

'And I'm telling you that something needs to be done.' It was Mrs Paxton's voice. 'How much longer are you going to let this situation continue?'

'If the blankers are finding it tough here, then maybe they should go elsewhere,' came Mr Costa's reply.

I froze, not even breathing as I waited to hear what was said next.

'Mr Costa, the *noughts*,' Mrs Paxton stressed the word, 'are being constantly picked on. It's only a matter of time before one of them retaliates.'

'Not in my school, they won't,' Mr Costa snapped back.

'All I'm saying is, it's up to us to lead from the front. If we teachers make it clear that such behaviour won't be tolerated, then our students will have to follow our example.'

'Mrs Paxton, are you really that naïve? Noughts are treated in this school exactly the same way as they're treated outside . . .'

'Then it's up to us to make this school a haven, a sanctuary for Crosses and noughts. A place where we provide equality of education, equality of opportunity and equality of treatment.'

'Oh, really. You're making mountains out of gnat bites,' Mr Costa dismissed.

'Better to over-estimate the problems than ignore them altogether.' Mrs Paxton was annoyed and making no attempts to hide it.

'Enough! No-one wanted them here in the first place.'

'I did,' Mrs Paxton shot back. 'And so did some of the other teachers and the government and . . .'

'The government did as the Pangaean Economic Community ordered. They were afraid of sanctions and that was the only reason they did it.'

'The reason doesn't matter. The point is, they did it. We'll reap what we sow, you mark my words. The noughts are here now and if we don't act soon, this whole scheme will fail.' Pause. 'Or is that the point?'

Mrs Paxton was fighting a losing battle and she didn't even know it. I couldn't bear to listen to any more. I turned and tiptoed out, careful to shut the door behind me without making a sound. Less than a minute later, Mrs Paxton came striding out of the secretary's office. She stopped abruptly when she saw me.

'Callum, what're you doing out here?' Mrs Paxton frowned. 'Callum?'

'Mr Jason sent me out of the class, miss.'

'Why?'

I bit my lip. My gaze dropped away from hers.

'Why, Callum?'

'We . . . we had an argument . . .'

Mrs Paxton waited for me to continue.

'. . . about history.'

'Oh yes?'

'It's not fair, Mrs Paxton. I've read thousands of history books and not one of them mentions us noughts, except to say how the Crosses fought against us and won. I thought history was supposed to be the truth.'

'Ah!' Mrs Paxton nodded. 'And you expressed your views to Mr Jason?'

I nodded.

'I see.'

'Callum, sometimes it's better to leave certain things unsaid . . .'

'But that's what everyone does . . Nearly everyone does,' I amended. 'And things that go unsaid soon get forgotten. That's why us noughts aren't in any of the history books and we never will be unless we write them ourselves. Mr Jason didn't like it when I said that us noughts have done things too. But then Mr Jason doesn't like anything I do or say. He hates me.'

'Nonsense. Mr Jason just doesn't want to see you fail. And being hard on you is his way of trying to . . .' Mrs Paxton sought for the appropriate thing to say, 'to toughen you up.'

'Yeah, right.' I didn't even try to keep the derisive scepticism out of my voice.

Mrs Paxton placed a hand under my chin to raise my head so that I had to look directly at her. 'Callum, a change of policy at this school and all schools was long overdue. Believe me, Mr Jason doesn't want to see you fail any more than I do. We don't want to see any of the noughts fail.'

'And he told you this, did he?'

Mrs Paxton's hand dropped to her side. 'He didn't have to.'

'Yeah, right.' I dismissed immediately.

Mrs Paxton looked thoughtful for a few moments. 'Callum, I'm going to tell you something in the strictest confidence. I'm going to trust you. D'you understand?'

I didn't, but I nodded anyway.

'Mr Jason isn't against you. And d'you know why?'

'No . . .'

'Because his mother was a nought.'

thirty-one. Sephy

'Don't treat me like this, Kamal. I won't stand for it.'

'Then go and have another bottle or eight of wine. That's about all you're good for these days.'

I winced at Dad's tone of voice, so utterly contemptuous and he made no attempt to hide or disguise it. Minnie sat on the stair above mine as we listened to one of our parents' rare arguments. Rare because Dad was never at home. Rare because on the very few occasions that Dad *was* home, Mother was usually too out of it to notice or too refined to start an argument. We'd just finished our dinner in the family room and both Minnie and I had been sent upstairs by Mother to do our homework. That alone was enough to tip us off that something was going on. Mother never told us to do our homework unless she wanted to get us out of the way.

'So you're not even going to deny it?' Mother asked.

'Why should I? It's about time you and I faced the truth. Past time in fact.'

'Kamal, what've I done to deserve this? I've always

been a good wife to you. A good mother to our children.'

'Oh yes,' Dad agreed. And if possible his tone grew even more sneering. 'You've been an excellent mother to *all* my children.'

I turned to give my sister a puzzled look. She was looking straight ahead. What did Dad mean by that?

'I did my best.' Mother sounded like she was starting to cry.

'Your best? Your best isn't up to much.'

'Was I supposed to let you bring your bastard into our house?' Mother shouted.

'Oh no! The great Jasmine Adeyebe-Hadley bring up her husband's child as her own? That would never do. I mean, God forbid that you should chip a nail or dirty one of your designer gowns looking after my son.'

'I should have let you bring your son into our house, I know that now,' Mother said. 'But when you told me, I was hurt. I made a mistake.'

'So did I, when I married you,' Dad shot back. 'You wanted to punish me for my son who was born before you and I ever met and that's what you spent years doing. Don't blame me if I've finally decided enough is enough.'

Dad had a son? Minnie and I had a *brother*. I turned to my sister. She was looking at me, her eyes narrowed. We had a brother . . .

'Kamal, I want . . . I was hoping that maybe we could start again,' Mother began hesitantly. 'Just you and me. We could go away somewhere and . . .

'Oh, Jasmine, don't be ridiculous,' Dad interrupted. 'It's over. Just accept the fact. Besides, look at you . . . You've really let yourself go.'

I gasped at that – and I wasn't the only one.

'You're a cruel man,' Mother cried.

'And you're a drunk,' said Dad. 'And worse than that, you're a boring drunk.'

Minnie stood up and headed upstairs. I didn't blame her. I knew I should do the same. Stop listening. Walk away. Just go, before I ended up hating both my parents – but I stayed put. Like a fool, I stayed put.

'If it wasn't for me you wouldn't be Deputy Prime Minister. You'd be nowhere.' Mother's voice trembled as she spoke.

'Oh please! Don't pretend you did it for me because we both know that you did it for yourself, then the kids, then our neighbours and your friends. What I wanted, what I *needed*, came a long way down your list.'

'I didn't hear you protest when my parties got you known by all the right people, started you moving in all the right circles.'

'No, I didn't complain,' Dad admitted. 'But you got just as much out of it as I did.'

'And now you're going to walk out on me and your children for that . . . that . . .' Mother's voice dripped with bitterness.

'Her name is Grace,' Dad interrupted harshly. 'And I'm not walking out on you now. I left a long time ago; you just refused to believe it. You and the children will get everything you need. You'll be well provided for. And I want regular access to my girls. I love them too much to let you poison their minds against me. But after the next election, I'm going to make it officially known that you and I are no longer together.'

146

'You won't get away with this. I'll . . . I'll divorce you,' Mother threatened. 'I'll tell all the newspapers . . .'

'You'll divorce me?' Dad actually laughed. I flinched, sticking my fingers in my ears, only to take them out again at once. 'Jasmine, the day you divorce me will be the happiest day of my life.'

'You can't afford the scandal of a divorce in your position. A position I helped you to get.'

'If I had a penny for every time you've said that, I'd be the richest man on the planet,' Dad replied.

Dad's footsteps sounded on the parquet floor. I jumped to my feet and darted upstairs, not stopping until I'd reached my bedroom. I leaned against the door and closed my eyes. I didn't cry. I wasn't even close to crying. I grabbed my jacket from over my chair and ran downstairs, heading out of the door before anyone could stop me. I needed to clear my head and our house wasn't the place to do it. I ran and ran, through the rose garden, across the wasteland, towards the beach. Maybe if I ran fast enough my thoughts would click into some sort of order.

Dad had found someone else. He was leaving. And I had an older brother, older than Minnie. Nothing in my life was a fact. There was nothing to cling on to, nothing to anchor myself to. I just whirled around and around and . . .

Callum . . .

Callum was already there – in our place. In our space. I ran along the beach the moment I saw him and plonked myself down beside him. Callum put his arm around my shoulders. We sat in silence, whilst I tried to straighten out my thoughts. I looked at his face which was in profile. But

I could see enough to realize there was something bothering him, something that was making him sad.

'I'm sorry about Mr Jason,' I said at last. 'I finally got what you were talking about in today's lesson.'

'Don't apologize for him,' Callum frowned. 'It's not your place to apologize for every moronic cretin in the world.'

'Only the moronic Cross cretins?' I asked with a brief smile.

'Not even those.' Callum smiled back. 'I'll tell you what, you don't apologize for every Cross who's an idiot and I won't apologize for every nought who's the same. Agreed?'

'It's a deal.' Callum and I shook hands.

Come on! Best to get it over with! I told myself. Taking a deep breath, I said, 'Callum, I've got a confession to make. About my birthday party.'

He became very still the moment the words left my mouth. 'Oh yes?' he prompted, his arm dropping away from my shoulders.

'It's just that . . . I wanted you there, but for mostly the wrong reasons.'

'Which were?'

'I wanted to upset Mum and my so-called friends,' I told him. 'I wanted to hit back at all of them.'

'I see.'

'No, you don't,' I said. 'I'm telling you now because I'm taking back my invite.'

'Why?'

'Because . . . because,' I said, hoping Callum would get my ridiculous attempt at an explanation.

He secret-smiled at me, saying dryly. 'Thank you.'

'You're welcome! We'll do something else for my birthday – OK?'

'OK.'

'Growing up is hard work,' I sighed again.

'And it's going to get harder,' Callum warned, his voice suddenly grim.

I looked at him and opened my mouth to ask what he meant. But I closed my mouth without saying a word. I was too afraid of the answer.

thirty-two. Callum

It was late at night, past eleven, as I lay on top of my bed, trying to make sense of what Mrs Paxton had told me. *Mr Jason's mother was a nought* . . . I was missing something somewhere. Mrs Paxton had been so sure that Mr Jason was on my side and yet every time he looked at me . . .

He hated me.

I was sure of it. I was *almost* sure of it. Maybe I was just being paranoid. Maybe I was just being a coward, assuming that every Cross was my enemy so that if it turned out to be the case I could say 'I told you so!' But Mrs Paxton wasn't my enemy. And Sephy certainly wasn't. I rubbed my hands over my forehead. My thoughts were spinning round so much they were giving me a splitting headache. I wasn't sure of anything any more.

Someone knocked on my door. I sat up.

'Who is it?'

'Lynny,' said my sister. 'Can I come in?'

' 'Course.'

Lynette came into the room, quietly shutting the door behind her.

'You OK?' I asked.

'No,' Lynny shook her head. 'You?'

'The same. But I'll survive.'

Lynny gave me a strange look at that. But then she smiled and the peculiar expression on her face vanished without trace. Since Lynny's and Jude's fight, neither of them had spoken to the other. Not one word. My sister sat down at the foot of my bed. She started picking at the loose threads on my duvet cover. I wasn't sure what to say, so I said nothing.

'How's school?'

'It's OK. I'm learning a lot.' And wasn't that the truth!

Lynny must've picked up on my tone of voice because she looked up and smiled dryly. 'Tough going, huh?'

'The toughest.'

'Reckon you'll stick with it?'

'I'm in now. Wild horses couldn't drag me out,' I said belligerently.

Lynny smiled, her face full of admiration. 'How d'you do it, Callum?'

'Do what?'

'Keep going?'

I shrugged. 'I don't know.'

'Yes, you do,' Lynny challenged, which kind of made me start.

I smiled at her total conviction that I knew what I was doing. 'I guess, I keep going because I know what I want.'

'Which is?'

'To be someone. To make a difference.'

Lynny looked at me and frowned. 'What if you can't do both?'

'Huh?'

'If you can only have one, which one means more to you? Being someone or making a difference?'

My smile was broad as I looked at her. I couldn't help it.

'What's so funny?' Lynny asked.

'Nothing. It's just that you and me talking like this, it reminds me of the old days,' I told her. 'We used to have debates about anything and everything. I've missed our talks.'

Lynny smiled back at me, her smile waning as she said, 'You haven't answered my question, and don't try to wriggle out of it! Which one means more – being someone or making a difference?'

'I don't know. Being someone, I guess. Having a large house and money in the bank and not having to work and being respected wherever I go. When I'm educated and I've got my own business, there won't be a single person in the world who'll be able to look down on me – nought or Cross.'

Lynny considered me carefully. 'Being someone, eh? I would've put money on you choosing the other one!'

'Well, what's the point of making a difference if you've

got nothing to show for it, if there's not even any money in it?' I asked.

Lynny shrugged. She had a strange expression on her face, like she was sad for me.

'What about you? What keeps you going?' I asked.

Lynette smiled, a strange, mysterious smile as her thoughts turned in on themselves and I was totally excluded.

'Lynny?' I prompted, uncertainly.

My sister stood up and headed for the door. I thought that was the end of the conversation but she turned to me, just before she left the room.

'D'you wanna know what kept me going, Cal?' Lynny sighed. 'Being bonkers! I miss being insane . . .'

'Lynny, don't say that.' I leapt up. 'You were never insane.'

'No? Then why do I feel so empty now. I know I was living in a fantasy world before, but at least . . . at least I was somewhere. Now I'm nowhere.'

'That's not true . . .'

'Isn't it?'

'Lynny, you are all right, aren't you?' But even as I asked the question, I knew the answer.

'I'm fine. I just need to sort myself out.' Lynny sighed deeply. 'Callum, doesn't any of this ever strike you as – pointless?'

'What d'you mean?'

'Just what I said. Our being here – it works from the Crosses' point of view, but what about our own? Because if this is all there is, we might as well be robots. We might as well not exist at all.'

'Things will get better, Lynny,' I tried.

'D'you really believe that?'

'Yeah. I mean, I'm at Heathcroft High, aren't I? A few years ago that would've been impossible. Unthinkable.'

'But none of their universities will take you.'

I shook my head. 'You don't know that. By the time I'm ready to leave school they might.'

'And then what?'

'I'll get a good job. And I'll be on my way up.'

'Doing what?'

My frown deepened as I glared at my sister. 'You sound just like Mum.'

'Sorry. I didn't mean to.' Lynny turned around to leave the room. 'Just remember, Callum,' she said, her back towards me, 'when you're floating up and up in your bubble, that bubbles have a habit of bursting. The higher you climb, the further you have to fall.'

Lynette left the room, without bothering to shut my door. I stood up and walked over to do it myself, still annoyed with her. Of all people my sister should not just understand my dreams but cheer them. Let down didn't even begin to describe how I felt. I was just about to slam my door shut when I caught sight of Lynny's face as she closed her own bedroom door behind her. She was hurting inside. Hurting badly and close to tears. I stepped out onto the landing, wincing as my bare feet struck a nail not flush with the greying, warped floorboards. By the time I'd rubbed my toe and looked up again, Lynny had gone.

thirty-three. Sephy

'Minnie, can I come in?'

'If you must,' my sister said grudgingly.

I walked into her room, only to stop short when I saw my sister's face. She'd been *crying*. I'd never seen my sister cry before. Ever.

'Minnie, are you . . ?' I didn't finish my question. I already knew the answer and besides, asking it would only have cheesed her off.

'How many times do I have to tell you not to call me Minnie?' my sister snapped. 'My name is Minerva. M-I-N-E-R-V-A! Minerva!'

'Yes, Minnie,' I said.

Minnie looked at me and smiled reluctantly. 'What d'you want, frog face?' she asked.

I sat down on the chair in front of her dressing table. 'I think Mother and Dad are going to get a divorce.'

'That won't happen,' said Minnie.

'How can you be so sure?'

' 'Cause Dad's been threatening Mother with a divorce for years – and it hasn't happened yet.' Minnie shrugged.

I thought for a moment. 'But it was Mother who threatened it this time, not Dad.'

Minnie's head snapped up at that. She stared at me.

'D'you think they might then?' I whispered.

Minnie shrugged and looked away again.

'And what about our brother?' I asked.

'He's not our brother. He's just our dad's son.' Minnie stood up and walked over to her window. 'And what about him?'

'How do we find him?'

'We don't.' Minnie looked at me like I'd lost my marbles.

'But don't you want to know who he is? What he looks like? Aren't you curious?'

'Of course not. I wasn't curious about him three years ago when I found out about him, so why should I be curious now?'

'Three years ago!' I said, aghast. 'You knew we had a brother three years ago? Why didn't you tell me?'

'Why would I do that?' Minnie frowned. 'What good would that have done? Dad had a fling before he met Mother and had a son. That's all I know or want to know.'

I stared at my sister. It was like we were having two different conversations. She couldn't see my point of view and I certainly couldn't see hers.

'Minnie, don't you even want to know our brother's name?'

'Stop calling him our brother. And no, I don't.'

'Well, I do. I'm going to ask Dad and . . .'

Minnie flew across the room and pulled me off my chair in about two seconds flat. 'You'll do no such thing, d'you hear?'

'But Minnie . . .'

'How d'you think Mother'd feel if you started asking about Dad's son? She's unhappy enough without you making it worse.'

'OK! OK!' Minnie let go of my arms. I immediately rubbed them to try to get the circulation going again.

'Is that why she's so unhappy? Because of . . . Dad's son?' I asked.

Minnie regarded me, considering her answer very carefully before she spoke. 'That's part of the reason.'

'And the other part?'

'She had an affair a while ago and . . .'

'*Mother?*' My eyes were open so wide they must surely plop onto my cheeks. 'Mother had an affair?'

'Don't sound so surprised.' Minnie smiled at my expression. 'I think she only did it to make Dad sit up and take a bit more notice.'

'Did it work?'

'What d'you think?' Minnie said, scornfully. 'If anything it drove them further apart. And then Mum felt even more alone. She hasn't got any friends, you know.'

'What're you talking about? She's got friends dripping out of cupboards,' I scoffed.

'Not close ones. Not real friends that she can tell anything and everything to.'

'She's probably driven them all away with her funny moods,' I sniffed. 'One moment she's pushing me away or acting as if I don't exist and the next she wants to know about every minute of my day. If I didn't have to live in the same house as her I wouldn't put up with her either.'

'She's lonely,' said Minnie.

'Why doesn't she just go out and make some new friends then?' I asked.

Minnie smiled, one of her superior smiles that instantly ruffled my feathers. 'You're very young, Sephy.'

'Don't be patronizing,' I fumed.

'I'm not. I'm just stating a fact. And d'you know what I wish for you?'

'What?' I asked, expecting something unpleasant.

'That you never grow older.'

thirty-four.   Callum

Well, Callum, this is it. Are you going to do it or not? Are you going to stand up for yourself? You've had more than half a term of this . . . this crap. Speak. Say something. Don't be such a wimp. DO IT!

'Excuse me, Mr Jason. May I have a word with you?'

'As long as it's a short, fast word,' Mr Jason replied without bothering to look up from fastening his bag.

I looked around, waiting for the last person to leave the classroom.

'Well?' Mr Jason snapped, as he headed for the door.

'Why . . . why did I get a C-minus for my mid-term grade when I got twenty-seven marks out of thirty in your last test and came first?'

'Your grade reflects other things besides how well you did in the test.'

'Like what?'

'Like your coursework and homework to date, not to mention your attitude.'

'I've never got less than nine out of ten for my homework.'

Mr Jason stopped in his tracks, just beside the door. I finally had his full attention. 'Are you questioning my judgement? Because that's exactly what I mean when I say your attitude leaves a lot to be desired.'

'I'd just like to know your reasons, that's all.'

'I gave you the grade you deserved – no more, no less.'

'Adotey got a B when my work so far this term has been getting better marks than his and I got five more in the test.'

'If you don't like the way I've graded you, you can always appeal,' Mr Jason challenged.

But I was ready for that one. 'OK, I will.'

I went to move past him but he slammed the door shut before I could leave.

'I see you've chosen this particular time to make a fool of yourself, McGregor. Your grade will not be altered, I can promise you that.'

I regarded him, Mrs Paxton's words still ringing in my ears.

'Why d'you hate me so much?' My words tumbled out in angry frustration. 'If anything you should be on my side.'

Mr Jason drew himself up to his full height, his eyes giving me frostbite. 'What're you talking about, boy?'

'You're half-nought so I don't understand . . .'

Mr Jason's bag dropped to the floor, forgotten. He gripped my shoulders and started shaking me. 'Who told you that . . . that lie?'

'I . . . no-one. I just thought . . . You're lighter than Mrs Paxton and all the others so I just thought . . .'

Mr Jason released me as suddenly as he'd grabbed me. 'How dare you? *How dare you?* Who else have you said this to?'

'No-one.'

'No-one?'

'I swear.'

'Every time I look at you, I thank God I'm not one of you. D'you hear me? I thank God.'

'Y-yes, sir . . .'

Mr Jason picked up his bag and marched out of the classroom. I didn't realize it until he was out of sight, but I was shaking. Actually, physically shaking.

But at least that question was answered.

thirty-five. Sephy

Mr Jason strode down the corridor with a face like a cold rice pudding. The man was *seriously* ticked off. I only noticed because I was looking at the faces of every male that passed me, wondering if this boy looked like my brother, or if that boy had the same eyes, the same nose, the same mouth as my brother. I'd been at it all day. I'd been at it ever since I'd heard I had a brother. *My brother.* I turned the corner and saw Callum standing in the door-way of our classroom. I was ready to tell him my news now. Quickly checking up and down the corridor to make sure we were alone, I said, 'Callum, guess what? You'll never believe what I found out from eavesdropping on Mother and Dad . . .'

'Not now, Sephy.'

'But Callum, this is important . . .'

'Sephy, I said not now. Can't you think of anyone else but yourself for a change?' Callum snapped.

And he strode off, in the opposite direction to Mr Jason. But not before I realized that the expression on his face mirrored that of Mr Jason. Exactly.

thirty-six. Callum

We were all sitting down for dinner and not one of us spoke. No-one had anything to say. Lynny kept her head bowed and concentrated on her plate of sausages and chips. Jude had the same sour, sullen look on his face that he'd worn since he and Lynny had had their fight. Dad's face was sad. Mum threw down her knife and fork, the clatter making us all jump.

'Goodness me! What's the matter with everyone?'

'Meggie . . .'

'Don't Meggie me.' Mum frowned at Dad. 'There's been a funny atmosphere in this house for a while now. What's going on?'

'I'm going for a walk.' Lynny sprang out of her chair.

'Lynny?' Mum wasn't the only one who was surprised. This was the first time Lynny had shown the slightest interest in leaving the house by herself since I don't know when.

'It's OK, Mum. I'll only be gone for a little while.'

'Where're you going?' asked Mum.

Lynny smiled gently. 'Mum, I'm a big girl now. Stop worrying.'

'Want some company?' I asked.

Lynny shook her head. She turned abruptly and headed upstairs.

'I thought you were going for a walk?' Mum called after her.

'I want to do something first,' Lynny called back.

I carried on eating my dinner for the want of something better to do.

'I'm going now. I'll see you all later,' said Lynny, when she finally came downstairs again.

And she grabbed her wraparound jacket and headed out of the door with all of us watching her. Lynny turned round. Mum half stood up, but then she sat down again, never taking her eyes off my sister.

'Bye, everyone,' Lynny smiled softly, the saddest, loneliest smile I've ever seen. And then she shut the door behind her and was gone.

'Ryan, I want to know exactly what's going on – and don't say it's nothing. That won't work this time. One of you had better start talking – and fast.'

Jude lowered his head. I looked at Jude. Dad looked at Mum.

'Meggie, it was when you last went to visit your sister,' Dad said at last.

'I'm listening,' Mum prompted sombrely.

And, as Dad told her exactly what had happened, we waited for the storm to hit.

Mum sat glaring at each of us in turn. I knew she was still doing it, even though I didn't dare look at her. After a lot of shouting, she'd spent the last three and whatever hours staring and glaring and scowling, until I don't know about the others, but I felt like a withered worm, twisting for her contemptuous inspection.

'Ryan, where's my daughter?' asked Mum for the umpteenth time.

Dad didn't answer. He couldn't. He just continued to hang his head.

'Jude and Lynette fighting . . . Ryan, I can't believe you let it happen. You are the most ineffectual useless man it's ever been my misfortune to come across,' Mum said with deep reproach.

'It's not Dad's fault, Mum,' Jude tried.

'And you can shut right up.' Mum turned on him like a cornered rat. 'I'm sick to the back teeth of this belief you have, that you and your opinions are always right and everyone else is wrong. You've been picking on your sister and goading her for months now.'

'Well, you've been doing the same to me, so that makes us about even,' Jude shot back bitterly.

'I've been picking on you – as you call it – because you're not doing anything with your life. You could work with your dad in the lumberyard or do an apprenticeship with Old Man Tony but . . .'

'Old Man Tony is always bombed off his trolley! Light a match in front of his mouth and the whole street would go up in flames. And I don't want to work in his ruddy bakery!' Jude shouted. 'If I get into that, I'll never get out again. I'll be covered with flour and baking bread till the day I die.'

'It's an honest job.'

'I don't want an honest job!'

'You don't know what you want,' Mum dismissed with a snort.

'Yes, I do. I want to go to school.' The words came out in a rush.

I stared at Jude. Since when had he wanted to go back to school? He'd always scorned me for having my nose in book after book. When I'd been studying for the Heathcroft High entrance exam, every word, every syllable he'd directed my way had dripped with sarcasm and contempt.

'Jude, we've been through this before,' Mum sighed her impatience. 'We didn't have the money to keep you in school. I lost my job – remember?'

'But you found the money for Callum to go to school,' said Jude. 'Every bit of care and attention in this house goes to Lynette and Callum. When is it my turn?'

'Boy, stop talking nonsense,' Mum snapped. 'You're

our son and we love you – just the same as the others – but at this precise moment I don't like any of you very much.'

'Then I won't inflict my presence on you any longer.' Jude sprang to his feet and headed for the front door.

'Jude . . .' Mum was also on her feet and moving forward.

Jude threw open the front door, but was halted in his tracks by the presence of two police officers, framed by the darkness outside. One of the officers had his arm raised, ready to knock on the door. They seemed as startled to see us as we were to see them. The officer in front was obviously the one in charge. A police sergeant, I think he was. A thin, reedy man whose uniform looked at least a size too big for him. The constable was almost the exact opposite. He was built like a brick outhouse. What he lacked in height, he made up for in width. Both of them were Crosses of course. Nought police officers were as rare as blue snow.

'Mr McGregor?' The senior police officer looked around the room. Dad stood up slowly.

'Lynette . . .' Mum whispered. Her trembling hand blindly sought and found the back of the sofa, her eyes never leaving the officers.

'May we come in?'

Dad's nod was brief. 'Please.'

They stepped into our living room, carefully shutting the door behind them.

'I'm Sergeant Collins and this is Constable Darkeagle,' said the senior policeman.

'Officers?' Dad prompted when no-one in the room

spoke. We were all wound so tautly that platitudes just made our torture worse.

'I'm so sorry, sir, ma'am. I'm afraid I've got some bad news.'

The officers had pitying, embarrassed looks on their faces. Dad swallowed hard, his expression carved in granite.

'What's happened?' he asked quietly.

Mum's grip on the sofa tightened, her knuckles whitening. I stared at the officers, telling myself that no matter what they said, it wouldn't, *it couldn't* be as bad as the thoughts racing through my head.

But it was.

'You have a daughter called Lynette McGregor?'

Dad nodded.

'I'm terribly sorry, sir, but there's been an accident – a tragic accident. I'm afraid she walked right into the path of an oncoming bus. Er . . . witnesses said she seemed to be in a world of her own. Maybe she had things on her mind?'

No-one answered his question. I don't think he expected an answer because he went on almost immediately.

'It was no-one's fault. If it's any consolation, she was killed instantly. She didn't suffer. I'm so sorry.

No-one spoke. I kept my eyes on the officer, the bearer of the bad news. I couldn't have looked at any other member of my family then if my life had depended on it.

It was all my fault.

That's how it felt. I remembered her staring at herself in the cracked living-room mirror, her hands bloody where she'd cut herself on the rough glass. Only a few days ago. Only a lifetime ago. Lynette . . .

'Your daughter is in the morgue of the local hospital if you wish to see her . . .'

'NO!' Mum let out a sudden howl like a wounded animal and sunk to her knees.

Dad was at her side at once. Jude took a step forward then stopped. The two police officers looked away, unwilling to be spectators at Mum's grief. I stood like a statue, frozen and mute. The seconds ticked past. Dad hugged Mum to him, rocking her. Mum didn't speak and she didn't cry. She didn't make another sound. Her eyes were closed as she let Dad rock her. Sergeant Collins stepped forward, a card in his hand.

'This is my number. If you need anything, anything at all, just phone me. I've written the number of a bereavement service on the back of the card in case you want to use it.'

Dad took the card. 'That's very kind of you, Officer. Thank you.' His voice shook as he took the card.

'I'm so sorry,' Sergeant Collins said one more time before ushering the constable out of the front door.

At the click of the closing door, I sank down onto the sofa. Lynette entered my head and filled my thoughts and spun around me and danced through me until it felt like she was swallowing me up. Jude stood quite still, looking utterly lost. Mum opened her eyes slowly. She pulled herself away from Dad, who reluctantly let her go, before turning to face us. A solitary tear trickled down her cheek.

'You must all be so proud of yourselves,' she said. 'I hope you're happy now.'

'Meggie, that's not fair,' Dad began. 'The officer said it was an accident.'

Mum looked at each of us in turn. 'Was it? Or did she have her mind on what you all said to her?' Then Mum buried her head in her hands, murmuring, 'My baby . . . my baby . . .'

And we could do nothing but stand and watch – all of us together, each of us utterly alone.

thirty-seven. Sephy

I flicked from channel to channel to channel, searching for something to watch. Looking for something to occupy my time. Nothing on that channel. Nothing on that channel either.

'For goodness' sake!' Minnie snatched the remote control out of my hand and threw it across the room.

'What's biting you?' I asked.

'Doesn't anything ever bother you?' Minnie asked, shaking her head.

'Lots of things bother me,' I frowned.

'But nothing that you actually lose any sleep over, eh?'

'What're you talking about?'

'Mother and Dad are splitting up. It's actually going to happen. Doesn't that mean anything to you?'

'It means a lot to me,' I protested. 'Dad's got someone else. Mother's drowning her sorrows even worse than before and you lash out at me all the time because I'm an easy target. But there's not a single thing I can do about any of it, is there?'

Minnie gave me a look that would've felled a giant redwood, before she marched out of the room. I stood up and hunted for the remote. I mean, jeez! Was it my fault?

What did she want from me, for goodness sake? If I could've done something about Mother and Dad then I would've. But one person, especially someone like me, never made a difference to a ruddy thing. At last I found the remote and sat back down on the sofa, growing more angry with each passing second. Minnie drove me nuts with her constant moods and her sulky behaviour. In fact, if she thought . . .

'Sephy, phone for an ambulance. Quick!'

I've never moved so fast in my life. I took the stairs, two and three at a time, following the sound of Minnie's voice. I ran into Minnie's bedroom but it was empty. I dashed into Mother's bedroom across the landing and stopped suddenly like I'd hit an invisible brick wall. Mum was slumped on the floor, a tablet bottle by her side with a few scattered pills on the carpet. A very few pills. Minnie cradled Mum's head on her lap, frantically stroking her hair and calling her name.

'An ambulance. Now!' Minnie screamed at me.

I ran along the landing to the phone, shock freezing my eyes wide open. Mother had tried to kill herself.

My mother had tried to kill herself . . .

thirty-eight. Callum

There was something wrong with me. I didn't cry. I couldn't. I sat on my bed and stared into nothing and I couldn't cry. I lay on my back with my hands behind my head – and nothing. I lay on my stomach, burying my face into my pillow, waiting for the tears to start. But they didn't. My sister was dead and I couldn't feel a thing. My head still buried in my pillow, I clenched my fists and stuck them under it so I wouldn't do something silly like punch the wall or the headboard. My fingers brushed against something cold and smooth. I sat up and lifted up my pillow. There was an envelope with *Callum* written on it in my sister's neat, tiny writing. Shock, hot and electric, shot through me. I picked it up. The letter dropped to the floor. I stared down at it, unable to believe my eyes.

'Lynny?' I whispered, confused.

I looked around, expecting to see her standing in my bedroom doorway, smiling at me, 'Gotcha!' all over her face. But the room was empty. What should I do? I bent down and picked up the letter between two trembling fingers. I was desperate to know what it said, but at the same time, I was terrified. Count to three and then do it. I got to two, then tore open the letter. My heart hammering, I began to read.

Dear Callum,

This is a very hard letter to write but I wanted you of all people to know the truth. By now, if I'm very lucky and God is very good, I won't be around any more. I'm tired and I want out, it's as simple as that. I've tried to think of the best way to do this and I think walking in front of a bus or a tram or a train is the easiest. A car is too hit and miss! See! My sense of humour has come back, along with my sanity. The return of my sanity, I can stand. It's the return to reality that I can't cope with.

I'll try to make it look like an accident so that I don't shame Mum and Dad but I wanted you to know the truth. I'm not ashamed of who I am any more, but I don't want to live in a world where what I am isn't good enough, where nothing I do will ever be good enough because I'm a nought and I always will be and nothing will ever change that. I hope you and Sephy have more luck than Jed and me – if that's what you want. Take care of yourself. And whatever life throws at you, be strong. Be strong for both of us.

All my love,
    Lynette

Lynny . .

I stared down at the letter in my hand. The words blurred and swam before me. I didn't have to read it a second or a third time. Once was more than enough. Crumpling the letter in my hand, I squeezed it smaller and smaller. I squeezed it like my heart was being squeezed. I sat perfectly still, for a minute, an hour, I don't know how long. Long enough for the pain in my throat to subside. Long enough for my eyes to stop smarting. And only when I could trust myself not to hurt so much, only then did I move. I tore the letter into a hundred pieces and let them fall to the floor like paper rain.

For the first time in my life I hated my sister. Hated her. She'd given in. She'd given up on life and left me to live it for the both of us. *All my love* . . . Was that all love did for you? Made you give up and give in? Left you open to pain and hurt? If it was, I swore that nothing would ever make me do the same as her.

Nothing.

thirty-nine. Sephy

Minnie and I sat together, her arm around my shoulder.

'Minerva . . ?'

'Shush!' Minnie whispered. 'Mother will be all right. You'll see. She'll be fine.'

I looked up and down the carpeted corridor. The place looked more like a hotel than a hospital. Did they really know what they were doing? And where was Mother? They'd only let us in the ambulance because Minnie had insisted and kept her hand in Mother's all the time. And the moment we arrived, Minnie and I had been ushered to a waiting area whilst Mother was put on a trolley and wheeled off somewhere else. The minutes ticked, ticked, ticked by – and still nothing. No word, no nurses, no doctors, nothing.

I looked down at my twisting hands in my lap.

Please, God . . . Please . . .

'Minerva? Persephone? Ah, there you are,' Juno Ayelette, Dad's personal secretary, marched along the corridor towards us.

Minnie sprung to her feet. Following her lead, I did the same.

'It's a shame you two didn't have your wits about you,' Juno told us.

Puzzled, I looked from Juno to Minnie, who was just as baffled as I was.

'You should've phoned me first rather than phoned for an ambulance on a landline. The story is already out that your mother took an overdose because your dad has found someone else.' Juno frowned. 'This is going to take some fancy footwork on my part.'

I shook my head, convinced that my mind was playing tricks. Surely I'd heard that wrong? I must've. No-one could be so thoughtless. So heartless.

'Mother tried to commit suicide . . .' Minnie whispered.

'Of course she didn't,' Juno scoffed, taking out her mobile phone. 'Anyone who tries to commit suicide takes a lot more than four sleeping tablets. She was just trying to get attention and sympathy.' She pressed a series of numbers on her phone.

I turned to my sister. 'Minnie, what . . ?'

'Hi, Sanchez?' Juno's voice cut across my own. 'Listen. We need to call in a few favours. I'm at the hospital and . . . yes, of course she's fine . . . it's nothing at all, I promise you, but we need to spread the word that it was an accident, nothing more . . . Yes . . . Yes . . .'

Minnie snatched the phone out of Juno's hand and threw it to the ground before grinding it under the heel of her boot. I stared at my sister, my heart racing, my eyes alight with new found admiration.

'How dare you . . ?' Juno began.

'You can go to hell,' Minnie screamed at her.

'You're a spoilt brat, Minerva Hadley.'

'And you're an insensitive cow!' And with that my sister marched off towards the casualty department.

I smirked at Juno before I ran to catch up with my sister. She glanced my way, her expression grim.

'Electric, Minerva. Just electric!' I told her.

And whilst she didn't smile, the grim expression on her face softened.

Slightly.

forty. Callum

It was the day of Lynette's funeral – a week after her 'accident'. A week of no school, no tears, no nothing. I'd gone for a late morning walk down to the beach. Alone. I stood on the sand, wearing my one and only formal blue suit and watched the waves lap back and forth, wondering why they did that. What was the point – if there was one? Did anything in this world have a point or was Lynette right? At last I walked home. Alone.

Only to find our house filled to overflowing with people. Friends, family, neighbours, strangers. I hadn't expected all these people. I couldn't cope with them. A quiet funeral, Dad had said. It looked like we had every nought in Meadowview struggling to get into our living room. I stood in a corner and watched for a while. Friends and strangers alike fought to be the first to say how sorry they were and spout on about 'tragic accidents' and 'wasted lives'. So many people had come to pay their last respects that our front and back yards were both full – never mind the house. The level of noise from all the chatter was incessant. I reckoned it wouldn't be long before I'd have to escape somewhere for some peace and quiet or I'd explode. Jude was with some of his friends, the now permanently sombre expression on his face. He wasn't saying much, but he was drinking. Lager, I think it was. And from the way he was swaying on his feet, it obviously wasn't his first. Well, if he wanted to be stupid, then I for one wasn't going to stop him. Let him make a fool of himself, for all I cared. The whole world could go to hell for all I cared.

What would Lynny have made of all this fuss? She'd probably have been as bewildered by it as I was. And what would Mum and Dad and Jude say if they found out that Lynny's 'accident' was anything but? Stupid question. I knew what they'd say, how they'd feel. So they would never know. I'd burnt the torn-up bits of Lynny's letter. No-one but me knew what had really happened. And I vowed that it would stay that way. I owed Mum and Dad that much. Especially Mum.

The noise around me was relentless. I rubbed my already throbbing temples. Had Mum and Dad really invited all these people? Where was Dad anyway? I hadn't seen him for a while. Nor Mum for that matter. I moved around the room as best I could, shaking hands and nodding my thanks at all the 'I'm so sorry's bombarding me from every direction. Just when I thought I'd have to duck out of there or burst, I finally saw Dad. He was huddled in a corner with two other men. One had untidy, wavy-blond hair tied back in a pony-tail and he wore a trim moustache. The other had dark chestnut-brown hair and the kind of tan that must've been paid for. He looked almost mixed race – lucky beggar. How I wished I could afford the treatment to make my skin permanently darker.

I started to walk towards them but the intense, solemn look on all their faces halted my steps. I watched, concentrating hard on trying to read their lips. Even though I'd never done it before, it was as if I'd somehow convinced myself that all I had to do was focus, to be the best lip-reader in the world. Well, the best nought lip-reader at any rate.

Dad wasn't saying much. He nodded, then nodded again. A word here, a nod there, that's all he did. It seemed to be enough for the two men though because as the conversation went on they began to smile and pat Dad on the back. Then one of them pressed something into Dad's hand. Dad didn't look at it, but immediately stuffed it into his jacket pocket. Out of the corner of my eye, I saw Mum enter the room. She looked around for Dad. She saw him and immediately starting making her way through the crowd in Dad's direction. Then she stopped. She'd noticed who Dad was with. Fury flashed across her face. She pushed towards them even more vigorously then. I was so busy watching Mum watching Dad that I wasn't aware of the silence sweeping through the room until it had reached and passed me. Looking around, I saw that every eye was on something going on behind me. No-one spoke. No-one moved. I turned, wondering what could've happened to cause such a reaction.

Seeing her was like a boxer's punch to my stomach. I was actually winded and breathless.

Sephy . . .

What was she doing here? Was she mad? Stillness rippled out from her, like the ripples when a stone is thrown into a pond. Sephy walked towards me, looking straight at me, but she didn't say a word. Then her gaze swept past me, her face set as she walked on by. I turned as did everyone else to see what she was going to do. She walked up to my mum who was only a couple of steps away from my dad by now.

'Mr and Mrs McGregor, I just wanted to come and see you to say how sorry I am about Lynette. I know what you're going through. My mother . . . I know . . .' Sephy's voice trailed off. She would've had to have the hide of a rhino not to pick up on the atmosphere in the room. 'I hope I'm not intruding or anything . . . I just wanted to say . . . I'm sorry . . .'

Mum was the first to recover. 'You're not intruding, Miss Hadley.' She stepped forward. 'Thank you for coming. Can I get you a drink?'

Sephy looked around at all the people staring at her,

most of the faces now suspicious and hostile. 'No, I don't think I should stay.'

'Nonsense. You've come this far, you can't leave without a drink. Can she, Ryan?' Mum spoke directly to Dad.

Dad was alone in the corner of the room. The two men he'd been talking to had vanished – seemingly into thin air. But it didn't matter. Sephy had all of Dad's attention. He was glaring at her like she was some kind of disgusting fungus he'd found growing in his navel. It was exactly like the look Mrs Hadley shot at me when I went to see Sephy after she'd been beaten up. *Exactly* like it.

'Ryan?' Mum's stern voice had Dad raising his head to look at her.

'Hello, Miss Hadley,' Dad managed to spit out.

'I'll go.'

'Sephy . . .' I stepped forward but Jude got in first.

'Yes, go!' he said furiously. 'Who told you to come here in the first place? You and your false sympathy aren't wanted.'

'Jude, that's enough,' Mum told him firmly.

'If she cares so much, where was she for the last three years when Lynette was out of her head and we didn't have two beans to rub together, never mind the money to get Lynny the help she needed? Where was this dagger when you got fired, Mum, and I had to drop out of school? Where was she when Harry over there got the boot?' Jude pointed to a man by the door. 'And all because she wanted to behave like a brat even though she knew it would get him into trouble.'

Sephy was staring at this guy, Harry, who was glaring right back at her. I'd never seen him before in my life. What did he have to do with Sephy?

'Our new chauffeur told me you'd decided to quit.' Sephy's voice was little more than a whisper but in the stillness of the room it was enough for everyone to hear.

'I got fired because you were left alone to face the riot at your school,' Harry called bitterly across the room. 'I begged you to stay in the car but you didn't want to – remember? When your face was plastered all over the TV screen and I was nowhere to be seen, your mother kicked me out so fast I'll have the imprint of her foot on my backside 'til the day I die.'

Whispered comments full of anger and antagonism swept around the room.

Sephy shook her head, shocked. 'I didn't know. I swear I didn't know.'

'Didn't take the trouble to find out either.' Harry turned away in disgust.

'You and others like you have brought us nothing but grief.' Jude pushed Sephy hard against her shoulder. Some of the others in the room gasped at his audacity. Shoving a Cross like that was just asking for trouble, but Jude was way past caring. 'And then you have the nerve to come over here . . .'

'Mrs McGregor, Mr McGregor . . .' Sephy appealed to them for help.

'Persephone, I think it's best you should leave,' Dad told her directly.

'But I haven't done anything . . .' said Sephy, bewildered.

'That's right, you haven't,' Dad agreed, pointedly. 'You come here in your fancy dress which cost more than I make in a year and we're supposed to smile and cheer? Is that how it's meant to work?'

'No . . .' Sephy whispered.

'Just go away,' Jude hissed at her. 'Go on, get lost before I do something I'll regret.'

Sephy looked around. Her eyes met mine. I tried to step forward but some woman behind me grabbed my arm and pulled me back.

'Let her go. Noughts and Crosses don't mix, boy,' the woman whispered to me.

Sephy shook her head and darted from the room. I could see only too well the shimmer in her eyes as she ran past me. Even though the room was full to capacity, a pathway opened up for her like Angel Shaka's parting of the Sea.

'You had no right to do that, Jude.' Mum waited until Sephy had gone before rounding on my brother.

'Oh yes he did,' Dad answered before Jude could open his mouth. 'She wasn't wanted here. Jude only told her the truth.'

Mum wasn't the only one to stare at Dad. Where had all that come from? I'd thought Dad's motto was to live and let live. When had that changed? When Lynny died . . ? Or maybe it was there all the time and I'd just chosen not to see it.

'Ryan . . ?' Mum said.

Around us, people started talking again – nervous, embarrassed chatter. I reached Mum's side at the same time as Dad.

He stopped and looked straight at Mum, a cold, hard expression on his face I'd never seen before. 'Meggie,' he said. 'My ineffectual days are over.'

Then he moved past her. Mum turned to stare after him. I watched Dad's retreating back. There was something about him, the way he walked, the way he talked . . . Something in his voice scared me. Scared the living daylights out of me.

forty-one. Sephy

It'd only been three years since Callum's mum had worked for mine. Three short years. Three years had passed like three minutes to me, but walking into Callum's house had been like walking into a room full of strangers. I remembered Callum's mum and dad so clearly but my memory of them was nothing like the reality. They hadn't wanted me there. Not one of them had. With everything that'd happened to my mother, I wanted to show them that I really did care, that I understood. Minnie and I could've so easily been in the same boat as Callum, no matter what Juno said.

Each move I made in Callum's direction just seemed to pave my way faster to hell.

forty-two. Callum

I went and sat down beside Sephy on the beach. Neither of us spoke. I was getting sand on my one good suit but I didn't care. I was past caring.

'I didn't mean any harm, Callum,' Sephy said at last.

'I know but . . .'

'But it wasn't the best idea I've ever had in my life,' Sephy sighed.

'Not as such – no,' I said.

'I can't seem to do anything right at the moment,' Sephy said at last. There wasn't a trace of self-pity in her voice, just the merest hint of sadness. 'I am sorry about your sister, Callum. I just wanted to show how much. I thought sending a card would be a bit . . . a bit . . .'

'Impersonal?'

'Exactly,' Sephy sighed again. 'It was just a spur of the moment thing to walk over to your house. I thought it'd make a difference somehow.'

I didn't know what to say to that, so I said nothing.

'This is growing up, isn't it?' Sephy asked.

'I think it is,' I nodded.

'Would you put your arm round me please?'

I hesitated.

Sephy sighed. 'If you'd rather not.'

'No, it's not that.'

Sephy gave me one of her looks.

'I just . . . never mind.' I put my arm around her. She put her head on my shoulder. And we both sat and watched the waves foam up on the beach and the shadows lengthen.

THE SPLIT

forty-three. Sephy

Minnie and I walked along the corridor towards Mother's private room. It'd been two weeks since Mother's accident. Karl, our chauffeur, brought us to see Mother each evening and although Mother was physically better, her behaviour was really making me worry. The mother I'd got used to over the last few years had disappeared, and in her place . . .

'Minerva! Persephone! I'm so glad to see you. I've missed you both so much. Come and give me a hug.'

Minnie and I glanced at each other before doing as we'd been asked. Mother hugged Minnie, then gave me a bear hug which left me breathless.

'I love both of you so much,' she told us, her voice trembling with emotion. 'You know that, don't you?'

Minnie nodded, embarrassed.

'We love you too, Mother,' I said, feeling very uncomfortable. I wasn't used to Mother saying such things. Jeez! I wasn't used to Mother saying much of anything.

'I know you love me.' Mother pulled me to her to kiss both my cheeks. It was only by a supreme effort that I didn't wipe my face the moment she released me.

'You're the only ones who care whether I live or die,' Mother continued. The gratitude in her voice made me feel incredibly uncomfortable – and guilty. Had Dad been to see her yet?

'Your friends would visit you too, if you told them you were in here,' Minnie pointed out.

'NO! No. I don't want anyone . . . No. I'll see them when I leave.'

'When will that be?'

'When I'm all better,' Mother announced brightly. Too brightly. Minnie and I exchanged another look.

'Are you coming to see me tomorrow?' Mother asked.

'Yes, of course,' Minnie said.

'Do me a favour? Could you bring me my make-up bag? I feel naked without my make-up.'

'OK, Mother,' Minnie said, quietly.

Mother was still smiling, a frantic almost manic look on her face. 'Oh, and a bottle of champagne – to celebrate my lucky escape,' Mother laughed.

'Champagne?'

'Yes, of course. Or failing that, some white wine will do.'

'Mother, I don't think that's a good idea . . .'

'Just do as you're told.' The first crack appeared in Mother's mask. She plastered it over with a broad smile. 'Sorry, love. I'm a bit on edge. If you don't help me Minnie, no-one else will. Y-your father hasn't even been to see me. Not a phone call. Not so much as a Get Well Soon card.' An even wider smile than before. 'So I'm celebrating. Today is the first day of the rest of my life. So bring me what I asked for – OK, sweetie?'

'OK, Mother.'

'Good girl.'

'I love you, Minerva.'

'Yes, Mother.'

'My two best girls.' Mother leaned back with a smile. Her smile faded into a look of such intense sadness that I could hardly bear to look at her. 'Here's a little life lesson for my two best girls. Never make a mistake because it will never be forgiven. Or forgotten. Never put a foot out and you'll never put a foot wrong.'

'I don't understand, Mother,' Minerva frowned.

'I made a mistake once.' Mother's eyes were closed now and her voice was faraway and dreamy. 'I did something I shouldn't've. But I was lonely. Your father was never at home and I was so tired of being alone. But he found out. I made a mistake you see. And I've never stopped paying for it.'

'Mother, it doesn't . . .'

'So don't be like me.' Mother opened her eyes and smiled brightly. 'Be perfect. My perfect little girls. I love you so much.'

I bent down, untying my shoelace so that I could tie it up again. A single tear splashed down onto my shoe. But Mother didn't see it.

So that was OK.

forty-four. Callum

'I'm going out.' Mum pulled on her jacket as she spoke.

'Where?' Dad stood up from the table where he'd been poring over some kind of map with Jude.

'For a walk.' The front door was now open.

'Meggie, how much longer are you going to carry on like this?' said Dad.

'Like what?' asked Mum, her back to us.

Jude and I exchanged a glance. Lynette's funeral was over three months ago now and Dad wasn't the only one who'd changed. Most nights Mum had taken to going for long walks, returning long after I'd gone to bed and was meant to be asleep. Crossmas had come and gone in our house without much cheer. The new year had started and here we all were, occupying opposite ends of the compass.

Dad sighed, exasperated. 'Meggie, why won't you talk to us? To me?'

Mum turned, her eyes ablaze. 'Will you give that up?' she asked, pointing to the long map spread out all over our table.

'No.'

'Then we have nothing to say to each other.'

'Meggie . . .'

Mum headed out of the door, slamming it shut behind her.

'What's going on, Dad?' I asked.

Dad was still staring at the front door. I doubt if he even heard me. I tried to move closer to the table but Jude rolled up the map before I had a chance to take a good look at it. I did see enough of it this time though to realize that it wasn't just a map; it was a blueprint.

'Come on, Jude, we've got work to do,' Dad said grimly.

'Where're you going, Dad?' I asked.

'Out.'

'Out where?' I asked.

'To a meeting.'

'What meeting?'

'None of your business,' Dad replied tersely, pulling on his coat.

'Where is it?'

'That's none of your business either.'

Jude ran a large elastic band around the now rolled up blueprint and went to join Dad. He put the blueprint down by his feet and put on his jacket which was hanging on a hook by the door. There was no way he was going to let that blueprint out of his sight. I regarded both Jude and Dad, standing together at the front door looking in every way like father and son – and I felt totally excluded.

'How come Jude gets to go with you and I don't?'

'Because you're not old enough,' said Dad.

Jude snorted and muttered something under his breath. At Dad's warning look he shut up. What were both of them up to? A house of secrets, that's what my home had become. Mum had withdrawn to a place where none of us were able to reach her. And on top of that, Jude and Dad were doing something where I wasn't wanted.

And I missed Lynette so much.

She never said very much and goodness knows she never did much but it was like she was the glue that kept our family together and now that she was gone we were each floating further and further away from one another.

Something else to hate my sister for.

'Please let me come with you,' I pleaded.

I didn't know where Mum was and I didn't want to be on my own. I needed to belong somewhere, to something, to someone.

'No way,' Jude shot out before Dad could open his mouth.

'I won't be any trouble.'

'Yeah, right!' Jude scoffed.

Dad walked over to me and placed a hand on my shoulder. 'Callum, where we're going you can't follow.'

'Why not? If Jude's old enough to belong to the Liberation Militia then so am I.'

'What?' Dad spun around. 'Jude, you stupid boy. What've you been saying? You know we're not meant . . .'

'I didn't say anything, Dad. I swear,' Jude denied vehemently.

'Jude didn't tell me,' I said.

'Then who did?' Dad asked brusquely.

'No-one. I worked it out for myself. I'm not stupid,' I told him. 'So can I come with you now?'

'No way. We're going to a Liberation Militia meeting

and you're too young. Besides, if you were seen it'd be the end of your school career. Is that what you want?'

'I don't care. I'm just wasting my time at Heathcroft and everyone knows it.' I shrugged away from Dad's hand. 'Colin's dropped out and Shania's been expelled for no reason and everyone's taking bets on how much longer Amu and I are going to be there. Besides, I was thinking of leaving anyway.'

'Over my dead body,' Dad flared up at once. 'You are going to school and you'll stay at school until you're eighteen and then you'll go on to university. Do I make myself clear?'

I looked away from him, my lips firmly together.

'Callum, I asked you a question.' Dad grabbed my chin and forced my face around till I had no choice but to look directly at him. 'You will not leave school without any qualifications. Understand?'

'Yeah, OK.' I mumbled.

Dad headed for the door, beckoning to Jude as he did so.

'And don't bother blabbing to your dagger friend about us being in the Liberation Militia,' Jude hissed at me. 'Not unless you want to put a noose around our necks.'

Both Dad and Jude left the house without a backward glance and once again I was alone.

forty-five. Sephy

Minnie was reading one of those 'ten ways to get your man' women's magazines that are incredibly, tediously boring! But Minnie's sixteen – two years older than me – so I guessed it was only a matter of time before I started reading that stuff too. Right now though, I had other things on my mind. I licked my lips, nervously.

'Minnie, what are we going to do?'

'What d'you mean?'

My sister was being either really thick or really evasive.

'Mother. Her drinking's getting worse,' I said.

'She's just smoothing out the rough edges,' Minnie smiled wryly as she answered with Mother's often repeated line, trotted out whenever we tried to bring up the subject of her drinking.

'Any smoother and she won't have to walk places, she'll just roll,' I frowned.

'You tell her that,' Minnie challenged.

My sister was no use at all. I huffed impatiently so she'd get the message, but her nose was already back in her magazine. Mum'd been at home for a while now and she was steadily getting worse. She spent a lot of time in her room. And when she did emerge it was always to smother us with kisses and tell us how much she loved us before she made her way to the wine cellar or the kitchen. Funny how she always reeked of expensive perfume as she smothered us with hugs and kisses. It was a close-run thing to say which was the most overpowering – her perfume or her kisses. Or maybe her attempts to prove to us that she wasn't drinking any more. She wasn't fooling anyone.

Because it was so obvious. She was growing more and more out of it. Sadder and lonelier – and worse.

And there wasn't a single thing I could do about it.

forty-six. Callum

Saturday. It was eighteen days and five months after Lynette's death. Funny I should think of it that way. The days before the months. My sixteenth birthday in February had come and gone, with a card and a book signed from both Mum and Dad, but bought and wrapped by Mum. It hadn't been much of a birthday. No-one had felt like celebrating. And sitting round the table cutting the birthday cake had been a silent affair – because Lynny wasn't there. The winter had come and gone and spring had arrived – and nothing had changed. Funny that not a single day passed without me thinking about Lynette. When she was here, she so often just seemed to fade into the background, like something that's always there but you never really think about. Like air. But now that she was gone . . .

Lynette's secret still hung heavily over me, like a shroud. No-one knew the truth about her death except me. And with each passing day, the longing to tell someone grew stronger. There was Sephy, but each time I tried to tell her the truth about my sister, the words just wouldn't come. It felt like I was being disloyal to not just Lynette but my whole family by wanting to tell Sephy and no-one else. On the spur of the moment, I headed for the phone and used our signal to phone Sephy's house. Within five minutes she was phoning me back.

'Hello you,' I said.

'Hello yourself,' Sephy replied.

'So what're you up to today then?' I asked. I had to keep my voice down because Mum and Dad were upstairs. Jude was out – as per usual – so I was taking this opportunity to use the phone. I was hoping Sephy wouldn't have anything planned so that we could spend this Saturday together.

'I'm going shopping! With Mother!' Sephy wailed.

'Poor you.' I had to struggle to keep myself from laughing out loud at Sephy's tone of voice. She hated shopping at the best of times. And as for shopping with her mum, that must be her idea of hell on earth.

'It's not funny!' Sephy snapped.

'Of course not,' I soothed.

Sephy gave a very undignified snort down the phone. 'You're laughing at me again.'

'As if.'

'What're you going to be doing with the rest of the day then?' Sephy asked me.

'I thought I might go to the park, or maybe the beach. Maybe I'll do both. I haven't decided yet.'

'That's right, rub it in.'

'Just think of all that lovely money you're going to spend,' I told her.

'Mother's going to spend it, not me. She's decided she needs some spending therapy,' Sephy replied.

'Well, if you can't get out of it, get into it!'

'I'd much rather be with you,' Sephy admitted.

There it was again, that familiar twist in my stomach whenever she said things like that to me.

'Hello?' Sephy said, uncertainly.

'I'm still here. Maybe we can meet up later this afternoon?' I suggested.

Sephy sighed. 'I doubt it. Mum wants to buy me some dresses and update my school uniform and she wants to buy herself an evening dress and some shoes. Just the shoes by themselves will take three or four hours at least.'

'Why? Has your mother got duck's feet or something?'

'No, just a duck's taste in shoes. I swear, Callum, it's going to be *torture*!'

'I might see you at the shopping centre actually. I've got to get some things for school,' I said.

'Like what?'

'Pens, rulers and I was thinking of buying myself a new calculator.'

'I'll keep my eyes open for you,' Sephy said. 'Maybe I'll see you at the café? You can stop me from going completely insane!'

'If I miss you at the centre, how about getting together this evening then? We could have a late picnic on the beach. Around six o'clock?'

'I'll try but I can't guarantee anything,' Sephy said.

'Fair enough.'

'Saturday in the Dundale Shopping Centre,' Sephy groaned. 'Just shoot me now and put me out of my misery!'

Laughing, I said bye and put the phone down. And then I thought of Lynette again — and the laughter stopped.

forty-seven. Sephy

'D'you like these shoes?'

'Yes, Mother. They're really nice,' I smiled.

'But those burgundy ones with the thin straps were better, weren't they?'

'What burgundy ones?'

'The ones we tried in Roberts & Miller,' Mum replied.

That was four shoe shops ago.

'Well, I really like these ones,' I tried.

'I think I'll go back to Roberts & Miller and try on those burgundy ones just once more.'

Aaaarrrrrgggggghhhhhh!

forty-eight. Callum

Lunch was over, without too much grief – for once. Jude had come home from heaven only knew where so we'd all eaten together – which made a change. Mum indulged in small talk, telling us all about what our neighbours and relatives and friends were up to, whilst Jude was his usual effervescent, scintillating self and didn't say one word. No-one was particularly bothered that I didn't have much to say either. Before I'd swallowed my last mouthful, my knife and fork clattered onto my plate and I jumped up. Grabbing my jacket off the back of the sofa, I headed for the door.

'Where're you going?' Mum asked with a smile.

'The shopping centre.'

Jude leapt up like a scalded cat. 'Oh no you're not.'

I frowned at him. 'I'll go where I ruddy like. Since when is it any of your business where I go?'

'Callum, you don't want to go there. Not today,' Jude said, nervously.

'Jude?' Mum stood up slowly.

A tense, watchful atmosphere entered the room like chilling fog.

'Why shouldn't I go?' I asked my brother.

He didn't answer.

'What's going on?' I persisted.

I turned to Mum. She was staring at Jude, a stunned look on her face. From her expression, she was obviously well ahead of me.

'Don't go there, Callum,' Jude told me, pointedly.

'But . . .' And only then did I click.

The Liberation Militia were planning something at the Dundale. Something Jude knew about. Something my brother didn't want me anywhere near. And then I remembered.

'Sephy's at the shopping centre,' I said, horror-stricken.

'Callum . . .' Jude began.

I didn't wait to hear any more. I ran out of the house, leaving the front door wide open as I raced for the shopping centre.

forty-nine. Sephy

Mother was driving me nuts! In our five long, *long* hours together, I'd bitten my tongue so many times it'd swollen up to the size of a football and was choking me. If she asked me for my opinion on one more pair of shoes, I couldn't be held responsible for my actions. I sipped my orange juice, grateful for the short but welcome break away from her. She'd gone back to the car park to pack away her various purchases. She was enjoying herself. I'm glad one of us was!

'Sephy! Thank God! You have to get out of here.'

'Callum!' I beamed. 'Where did you spring from?'

'Never mind that. You've got to leave this place now.'

'But I haven't finished my drink . . .'

'Never mind your ruddy drink. You have to leave – NOW!'

I looked at Callum then, really looked at him. He was scared. No . . . he was terrified.

'What's going on?'

'Don't argue. Out!' Callum told me grimly. 'Come on.'

Callum dragged me out of my seat and towards the café door.

'Excuse me, love, but is this boy troubling you?' a stranger asked as I was dragged past his table.

'No! No, he's a friend of mine,' I called back. 'He wants to show me something . . .'

Callum dragged me out of the café and along the concourse and then every alarm in the world went off, at least that's what it sounded like.

'What's going on?' I asked, looking around.

'Move it. Come on.'

And we were running towards the nearest exit. Others around us were looking around and frowning, wondering what was going on. Maybe they saw Callum and I racing for the nearest exit, maybe we started it. I don't know. But it seemed like moments later, everyone was shouting and racing for the exits. We were amongst the first ones out of the Dundale. We stumbled out into the spring sunshine and still Callum had hold of my hand and was pulling me after him.

'Where're we going?' I asked breathlessly.

'Run. Come on,' Callum puffed from beside me. 'I thought I'd never find you. It took me almost half an hour to find you. Move.'

'Callum, I'm getting a stitch,' I protested.

'Tough. We've got to keep going.'

'Callum, enough!' I pulled my hand out of his. 'You're . . .'

Then there was a flash like the very air was alight, followed a fraction of a second later by the most colossal boom. I was blown off my feet and into the air like a dry leaf in a high wind. And even from where we were, I could feel an intense heat on my back. I landed flat on my face, my arms outstretched. There was a strange ringing sound in my ears and it wouldn't stop. For I don't know how long, I lay in a daze. Was I dead? Was this what it felt like to die? I closed my eyes tight and covered my ears, trying to block out the incessant ringing sound – only it was inside my head, not outside. I swallowed hard and my ears popped, and the ringing stopped. Twisting around, I turned to see what on earth had happened. Billowing smoke shot out of the shopping centre. For a moment it was eerily quiet, like the end of the world. I wondered panic-stricken if the explosion had deafened me. And then I heard screaming and sirens and all hell was let loose.

I turned to Callum, who lay stunned beside me.

'Are you OK?' You're not hurt?' Callum asked anxiously, running his hands up and down my back and arms.

'Y-you *knew* that was going to happen . . .' I realized,

aghast. 'You didn't . . . Tell me you didn't . . .' I shook my head. No, that was preposterous. Callum had nothing to do with whatever that explosion was. It must've been a bomb. But Callum didn't do that. He wouldn't. He *couldn't*.

But he *knew*.

'Mother! Oh my God!' I jumped to my feet and raced towards the car park across the street from the shopping centre.

I was almost across the street when I remembered Callum. I turned around.

But he was gone.

fifty. Callum

I'd barely got the key in the lock before the front door was flung open and Mum pounced on me.

'Where've you been? You look terrible. Are you all right? Where's Jude? Isn't he with you?'

'I thought he was here,' I said wearily, closing the front door behind me.

'No, he left almost as soon as you did,' said Mum. 'What happened?'

'Didn't you hear?' I asked, astonished.

'Hear what?'

She should've heard the explosion from here. But then

again, maybe not. Our house was right across town from the shopping centre.

'It hasn't been on the telly?' I turned to the TV, perplexed. The news wasn't on, just a rerun of some ridiculous detective programme where practically every low life in it was a nought. I recognized this episode. A cop was chasing a nought scumbag who'd shot and killed his partner.

'Callum, talk to me. What happened?'

'Mum . . .'

'We interrupt this programme to bring you a news-flash,' a voice suddenly declared.

My head whipped up. The telly's most popular news-reader appeared, his expression grim. My heart began to thump in a crazy way that made me feel physically sick.

'Please don't let it be something bad about us noughts,' Mum breathed.

'Just under thirty minutes ago, a bomb exploded at the world-famous Dundale Shopping Centre. At least seven people are known to have been killed outright with scores more wounded. Casualties are being taken by ground and air ambulances to the local hospitals. All hospitals in the immediate area have been put on full alert. A warning was received from the nought group calling itself the Liberation Militia only five minutes before the bomb actually exploded.'

'That's a lie,' Jude said.

Mum and I turned as one to see Jude standing in the doorway with Dad beside him. We turned back to the TV screen as Dad shut the front door.

The newsreader's face was replaced by a TV camera at the scene. It swung around this way and that, filming the carnage of people lying on the ground, windows shattered, blood on the concourse. There was no voice-over to accompany it. No voice echoing sorrow at the devastation. No voice filled with indignation. No sound at all. Just silence.

Which made it worse.

The camera focused on one woman sitting on the ground, rocking back and forth, blood running down her forehead and into her eyes. On to the next atrocity. The camera moved in a jerky fashion as if the person holding the camera was shaking, trembling, which he or she probably was. A child knelt by a man's side. The child was crying. The man was still. The camera was only on them for a second or two, but it was enough.

The Prime Minister appeared on the screen, his expression angry and forbidding.

'If the Liberation Militia think this cowardly, barbaric act of terrorism is going to win over the vast population of this country to their way of thinking, then they are very much mistaken. All they've done is strengthen our resolve not to give in to such "people" or tactics.'

'Dad . . .' Jude whispered.

'Shush.' Dad focused on the telly and nothing else.

The newscaster's face re-appeared. 'A senior police officer on the scene believes that the bomb was planted in a café bin inside the shopping centre but stated that it was too early to speculate. He did promise however that the perpetrators of this crime would be brought to swift justice. There will be more information about this in our main news bulletin after the current programme. Once again, a bomb has gone off in the Dundale Shopping

Centre, killing at least seven people.'

The detective programme returned just as the cop gave a flying tackle and brought the killer nought to the ground.

'Dad? What happened? You said . . .'

'Shush, boy,' Dad admonished, looking at Mum.

Mum used the remote to switch off the telly. Then she turned to look directly at Dad. 'I'm going to ask you something, Ryan, and I want your solemn promise that you're going to tell me the truth.'

'Not now, Meggie.' Dad headed for the stairs. Mum instantly moved to block his way.

'Yes, *now*. Did you or Jude plant that bomb?'

'I don't know what you're talking about.'

'Damn it, Ryan, don't treat me like a cretin. Promise me you had nothing to do with this business.'

Dad didn't speak. He regarded Mum, defiance in every bitter twist and turn of his expression. 'What I did or didn't do is none of your business,' Dad said at last.

I'd never heard Dad speak to Mum like that before. The pinched, angry look on Mum's face was an indication she'd never heard that tone of voice from Dad either. Mum and Dad regarded each other, their expressions setting harder and harder. They were standing perfectly still and moving further and further apart. Mum deliberately turned her back on Dad to face Jude.

'Jude, did you plant that bomb? NO! Don't look at your father. I asked you a question – now answer it.'

'We . . .'

'Jude, keep your mouth shut, d'you hear?' Dad ordered grimly.

'Jude, I'm still your mother,' Mum said very, very quietly. 'Answer me please.'

Desperately, Jude looked from Mum to Dad and back again.

'Jude . . ?' said Mum.

'We had to, Mum. Our cell was ordered to do it. Some of us set it up last night, but they said they'd phone through with the warning an hour before it went off. I swear they did. They said that everyone would be evacuated in plenty of time.' The verbal waterfall tumbled from Jude's mouth.

'You killed, you *murdered* all those people . . .' Mum whispered, appalled.

'Dad said they would phone through with a warning. That's what he said. I don't understand.' Jude turned bewildered eyes towards Dad.

Mum's whole body was shaking, heaving. Her lips clamped together as she struggled to stop herself from retching.

'Meggie . . .' Dad's mask slipped for the first time that evening. He looked so forlorn. He touched Mum's arm. She spun around and slapped his face so hard, there was a crack as her fingers bent right back.

'You murdering, lying . . . You promised me there'd never be anything like this. You promised you'd only be involved in the background, in planning. You *promised*.'

'I didn't have any choice. Once you're in, they've got you – and you have to do as you're told.'

'You don't. You could've said no. You *should*'ve said no.'

'I was protecting you, Meggie. And our sons. I had no choice.'

'Protecting us from what? From something you inflicted on us in the first place?' Mum dismissed.

'Who d'you think I'm doing all this for?' Dad cried.

'I know exactly who you're doing all this for. But she's dead, Ryan – and murdering innocent people won't bring her back.'

'You've got it wrong, Meggie.' Dad shook his head.

'Have I? I warned you, Ryan. I begged you not to involve Jude in all this.' Mum cradled her now-limp right hand in her left. One of her fingers was bent back on itself in a definite V-shape.

'I'm sorry . . .' Dad began. But if anything that just made things worse.

'Sorry? *Sorry?* Say that to the families of all those people you murdered,' Mum yelled at him. 'How could you? I can't bear to look at you.'

Dad straightened up. His eyes flint-like again. The mask was back – with a vengeance. 'At least now the Crosses will know we mean business.'

'All those people killed and maimed and that's all you have to say about it?' Mum's voice dropped to a strange hush.

'They were legitimate targets,' said Dad.

Mum stared at Dad like she'd never seen him before. Silence. She turned away, wearily. 'In that case we have nothing more to say to each other. Jude, could you take me to the hospital please? I think I've broken one of my fingers.'

'I'll take you,' Dad insisted.

'I don't want you anywhere near me. Don't you ever come near me again,' Mum hissed. 'Come on, Jude.'

Jude looked at Dad, unsure of what to do. Dad nodded and turned away. Jude took Mum by her left arm and led her out of the house. Only when the door shut, did Dad let go. Closing his eyes, he wrapped his arms around himself and bent his head, almost like he was praying. Except I knew he couldn't be because Dad doesn't believe in God. He began to tremble like Old Man Tony when he's got the DTs.

'Dear Lord, please . . .' Dad began. But then he opened his eyes and saw me watching him. He started with surprise. A second or two passed before I saw recognition on his face. In everything that had happened, I'd been completely forgotten. By everyone.

'I'll . . . I'll just go and see if Jude and Mum n-need my help,' I stammered.

It wasn't that I wanted to be with them so much. I just needed to get away, to be somewhere else. Dad didn't try to stop me. I grabbed my jacket and headed out, shaking as the door shut behind me. The evening air was warm and welcome on my skin. Was I going to try and catch up with Mum or Jude or just run and run and keep going – for ever and ever, amen? I looked left, then right. My conscience made up my mind for me. I followed after Mum and Jude.

fifty-one. Sephy

If only I could stop my mind from spinning. If only I could shut out everyone and everything for just a few hours. Just long enough to get some sleep, so that I could think clearly afterwards. But I couldn't switch off.

After two fruitless hours of tossing and turning and counting everything from sheep to ring-tailed lemurs, I gave in and sat up, as wide awake as I'd ever been. I glanced at the silver clock on my bedside table – a fourteenth birthday present a few months ago from my father. A present he'd probably never even seen. It was still quite early. I'd gone to bed early, mainly because Mother had insisted, but even the regular beat of the second hand counting away time couldn't lull me off to sleep tonight.

Thank goodness Mother was OK. She was still packing away her shopping when the explosion went off. Glass from the centre was everywhere, scattered across most of the car park. And Mother was in a mad panic, screaming out my name over and over. The moment she saw me, she rushed towards me and gave me a hug which lifted me right off my feet. But we were OK – which is more than could be said for a lot of poor people still caught inside the Dundale when the bomb went off.

'We should see if we can help,' I'd said.

'No way. We're leaving now. At once,' Mother insisted.

And no amount of arguing on my part could change her mind. She wanted to put as much space between us and the Dundale Centre as fast as possible. I wasn't sure about the wisdom of her driving us home but we'd managed to get back home OK. Mother then insisted on checking me over properly but apart from a bruise on my forehead and a couple of grazes on my knees and hands I was fine – outside.

Inside, I couldn't get it out of my head that Callum had known about the bomb. He'd probably saved my life. But I almost wished he hadn't. Almost.

With a sigh I got up and headed downstairs to the kitchen. There had to be something I could do to help me get to sleep. A glass of warm milk perhaps. Mother was in her room and Minnie was away, spending the weekend with her best friend.

The kitchen was dark and silent and strangely comforting. I got myself a glass from one of the cupboards and headed for the fridge. The moment I opened it, I was instantly flooded with light.

What to drink? Warm milk or cold orange juice? In the fridge door was a half-full bottle of Chardonnay. I took out the bottle and swirled around the golden liquid. My mother lived in this bottle – and others like it. She was probably upstairs now, drinking to forget today's events. Drinking to forget a lot of things. After a moment's hesitation, I poured myself just enough to cover the bottom of the glass. The first sip almost made me gag. It tasted like refined vinegar. What did Mother see in this stuff? I took another sip. After all, there had to be something to it if Mother liked it so much. Another sip. Then another. And another. I poured out a bit more, half a glassful this time. I drank slowly but steadily. By the time I'd finished, Chardonnay didn't taste quite so bad. And it made me feel funny, pleasant inside. Sort of warm and squishy. Pouring out a whole glassful, I headed back to my bedroom. I sat up in bed, sipping at my wine, feeling very grown-up as I let it wash over me and through me and into me. My head started to sway from the inside out. Backwards and forwards, rocking me gently.

At last, I put down the empty glass and curled up in bed. This time I didn't even have to think about trying to sleep. This time I left the world behind the moment my head touched the pillow.

And I slept like a log.

fifty-two. Callum

Mercy Hospital was a sad joke. The rundown accident and emergency department was busting at the seams, and then some. It looked like many of the people there were nought casualties from the shopping centre. The walking, walk-in wounded. There were people crying, shouting, one woman was screaming at regular five-second intervals and no-one was taking the least notice of her. The air smelt of strong, cheap disinfectant. It was so strong I could almost taste it as it caught at the back of my throat, but it still couldn't quite mask the nastier smells of vomit and blood and urine it was trying to disguise. The whole place reeked of barely organized chaos. All the nurses were noughts and all but one of the doctors. I wondered what a Cross doctor was doing at a nought hospital. Building his stairway to heaven no doubt. I looked at my brother. He'd been involved in all this chaos and carnage around us. How did it make him feel to see the result of his handiwork? But he wasn't looking around. He was looking down at the ground, like his gaze was permanently stuck there.

'Are you all right, Mum?'

'I'll survive.'

Mum sat on one of the rock-hard benches, her face rigid and set as she cradled her purple-blue, swollen finger. It looked awful. I kept stealing glances at Mum, wondering why she wasn't crying. It must've hurt like blazes.

'Are you sure you're OK, Mum,' Jude asked, looking up at last.

'Yes.'

Ten seconds later. 'Are you all right, Mum?'

I wasn't surprised when she finally barked at him, 'No, I'm not all right, Jude. I've broken my finger, it hurts like hell and I'm sick of your stupid questions. So just shut up, OK?'

Everyone around us turned to look. Jude lowered his head, his cheeks flaming.

Mum looked at Jude's bent head and sighed. 'Look, I'm

sorry, love . . .' She carefully removed her good hand from underneath her bad and tried to put it on Jude's shoulder. Jude shrugged her off.

'Jude, I'm mad at your dad and I'm taking it out on you. I'm sorry. OK?' Mum put her hand on Jude's shoulder again. This time he didn't try to remove it.

'OK?' Mum said softly.

Jude shrugged and nodded at the same time.

'Callum, go and get yourself a drink or something,' said Mum.

'Why?'

'I want to talk to your brother in private. I have something to tell him.'

'Mum, please . . .' Jude began.

'This has nothing to do with the L.M.,' Mum told him. 'This is about you and me.'

'Can't I stay?' I asked.

'No. Do as you're told,' Mum ordered.

I walked over to the vending machine on the other side of the waiting room, but I wasn't thirsty. Besides which, I didn't have any money. Besides which, it was out of order anyway. It looked like someone had given it a good kicking – or tried to at any rate. I leaned against it, watching Mum speak earnestly to Jude.

Then even from where I was standing, I saw all the colour drain from Jude's face as he stared at Mum. He leapt up, profoundly shocked. Mum pulled him back down to sit next to her and carried on talking. She leaned forward towards Jude, speaking rapidly with an animation and urgency that showed she was telling Jude something serious. Very serious. I straightened up as I watched them, wondering what on earth was going on. Jude started shaking his head, slowly at first, then more and more quickly. Whatever Mum was telling him, he didn't like it. He didn't believe it. Or maybe he didn't want to believe it. I couldn't stand it any longer. I started walking back to them. By the time I reached them, Jude was looking straight ahead, his face pale, his eyes almost feverishly bright.

'Mum?'

'Sit down, Callum.'

I sat down next to my brother. Mum put her hand on Jude's shoulder. He turned to look at her, still stunned.

'Jude, darling, I . . .'

'Excuse me.' Jude jumped up and headed for the exit without a backwards glance.

'Where's he going?' I asked.

'I don't know,' Mum replied unhappily.

'Is he coming back?'

'I don't know.'

'Why's he upset?'

'Not now, Callum. OK?'

It wasn't, but I let it drop. Almost half an hour later, Jude came back. He sat down in his original place without saying a word.

'Are you OK, love?' Mum asked, gently.

Jude gave her a look like nothing I've ever seen before. Full of hurt and love and anger. Mum actually blushed and turned away. Seconds later, Jude did the same. It was obvious, neither of them was going to tell me what was going on. The minutes crawled by as we all sat in stony silence.

'Mrs Margaret McGregor?' A nurse finally called out from outside the room next to the reception desk.

Mum stood up slowly, doing her best to protect her finger.

'Mrs Margaret . . .'

'She's here,' I called out. 'She's just coming.'

Mum tried to stand up. I attempted to help her but it was hard going.

'Are you trying to melt into that chair or are you going to get up and help?' I snapped at my brother.

In a daze, Jude stood up. We steadied Mum between us and all walked into the nurse's little cubby-hole.

'My mum needs to see a doctor,' I said when we'd barely got our feet into the room.

'All patients are assessed here first before they see a doctor,' the nurse informed us.

'That's fine,' Mum said, casting a warning look at me.

The nurse shut the door behind us as Mum and Jude sat down. I stood up behind him. The nurse headed back to her chair stating, 'I'm Nurse Carter. I'll be your primary nurse whilst you're at the hospital.'

'Good. Fine.' Mum nodded.

'Formalities first, I'm afraid. Before we can administer any kind of medical care, I'll need to see your ID cards.'

'Sorry?' Mum frowned.

'It's the new government ruling. All patient IDs have to be checked and registered. I think it's their way of trying to stop benefit swindles.'

'I beg your pardon?' Mum's frown deepened. 'I'm not even on benefits.'

'It doesn't matter. This hospital and every other nought

hospital in the country gets a certain amount of money per patient we treat. The government are claiming that some hospitals have been trying to abuse the system. So the government's foolproof plan,' the sneer in Nurse Carter's voice made it only to clear what she thought of this so-called 'foolproof' plan, 'is to check each patient's ID card photo and fingerprint, so that patients can't hop around from hospital to hospital getting sickness certificates and hospitals can't lie about the numbers of patients they treat. That's the theory anyway.'

'And if I refuse to hand over my ID card?' Mum asked.

'Then we can't treat you,' Nurse Carter shrugged, regretfully.

'I don't think I have it. I left it at home.'

Nurse Carter sighed. 'Then I'll need the ID cards of at least two other people who can vouch for you.'

'I resent this. I'm not trying to defraud anyone,' Mum fumed.

'I know. And no-one here is accusing you of anything of the kind. But unfortunately we have no choice.'

Mum lifted up her hand. Although her palm was facing down and the back of her hand upwards, Mum's index finger was a V pointing up at the yellowing ceiling.

'Why don't you just chop off my finger and hold it to ransom until I can prove I'm who I say I am?'

'That won't be necessary,' the nurse smiled. She turned her gaze on Jude and me. 'These are your sons?'

'Yes,' Mum answered brusquely.

'They're fine boys.'

'I think so.' Mum allowed herself a faint trace of pride as she looked straight at Jude. 'Very fine boys.'

As Jude blushed, I ruffled his hair.

'Get off,' he scowled at my grinning face.

'Which one's the oldest?'

Mum paused for only a moment as she remembered Lynette. 'Jude here,' she supplied before my brother could. 'And this is Callum, my youngest.'

'OK, Jude,' Nurse Carter smiled. 'May I see your ID card?'

Jude dug into his jacket pocket and pulled it out. I did the same. Nurse Carter swiped them through something attached to her computer. It looked a bit like a machine for checking credit cards.

'What's that for?' Jude asked.

'All done.' The nurse handed Jude's ID back to him. She held out her hand to give back mine.

'What is that?' I asked. I hadn't failed to notice that she hadn't answered Jude's question.

'It just stores your ID details and thumbprints on our hospital database.'

'I don't want my sons' fingerprints stored,' Mum leapt to her feet, her face pale. 'Wipe it off – NOW.'

'Don't worry, Mrs McGregor. As soon as you're able to bring your ID card, your sons' details will be deleted.'

'You're sure?' Mum said slowly, sitting back down.

'Positive. That's standard hospital procedure.' Nurse Carter looked from Mum to Jude and I and back again. She was trying – and failing – to keep the curiosity out of her expression.

Jude looked down at his hands. And then I realized what was going on. So much for my so-called intelligence. I hadn't realized until now why Mum had panicked at the thought of Jude's prints being on file somewhere. Today was obviously my day for being incredibly slow on the uptake.

Nurse Carter lifted Mum's right hand by the wrist. 'How did you do this anyway?'

'It was an accident,' Mum mumbled. 'I hit something I shouldn't've.'

Nurse Carter gave Mum a considering look. 'I see,' was all she said.

The nurse examined Mum's hand very carefully, turning it this way and that as gently as she could. But even at her gentlest, the nurse still made beads of sweat break out over Mum's forehead and brought a pained shimmer to her eyes.

'Well, you've definitely dislocated something in there!' Nurse Carter said at last.

I mean – duh! We knew that already. And the look Mum gave the nurse said as much.

'Yes, I know! But it never hurts to get a second opinion on these things! You'll need an X-ray and then we'll get a doctor to sort you out. OK?'

Mum nodded.

We had to wait an hour before one of the only two X-ray rooms in the entire hospital became available. And then we had to wait another forty-five minutes before a doctor came to see us. The doctor finally gave Mum two injections at the base of her finger to numb any pain she might feel whilst he reset her bone, but he wriggled the needle around so much each time, that poor Mum was almost biting a chunk out of her lip by the time he'd finished. He prodded it a few times.

'Does that hurt?' the doctor asked.

'No.'

'You're sure.'

'Of course I'm sure. I'm hardly going to say no otherwise, am I?'

The doctor acknowledged Mum had a point with a nod of his head. He carefully manipulated her finger, feeling along it on both sides before giving it a hard tug. Jude and I winced and I for one closed my eyes. He should've given us some warning. I didn't realize he was going to just yank it.

'Did that hurt?' he asked, immediately.

Mum shook her head. 'The injections did,' she said. 'That didn't.'

'Good,' the doctor smiled. He took a bandage out of his pocket and started binding Mum's index finger to her middle finger. 'You'll need to keep this out of water and bandaged for the next three weeks.'

'Three weeks! I can't keep my fingers bandaged up for that long. I'm a housemaid. How can I clean anything with my fingers like this?'

'You either keep them bandaged for three weeks or you can forget about being able to use them at all,' the doctor warned. 'You must give your finger a chance to heal.'

'But, Doctor . . .'

'I mean it, Mrs McGregor. If you don't take my advice, you'll regret it.'

Mum scowled at him, but she got the message.

'You OK, now Mum?' I asked as we left our curtained cubicle.

'I'll live.' Mum's voice was clipped with worry. She headed straight back to Nurse Carter's station. Using her left hand, she knocked on the door – three smart taps that signalled business. The door opened almost immediately.

'I'll be back first thing tomorrow morning with my ID and I'm going to trust you to delete my sons' ID info from your database,' Mum said.

'Which son?' Nurse Carter asked.

'Both of them,' Mum declared.

'Don't worry,' Nurse Carter smiled gently. 'It's as good as done already. You have nothing to worry about.'

Mum visibly relaxed. 'Good. Good! Thanks for all your help.'

'My pleasure.' Nurse Carter shut the door as Mum turned to leave.

Moments later we were out of A&E – thank goodness – and on our way home. It was a good forty-minute walk back home, but the early April night wasn't too chilly. I looked up and made a wish on the first star I saw – something Sephy had taught me. The same wish made on every star I saw.

'Is your finger still OK?' Jude asked Mum.

'Yes. The injections haven't worn off yet.' Mum smiled.

They walked side by side back home, with me trailing behind them.

Our IDs were on the hospital database. Why did that worry me so much?

Don't be silly, I told myself. *You're agonizing over nothing.*

How did the saying go? If you go looking for trouble, you will surely find it.

fifty-three. Sephy

I limit myself to a glass a night, just enough to warm me up and chill me out. Waking up the following morning after my first night's drinking had taught me not to overdo it. Each minute sound, each tiny movement had set off a series of massive explosions in my head like nothing I'd ever experienced before – and I never wanted to go through that again either. All things in moderation. I'm not a drunk, not like Mother. I just drink because . . . Well, because.

I don't like the taste of this stuff particularly. And God knows it still gives me the worst morning headaches I've ever had in my life. But it makes me feel OK when I'm drinking it. Kind of warm and careless. It smooths out the rough edges – as Mother says. I don't mind so much about Mother any more. I don't even mind so much about Callum. A couple of drinks and I don't mind about anything.

Isn't that cool?

fifty-four. Callum

Mum went back and had our information deleted off the hospital database but she's still not happy. The slightest noise outside, the lightest knock at the door and we have to scrape her off the ceiling.

'Why don't you just walk around with an "I am guilty!" sign wrapped around you?' Dad snapped.

I winced the moment he said it, as did Mum.

'I'm sorry, Meggie,' Dad sighed.

Mum turned and walked away from him, without saying a word. Dad slammed out of the house. Jude turned up the telly volume, even though it was fine as it was before. I bent my head and carried on with my homework.

But we couldn't go on like that.

We were all sitting down for Sunday lunch of mince and spaghetti when Mum suddenly threw down her fork.

'Ryan, I want you out of this house,' Mum declared.

The floor beneath my chair disappeared and I started free falling.

'W-what?' Dad frowned.

'I want you out of this house by morning. I've thought about it and this is the only way,' said Mum. 'It's too late for you and me, but it's not too late for Jude. I'm not going to let you drag a noose around his neck. I love him too much to let you do that.'

'I love him too,' Dad stared at her.

'I don't like the way you show it,' Mum told him. 'So you must leave.'

'I'm damned if I'll leave my own house,' Dad declared.

'You will if you love any of us as much as you say you do,' Mum said.

I looked from Dad to Mum and back again, horrified. I wasn't the only one at the table who knew that Mum meant every word.

'You've never understood why I'm doing this,' Dad said bitterly. 'I want something more for my sons. Something better.'

'And the end justifies the means?'

'Yes. In this case it does. Especially when the daggers haven't left us with any other option.'

'I'm not arguing with you, Ryan. Just pack your b-bags and leave. OK?'

'No, it's not OK,' Dad shouted, making us all jump.

'If Dad leaves, then so do I,' Jude piped up.

'No, you won't,' Mum and Dad spoke in unison.

Jude looked at Dad, bewildered. 'But you can't stop me from belonging to the Liberation Militia. I'm not going to bow out now.'

'Jude . . .' Mum said, intensely hurt.

'Mum, for the first time in my life I'm doing something I totally believe in. I can actually do some good, make a difference.'

Make a difference . . .

'I'm sorry if that upsets you but sending Dad away

won't change my mind. I'll just go with him, that's all.'

'And if I don't take you?' Dad asked.

'Then I'll find somewhere else to stay. But I'm not giving up the L.M. I'm not.'

'Then you can both leave,' Mum said, stonily. 'And I'll do whatever I have to do to protect Callum. If I can only save one of my children then so be it.'

They all started shouting and screaming at each other at that. I stood up and headed for the door. I had to get out of there. Fast. They were all too busy hating each other to notice me. I slipped out of the front door and ran.

fifty-five. Sephy

'Hi Callum, old friend! Old buddy! Old pal! How are you on this glorious day? Isn't it a beautiful Sunday? The birds are singing. Not over here, but somewhere they must be singing, don't you think? Don't you think, old buddy? Old pal?' I burst out laughing.

Callum had a very strange look on his face as he watched me. He wasn't laughing though. Why wasn't he laughing? I tried to stop, but the look on his face made me laugh even harder. He leaned forward and sniffed at my breath. The look on his face made me laugh until my eyes began to water.

And the next thing I knew, Callum had me by the

shoulders and was shaking me like a country dog shakes a rabbit.

'S–s–stop i–it . . .'

'What the hell d'you think you're doing?' Callum shouted at me.

The look on his face scared me. Actually scared me. I'd never seen him so furiously angry before. 'L–let go . . .'

Callum let go of me almost before the words were out of my mouth. I stumbled backwards and fell in a heap. I tried to scramble to my feet but the beach was swaying. If the beach would just stop swaying for two seconds . . .

'Look at you, Sephy,' Callum said, his voice ringing with disgust. 'You're drunk as a skunk.'

'I am not. I've had just one glass of cider today, that's all. Or maybe two,' I giggled, adding conspiratorially. 'It would've been wine, but I don't want Mother to get suspicious . . .'

'How could you be so *stupid*?' Callum roared. I wished he'd stop. He was making my head hurt. 'You want to end up like your mother?'

'Don't be ridiculous.' I finally managed to get to my feet, but the whole world was rocking beneath them.

'I'm not. I can't stand your mother but at least she had a reason to start. What's your excuse? Not enough attention? Daddy's allowance not big enough? Mummy not giving you enough love? Bed not wide enough? Bedroom carpet not plush enough?'

'Stop it . . .' I was sobering up fast. Callum was being *horrible*. 'Don't stand there and judge me. How dare you?'

'If you behave like a complete moron, don't bleat when that's how others treat you.'

'I'm not a moron.'

'No, you're worse. You're a drunk. A lush. An alcy.'

I covered my ears. 'Don't say that. That's enough . . .'

'Is it? Come on then. I'm waiting to hear your reasons. I'm all ears.'

'You wouldn't understand.'

'Try me.'

'I'm tired, OK,' I shouted at him, shouted for the whole world to hear.

'Tired of what?'

'Of my mother and father, my sister, of you too if you must know. I'm tired of the way you all make me feel. This is it for me, isn't it? Be a good girl, study at school, study at university, get a good job, marry a good man, live a good life and they all lived happily ever after. The whole thing just makes me . . . makes me want to puke. I want something more in my life . . .'

'And you reckon you'll find it in a wine bottle?'

I kicked at the sand beneath my feet. 'I don't know where else to look,' I finally admitted.

'Sephy, don't follow your mother, OK? She's headed for a mental home – or a coffin. Is that really what you want?'

That made me start and no mistake. Was that really where Mother was going? I didn't want her to die like that. *I* didn't want to die like that. I regarded Callum, seeing myself as he must see me. A silly, pathetic child who thought that drinking was a way to grow older faster. A way to stop feeling, 'cause then nothing could hurt me.

'I should be getting back,' I said at last, massaging my throbbing temples.

'Sephy, promise me you won't drink any more.'

'No,' I said at once.

Callum looked so hurt and unhappy, that I couldn't leave it there. I just couldn't.

'But I promise I'll try,' I added.

On the spur of the moment, I leaned forward and kissed Callum on the lips. He moved back.

'Don't want to see what kissing is like any more – huh?' I tried to tease.

'You stink of alcohol,' Callum told me.

My smile vanished. 'D'you know something, Callum? Sometimes you can be just as cruel as my dad is to my mother.'

'Sorry.'

I turned to walk away.

'Sephy, I'm sorry.' Callum pulled me back.

'Just get lost.'

'Not without you.' Callum gave a pathetic attempt at a smile.

'Leave me alone,' I screamed at him, knocking his arm away. 'I should've known you wouldn't understand. I should've realized. Besides, you have other fish to fry now. You're part of the Liberation Militia. You must be so proud of yourselves . . '

'I'm not a member of the L.M. I never have been,' Callum denied harshly.

'How did you know about the bomb at the Dundale then?'

Callum pressed his lips firmly together. I recognized that look, he wasn't going to say a word.

'You should've let me get blown up, Callum. Sometimes . . . sometimes I wish you had . . .'

Callum kissed me then. And it wasn't like the first time we'd kissed either. He wrapped his arms around me and closed his eyes and kissed me. And after a startled moment, I did exactly the same.

And it wasn't bad, either.

But it wasn't enough. Our kiss deepened and his hands began to wander, and so did mine.

And it made things better. But it wasn't enough.

fifty-six. Callum

Of course I admit it. Things went too far. We didn't go all the way. Not *all* the way. But I'd only meant to kiss her to show that I didn't care if she reeked of ruddy cider. I wouldn't even care if her face was covered with puke . . . well, maybe that's going a bit far! But I wanted to show her . . . Anyway. I'm going to have to be more careful. Sephy's just a kid really. We both stopped in time. Not just one of us. I think we both realized we were moving too far too fast.

But now, the thing is, I'm doing my head in thinking about her. Jude would bust a gut if he could read my mind. He'd probably literally do it too. I'm only sixteen and Sephy's not even fifteen yet. In my world the trouble never stops. In hers, it never starts. This drinking nonsense is just her way of getting attention. I mean, it's not even as if she's getting drunk on proper booze. Not whisky or gin or vodka but cider, for goodness' sake! She's bored, that's all it is. I wish she could live half my life. Just half. That'd soon give her something to occupy her time.

Come on, Callum, think of something else or you'll never get any sleep. I wonder what she's doing at this precise moment. Lying in bed thinking of me? I hope so.

Dear God, if you really are out there, somewhere, please find some way for Sephy and I to be together when we're older. For good and all when we're older. Together for ever. Dear God, please. If it's not too much to ask. If you're out there . . .

Callum for goodness' sake, stop daydreaming and get some sleep. You're being totally pathetic. Stop it!

There was no warning. No knock at the door. No warning shouts. Nothing. The first I knew about it was the CRASH when our front door was battered in. Shouts. Calls. A scream. Footsteps charging. Doors banging. More shouts. More footsteps – pound, pound, pound up the stairs. By the time I was fully awake and had swung my legs out of bed, smoke was everywhere. At least I thought it was smoke. I dropped to the floor.

'Jude? JUDE!' I yelled, terrified that my brother was still asleep. I jumped up, looking around for him.

It was only then that I realized it wasn't smoke filling my room, filling the house. The strong smell of garlic caught in the back of my throat and brought instant tears to my eyes. I coughed and coughed, my lungs threatening to explode from my body and my eyes were streaming. *Tear gas.* I struggled to my feet and groped my way to the front door.

'DOWN! GET DOWN!' A voice, no, more than one voice, screamed at me.

I turned in the direction of the voice, only to be pushed to my knees, then down to the ground. My chin hit the hard floor, making me bite down on my tongue. My arms were jerked behind my body. Hands bent back. Cold, hard steel cutting into my wrists. My eyes hurt. My lungs hurt. My tongue hurt. I was pulled to my knees, then yanked up. Pushed and pulled and punched forward. I couldn't see. I closed my burning eyes – and I admit, I was crying by now, trying to clear the tear gas, desperate to stop the pain. My lungs were being filed with sandpaper. Stop breathing. Just stop. But I couldn't. And each breath was strong as ammonia, sharp as a razor.

'JUDE! MUM! DAD!' I called out, only to choke over the words. Only to choke. I couldn't take much more. My body began to seize up, curl in on itself. And suddenly we were out. Out of the house. Out into the cool, night air. I tried to draw a breath. My lungs were being sliced. I gasped. More air – clean, fresh air. Just as I was pushed into the back of a car, I heard my mum crying.

'MUM!' I called. I blinked, and blinked again, looking around, trying to see her. Shapes and shadows swam before me. The car took off. My hands were still handcuffed behind my back. My whole body hurt.

And I still didn't know why.

fifty-seven. Sephy

I can't keep doing this, bouncing between Mother and Minnie and school and Callum like a pinball. Everyone's controlling my life except me. And I can feel it's going to get worse, not better. I need to do something. I need . . . I need to get out of here.

But Callum . . .

I don't want to lose him. I don't want to leave him. But I must. Callum's a survivor. I'm not. He'll understand if I explain it to him. I can't think when I'm around him. He confuses me. Around him, all I do is think about him. Sad, but true! Pathetic, but true!

He kissed me tonight. And held me. And ran his hands over my back and my bum and my waist. And pressed me against him. And it felt so strange. Like I belonged right there with him. Except I didn't. I wish I knew why he did it. If only I could read his mind.

Wouldn't it be wonderful if Callum and I . . ?

STOP!

Don't be ridiculous. You're fourteen, for goodness' sake. Sephy, you need to get a life − literally! By the time you're ready to settle down, Callum will probably be married with six kids. Sort yourself out first, your life out second, and your love life out last! As if Callum would be interested in a kid like you anyway?

But he did kiss me . . .

Listen to me, talking to myself. Telling myself off. I'm really losing it. But I need to take my own advice. Get away. Get a life. Start now, before it's too late.

'Mother, I want to go away to school.'

Mother opened her eyes and blinked at me like a stunned owl. 'W-what, sweetie?'

'I want to go away to school. I need to get away from here, from . . . everything.'

'W-where would you go?' Mother struggled to sit up on her bed. Her eyes were vampire red. There was a tell-tale smell in the room. I looked at Mother and it was like looking in a mirror that foretold the future. But only for an instant. The smell was vile, the sight was worse. And the mirror cracked.

'I want to go away to school. A boarding school some-where . . .'

Callum . . .

'I was thinking maybe Chivers Boarding School 'cause it's not too far away.'

Just far enough away to keep me away from here. Too far for weekend visits in either direction. Far enough away to find something I liked about myself. Far enough away to grow up.

'Only about one hundred and fifty kilometres,' I continued.

Callum . . .

'But . . . what would I do without you?'

I could see from Mother's eyes that our conversation

was finally beginning to sink in.

'You'll have Minnie. And the servants. And all your friends and your parties and . . . everything.' I forced a smile. 'I want to go. Please, Mother?'

'You really want to leave?'

'Yes.'

Mother looked at me. A moment of perfect understanding between us. And it made me so sad. I almost changed my mind then. Almost. But not quite.

'I can see you've made your mind up about this.'

'I have.'

'And when would you want to start?'

'Now. Or in September at the latest.'

'But September's only a few months away.'

'I know.'

Mother looked at me, then lowered her gaze. 'I don't think so, sweetie,' she said, sombrely.

'Mother, I want to go.'

'I don't think it's a good idea,' Mother said, shaking her head.

'For who? You or me?'

'I said no, Sephy.'

I turned and slammed out of her room, grimly satisfied at the muffled wail Mother let out at the noise. I leaned against the wall, trying to figure out what my next move should be. In a moment of pure clarity I realized there was only one thing holding me back. One person stopping me from packing my bags and walking to Chivers right now. I had no idea how I was going to explain my plans to him but I had to. Callum would understand. He'd be on my side once he understood my reasons. Callum and I were like two sides of the same coin.

If Mother thought I was going to let the matter stop and drop here, she had another thought coming. I needed to get away. Get out.

Before it was too late.

fifty-eight. Callum

'Tell me about your brother's involvement with the Liberation Militia.'

'My brother's not in the Liberation Militia,' I denied, the words coming out as little more than a slur. I was so tired. How long had we been doing this? One hour? Twenty?

Two plain-clothed officers sat at the table opposite me. Only one of them was doing the talking though. This was obviously their version of bad cop, silent cop. 'I'll ask you again, which L.M. cell d'you belong to?'

'I don't. I don't. I don't.'

'When did Jude join the Liberation Militia?'

'He didn't – as far as I know.'

'When did your mother join the L.M.?'

'She didn't. She hasn't.'

'You sound very sure.'

'I am.'

'You weren't that sure about your brother.'

'I . . . I am.'

'What L.M. cell does your father belong to?'

'None of them.'

'Come on now. We know all about your family's involvement with the L.M.'

'What d'you need me for then?'

The two officers exchanged a look. I was cheesing them off. Good.

'Corroboration,' said the silent one at last. 'Confirm what we know already and we'll go easy on you.'

'I don't know anything.' I tried to rest my head on my arms on the table but the one who'd done most of the talking pushed my head back up. I sat back in my chair, utterly weary and something else besides. But I wasn't going to show them that.

'Don't mess us about, son.'

'I'm not your son.'

'And I'm not someone you want to make an enemy of,' said the non-talkative officer.

'Whose idea was the Dundale bomb? Your brother's or your father's?'

'You all hate Crosses, don't you?'

'You'd all do whatever it took to annihilate the lot of us. That's true, isn't it?'

'How old were you when you joined the L.M.?'

And on. And on. And round. And round. Question after question. No rest. No peace. No respite. Until my head was spinning giddy and each question echoed with the one before it and the one before that. Until I thought, *So this is what it's like to go crazy . . .*

And what about Mum and Dad and Jude? Where were

they? What were they doing? Why were the police so intent on my brother? I bit down hard on my bottom lip, terrified that I was actually voicing my thoughts, terrified of what I might give way. Think of something else. Think of nothing at all. Think of nothing. And that's when my mind closed down and the world stopped spinning.

I opened my eyes slowly. Please, no more questions. I couldn't take any more questions. I wasn't in the interrogation room any more. I was back in my cell, with Mum sitting on the bed beside me, stroking my hair back off my face.

'Callum? Thank goodness. Are you OK? They didn't hurt you.'

I took my time to sit up, shaking my head as I did so.

'W-where's Dad? Where's Jude?' I asked.

'Your dad's still being questioned and,' Mum took a deep breath, 'I don't know where Jude is. He wasn't in the house when those animals came crashing in.'

'He wasn't? What's going on? What do they want? Why're they going on and on about Jude?'

'They found an empty can of drink near to where the Dundale bomb went off,' Mum said grimly.

'So?'

'So, the can had Jude's prints all over it. So they say. It's a damned lie of course but they reckon they cross-referenced it with the print on his ID card.'

'But how did they get hold of his ID card . . ?' And then I realized.

Mum nodded. 'They scanned in his card when we were at the hospital. I guess they got the information from the computer before the nurse had a chance to delete it – if she ever really did.'

'But Jude didn't . . .' I looked straight at Mum. 'Did he?'

'They're saying he planted the bomb. They're saying w-when they catch him, he'll . . . he'll hang.' And Mum's face dissolved into a stream of tears.

'They won't get him. Once Jude knows they're looking for him . . .' I said, frantically.

'It's just a matter of time.' Mum shook her head. 'We both know that. And they've already issued a reward for information leading to his capture.'

'What kind of reward?'

'Fifty thousand.'

There was nothing to be said at that. Words and tears and prayers were useless. With that kind of money up for grabs it was just a matter of time before Jude was arrested.

'They've probably planted the evidence themselves. They don't have a clue who planted that bomb and they're just looking for a scapegoat.' My voice was barely above a whisper. I couldn't take it all in. They wanted to *hang* my brother. Nothing on this earth would make me believe he'd actually planted that car bomb. He might've been there, but he wouldn't've been the one to put it together and set it to go off. Jude wouldn't do that. He wouldn't. 'If they only want Jude, why're they still questioning Dad?'

'Dad demanded to see them once we knew why they were after Jude,' Mum told me.

'Why? What's Dad doing?'

'I have no idea.' Mum wiped her eyes with the back of

her hand. 'Probably saying the same as you, no doubt. I just hope he's careful.'

I stared at Mum. 'What d'you mean?'

Mum just shook her head. Before I could speak, the cell door clicked open. An officer I hadn't seen yet, opened the door wide. He was a slim man with cutting eyes who looked at us like we were worse than nothing.

'You two can go now.'

'Where's my husband?' Mum asked at once.

'He's being held, after which he'll be formally charged,' the officer told us.

'Charged with what?' I asked.

'My husband has done nothing wrong. Why's he being held?' Mum asked, her voice shaking, but it was hard to tell whether it shook with fear or anger.

'Get your things and leave,' the officer said. 'I haven't got all day.'

'I demand to know why you're holding my husband. I want to see him – now.' Mum exploded.

One look at the officer's furious expression was enough to tell me that there'd be snowball throwing contests in hell before this guy helped us in any way.

'You can leave or you can spend the rest of the night in this cell,' the officer's voice dripped ice. 'It's your choice.'

'May I see my husband please?' Mum forced herself to be civil. But it was too late.

'I'm afraid not. No-one but his lawyer will be allowed to see him until after he's formally charged,' the officer told us.

'What is he going to be charged with?' I asked again, desperate for an answer.

'Political terrorism and seven counts of murder.'

fifty-nine. Sephy

'Come on, Callum! Pick up the phone.'

Nothing doing. It just continued to ring. I glanced down at my watch. Where was everyone? Someone should've picked up the phone by now. It was almost nine o'clock in the morning for goodness' sake!

I put the phone down, trying to swallow down the uneasy feeling in my stomach.

Wait till later, then tell him your news in person. Tell him that come September, you'll be gone.

Will he try to persuade you to stay? Will he even care?

Wait till later and find out.

sixty. Callum

The offices of Stanhope and Rigby were every shade of dingy grey and dirty white imaginable. The waiting-room chairs were more like benches, made from the hardest –

and I do mean *hardest* – oak. The coffee machine had scum marks all over it. And the windows were so dirty it was impossible to make out anything beyond them. This was the fifth solicitor's office offering free legal aid that Mum and I had tried. Once the other solicitors had learned about Dad's case, we'd been shown the door so fast I was beginning to suffer from jet lag. But this office was by far the seediest. I told myself that beggars couldn't be choosers, but it didn't help.

'Mum, let's go,' I said, standing up. 'We can find better solicitors than this.'

'What d'you mean?' Mum frowned.

'Look at this place. I bet even cockroaches avoid this dump.'

'Don't judge by appearances.' A voice from behind made me jump. Mum stood up as I turned around.

A middle-aged man with jet black hair, silvering at the temples, stood in the doorway. He wore a checked shirt and denims and an expression on his face that was harder than titanium nails.

'And you are?' I asked.

'Adam Stanhope,' the man replied.

'This is your company, Mr Stanhope?' Mum asked.

'My father started it. I've carried it on,' he said.

I was impressed with that, for a start. Only one of the other solicitors we'd tried had been a nought. The rest had been Crosses. I knew there were no nought barristers but I hadn't expected to come across a nought solicitor whose father had been a solicitor before him. 'Where's Mr or Ms Rigby then?' I asked, still not sure whether or not I liked this guy.

'Dead. This way please.' Mr Stanhope turned and led the way out of the waiting room.

Mum gave me one of her warning looks as we followed him. We walked behind him, our footsteps not so much clicking as crunching on the cracked lino. Goodness only knew what it was covered with. A thin coating of honey-flavoured cereal from the sticky feel of it. We stopped outside a door which looked like a reinforced toilet cubicle door. Mr Stanhope flung open the door and – wow!

Polished wooden floor, creamy-white walls, mahogany furniture, leather sofa, every thing in the room spelt class with a capital C! I stared at Mr Stanhope, amazed.

'I thought you'd like my office!' Mr Stanhope said dryly. 'Tell me, d'you think this room makes me a better solicitor or a worse one?'

I got the point. 'Why is your waiting room so grotty then?'

'Let's just say that Crosses are shall we say, reassured by its appearance,' said Mr Stanhope. 'It doesn't pay to appear too successful. Please take a seat, both of you.'

I waited until Mum sat down first before doing the same.

'How can I help you, Mrs . . ?'

'Mrs McGregor,' Mum supplied. 'It's about my husband, Ryan. He's being held by the police.'

'Has he been formally arrested?'

'Yes.' Mum lowered her head, before forcing herself to look Mr Stanhope straight in the eye. 'He's been charged with murder and political terrorism.'

'The Dundale bombing,' Mr Stanhope sat back in his chair.

'That's right,' Mum replied. 'But he didn't do it. I know he didn't do it.'

'He told you that, did he?'

'The police won't let me talk to him. I need a lawyer, someone who can get in to see him on my behalf.'

'I see.'

'I don't have much money.'

'I see.'

'I saw in the telephone directory that you do legal aid work?'

If Mr Stanhope leaned any further back his whole body would sink right through the chair. Did he think bad luck was contagious then?

'Can you help us?' Mum asked, a tinge of impatience in her voice.

Mr Stanhope stood up and went to look out of his crystal-clear window. Venetian blinds were positioned to let in optimum light while still keeping the room private. I wondered what he could see. I wished I knew what he was thinking.

'Legal aid wouldn't begin to cover the costs in a case like this,' Mr Stanhope began. 'I can't work for free, Mrs McGregor . . .'

'I'm not asking you to,' Mum replied rapidly. 'I'll pay you whatever it takes. I just want my husband's name cleared.'

Mr Stanhope gave Mum a long hard look before answering. 'I'll go and see your husband first. Then I'll make a decision.'

Mum nodded and stood up.

'But from this moment on, you talk to no-one but me. Understood?'

Mum nodded again.

I stood up and asked, 'Mr Stanhope, are you any good?'

'Pardon?'

'As a lawyer, are you any good?'

'Callum!' Mum admonished.

'No, Mrs McGregor, it's a fair question.' Mr Stanhope turned to me. 'I've won far more cases than I've lost. OK?'

'OK.' I nodded.

We left the office.

Mum and I sat in the police-station waiting room for ages and ages. No-one offered us a coffee. A couple of times we got a 'Can I help you?' from officers entering the station, but that was all. Mr Stanhope had disappeared to talk to Dad and 'review the police case'. They didn't have a case, so what was taking so long? I wanted to see Dad. I wondered where Jude was. I wanted to go home and wake up and find that the last year hadn't happened. I wanted too much.

Mum stared ahead, twisting her thumbs around each other whilst we waited. I was beginning to wonder if Mr Stanhope had just given up and gone home and we'd been forgotten, when he finally made an appearance. And from the look on his face, I could tell right away that it wasn't good news.

'What's the matter? Is he all right?' Mum leapt to her feet. 'What have they done to him?'

'Could both of you come with me please?' Mr Stanhope said grimly.

After exchanging a worried look, Mum and I followed

the lawyer without a word. A police officer held open one of the heavy double-doors which led to the cells.

'Thank you.' Mr Stanhope acknowledged the gesture, as did my mum.

I didn't. The officer walked behind us. When we got to the last cell on the left, we all stood to one side as the officer opened the door. The moment the door was open, Mum flew into the room. I hadn't blinked before Dad and Mum were hugging each other as if they were glued together.

'Ryan, what's going on?' Mum whispered. 'Are you OK? You're not hurt . . ?'

Dad turned to beckon to me. Slowly, I walked over to him, knowing that he was going to hug me too. I wasn't wrong either. I wanted to be hugged by him. I didn't want to let him go because I was so scared. He hadn't done anything. Why was he still being held?

'Mr McGregor, would you like to tell your family what you told me?' Mr Stanhope asked.

'Never mind that,' Dad dismissed. 'Where's Jude? Have they let him go? Is he safe?'

'Jude? The police never had him. He wasn't in the house.' Mum frowned. 'I have no idea where he is.'

Dad stared, then he looked so furiously angry that I found myself taking a step backwards.

'Those bastards! They said they had him. They said Jude was as good as hanged . . .' Dad swallowed hard and turned away from Mum and me. Now he looked like the whole world had descended onto his shoulders.

'Ryan, w–what did you do?' Mum whispered.

Silence.

'Ryan . . ?'

'I signed a confession admitting to all the charges . . .' Dad's voice trailed off.

'What?' Mum breathed. 'Are you crazy?'

'They said they had Jude — and proof he was the bomber. They said someone had to take the blame for the Dundale bomb and it was up to me who took the fall.'

'And you believed them?' Mum asked furiously.

'Meggie, they threatened that you and Callum would also go to prison for conspiracy. It was my life or the lives of my entire family.'

'Did you do it? Did you plant the bomb that killed all those people?'

Dad looked straight at Mum. He didn't even blink. 'No.'

'Then why . . ?'

'I had no choice,' Dad repeated. Anger held his body tense and rigid. He looked like he was about to snap in half.

Mum blinked, totally bemused. 'If you put your hand up to the Dundale murders, you'll hang.'

'I know,' said Dad quietly.

I looked at Mr Stanhope, as if his face could tell me what I couldn't understand on Dad's.

'You want to die?' Mum asked, bewildered.

'Don't be stupid.'

'Mrs McGregor, the moment Detective Inspector Santiago told your husband the identification of the person whose prints were found, your husband confessed to everything. And his dictating and signing of the confession were videotaped. The tape will clearly show his confession was made without duress,' said Mr Stanhope softly.

Dad lowered his head and lowered his voice to match, until it was barely above a hushed whisper. 'Meggie, they found two of Jude's fingerprints on a cola can fragment in the bin where the bomb went off . . .'

'That doesn't prove anything . . .' Mum interrupted, her voice harsh. 'That just means . . .'

'A print was also found on part of the bomb casing that survived the explosion,' Dad cut across her. 'And the prints match . . .'

The world flipped crazily and I started to fall faster and further away from sanity.

Jude was the bomber . . .

That couldn't be right. The Crosses had set him up, framed him. My brother wasn't a bomber. He wouldn't do anything like that. And he certainly wouldn't be stupid enough to leave his fingerprints all over the bomb casing – unless he thought there wouldn't be anything left of the bomb to identify one way or another so why bother to wear gloves? Jude was the bomber . . .

'I told the police the truth.' Dad raised his voice to its normal level. 'I brought the cola from home. I didn't want to risk anyone seeing me if I went into the shops to buy one. That's the only reason it's got Jude's fingerprints on it. He must've handled it and put it back and I didn't realize. And as for the casing, I kept the . . . the necessary equipment around the house. Jude must have handled that as well. He obviously didn't realize what he was touching, he was just curious.' Dad raised his head and spun around, shouting into each corner of the room in turn, 'Jude had nothing to do with this, d'you hear? I'm guilty. No-one else.'

They didn't believe that, did they? No-one in his or her right mind would believe that ridiculous cock-and-bull story.

'Ryan . . .' Tears flowed down Mum's face.

'No, Meggie. I'm guilty. That's the truth and I'm sticking to it. I won't let them put you and Callum in prison for this. Or Jude,' Dad interrupted. He lowered his voice again. 'Just make sure that Jude stays lost so the daggers can't get their hands on him. If they find him, he'll rot in prison.' A tiny, sad smile played over Dad's face, but it was gone in an instant. 'But at least my confession means he won't die.'

sixty-one. Sephy

'*Today, Ryan Callum McGregor of 11, Hugo Yard, Meadowview was formally charged with Political Terrorism and seven counts of murder for the bombing outrage at the Dundale Shopping Centre. He has confessed to all charges so the court case against him will be a mere formality. His family consisting of his wife Margaret and two sons, Jude and Callum, are said to be in hiding.*'

Every word was an arrow pinning me to my chair.

But he didn't do it. I knew that as surely as I knew my own name. Callum's dad was no more the bomber than I was. Of course, he didn't do it. I had to help. I had to prove that. But how? There had to be some way. Something I could do. What could I do to help him?

Think. Think . . .

'Blanker scumbag!' Minnie hissed from across the room. 'His whole family should swing, not just him.'

'Minerva, I won't have language like that in this house, d'you hear? You don't live in Meadowview.'

'Yes, Mother,' Minnie said, chastened. But it didn't last long. 'And to think we've had him here, in this very house. And his wife actually used to work here. If the press get hold of that little bit of info, they're going to have a field day – and Dad's going to have kittens.'

'What d'you mean?' I asked.

'Oh Sephy, use your brain. If Ryan McGregor gets off, Dad will be accused of favouritism and protecting his own and all sorts, whether or not it has anything to do with him.'

'But the Dundale bomb had nothing to do with Mr McGregor . . .'

'Nonsense. He's confessed, hasn't he?'

I turned to Mother. She looked very thoughtful.

'Mother, they won't really hang him, will they?'

'If he's guilty . . .' Mother shrugged.

'And Callum goes to our school,' Minnie continued. 'Dad's going to get it in the neck for that as well.'

'Callum has absolutely nothing to do with this.'

'An apple never falls far from the tree,' Minnie nodded.

'What a pile of . . .'

'Persephone!' Mother's harsh warning had me biting back the rest of what I wanted to say.

'Even if Ryan McGregor is guilty – which I don't believe for one second – that doesn't mean that Callum . . .'

'Oh, Persephone. Grow up.' The rebuke didn't come from my sister. Mother shook her head at me before she stood up and left the room.

'You haven't a clue about the real world, have you?' Minnie said, her voice dripping with contempt.

'Congratulations! You sound just like Mother,' I took malicious delight in telling her.

Minnie said something incredibly unladylike and flounced out of the room. I smirked at her disappearing back until the door was shut. Then my smile faded. I stared at the closed door, feeling totally alone. What was it about me that made everyone do that? Walk out. Leave. Abandon me. After dismissing me. Why did what I said and did invariably drive everyone away.

Mother. Minnie. Even Callum.

But I was right about this one. Callum's dad wasn't the Dundale bomber.

Mother and Minnie were wrong. And I was going to prove it. I just had to figure out how.

sixty-two. Callum

After only about five minutes of waiting, Mum and I were shown in to Mr Stanhope's plush office. His secretary had told Mum that it was 'urgent' and 'about the case' but that was all she said. Mum and I both had the same question – 'What case?' The last time we'd seen Mr Stanhope, which was three days ago now, he'd told us quite categorically that he wasn't going to take the case.

'Mrs McGregor, Callum, please take a seat.' Mr Stanhope was all smiles from the moment we set foot inside his hallowed walls. One look at his face and my heart began to thump with painfully suppressed hope.

'You have some news?' Mum asked eagerly. 'Are they going to let Ryan go?'

'I'm afraid not.' Mr Stanhope's smile faded slightly, his voice full of regret. 'Your husband still insists that he's guilty.'

And just like that the hope inside was all but snuffed out. Again. Why had he asked us here then?

'I've been trying to get in touch with you at your home address but there's been no reply,' Mr Stanhope told us.

'We're not at our house any more,' Mum glanced at me. 'We're staying with my sister, Charlotte, on the other side of Meadowview.'

'You've been getting hate letters?' Mr Stanhope asked sharply.

'Amongst other things,' I scoffed. Like bricks through the window and death threats.

'Well, I'm happy to tell you that I will now be able to take on your husband's case,' Mr Stanhope told Mum. 'And the really good news is, I've persuaded Kelani Adams QC to take the case – not that she took much persuading.'

'Kelani Adams!' Mum was astounded. And she wasn't the only one. Kelani Adams was not just a nationally renowned but a world-renowned barrister. A Cross barrister. Why would any Cross take on Dad's case? 'I can't afford a lawyer like Kelani Adams.' She shook her head.

'Don't worry about that. That's all taken care of.'

'What does that mean?' I asked, before Mum could.

'It means, it's all taken care of,' Mr Stanhope frowned at me.

Mum and I exchanged a long look.

'I'd appreciate it if you answered my son's question properly,' Mum said.

'An anonymous benefactor has stepped forward with a very generous sum of money, and a promise of however much more is necessary to ensure that your husband gets the fairest trial possible.' Mr McGregor picked his way carefully through the words.

'We don't take charity, Mr Stanhope,' Mum said, tight-lipped.

'It's not charity,' Mr Stanhope shot back. 'I was told to inform you of that in the strongest possible terms.'

'By who?' Mum asked.

'As I said, I received a banker's cheque and a typewritten, unsigned note with certain instructions,' said Mr Stanhope.

'May I see the note?'

'I'm afraid not. One of the conditions on it was that you shouldn't be allowed to see it.'

'I see.'

I'm glad she did, 'cause I sure as hell didn't.

'Mrs McGregor, this is your husband's one and only chance to emerge from this case a free man. I would strongly advise you to take it.'

'Let me get this straight,' Mum said slowly. 'The only reason you're still involved in this case is because someone has paid you to stay involved – is that right?'

'Well, I wouldn't put it quite like that . . .'

'And the only reason Kelani Adams is involved is because she's being paid a great deal of money – is that right?'

'No,' Mr Stanhope said at once. 'The money allowed me to approach the best and she's it. The best does not come cheaply. Once she'd read your husband's file, she was more than prepared to take the case.'

'And I'm meant to be grateful for that, am I?'

'If gratitude is too much to ask, then your acceptance of the situation is all that will be required,' said Mr Stanhope.

Mum turned to me. 'Callum?'

It was hard to be asked for my opinion. Part of me wanted to leave it all down to Mum. Lynette was gone, Jude had disappeared, Dad was in prison and Mum and I were left floundering on our own. I wanted Mum to turn to me and tell me that everything would be OK again. I wanted her to make all the decisions, even the wrong ones. Especially the wrong ones.

'Mum, I think we should do whatever it takes to get Dad out of prison,' I said at last.

'OK then,' Mum said to the solicitor. 'I'll go ahead with whatever you and Ms Adams suggest. But first of all I'd like to speak to my husband as soon as possible.' She looked from me to Mr Stanhope. 'Alone.'

'I'll see what I can do,' came the solicitor's reply.

And all I could do was hope that Mum and I weren't making a big, big mistake. Not just for our sakes – but for Dad's as well.

But for me the most sickeningly humbling thing of all was I knew who had sent the money to Mr Stanhope.

Sephy.

I had no idea how she'd done it. And I had even less idea how I was ever going to thank her, never mind repay her. But I would. I sat in Mr Stanhope's office, on his expensive brown leather chair and swore an oath before God that I would pay her back. If it took me every penny I earned for the rest of my life, I would repay her.

sixty-three. Sephy

I came home from school and got the shock of my life. Dad's suitcases were in our hallway.

'Dad? DAD?'

'I'm in here, Princess.'

I raced into the family room, following Dad's voice like I was tied to it.

I leapt into his arms.

'Dad! I've missed you.'

'I've missed you too.' Dad swung me around – at least he tried to. 'Good grief! What have you been eating?' he exclaimed, dropping me. 'You weigh a ton!'

'Thanks!' I giggled with pure joy. Dad was home. Dad was *back*. 'Are you staying for good?'

'For a while at least,' Dad nodded.

But not in my direction. For the first time I saw that we weren't alone.

Mother was sitting in her rocking-chair, moving slowly backwards and forwards as she watched us.

'What . . . what's going on?' I asked.

'Ask your father. He has all the answers,' Mother replied.

I clicked then. Clicked on and died inside. Dad wasn't back for Mother. He wasn't back for any of us. Ryan

McGregor and politics were the ones who'd brought him home – nothing else.

'You're only here until after the trial, aren't you?' I asked Dad.

'The trial of the century' was what the newspapers and the telly were calling it. They should call it the miracle trial of the millennium if it managed to bring Dad back home.

'It's all up in the air,' Dad smiled, stroking my cheek. 'Nothing's decided.'

I took one look at Mother and I knew that was a lie. At least, she believed it was a lie, which was probably the same thing.

sixty-four. Callum

'Ah, Callum. Come in.'

I was seeing a lot of plush offices this week. First Mr Stanhope, now Mr Costa, our headmaster. It was only the second time I'd been in Mr Costa's office. Crosses seemed to be big on mahogany! And his carpet was like walking on spring grass, soft and bouncy and lush. Mr Costa sat down behind his mahogany desk and leaned back, then leaned forward, his elbows on his table as he tried to figure out which would be the most favourable position. His chair was more like a throne than otherwise, making the headmaster seem even more imposing. The sunshine shone through his crystal-clear windows behind him, making him even darker, like he was a powerful silhouette.

'Sit down please.'

I sat down in one of his squeaky leather chairs.

'Callum, there's no easy way to say this, so I'm going to get right to the point.'

'Yes, sir?'

'Until the matter regarding your father is satisfactorily resolved . . .'

The alarm bells now pealing in my head were deafening.

'The governors and I have decided that it would serve everyone's best interests if you were suspended for a while.'

So that was that. I was out.

'I'm guilty until my dad's proven innocent? Is that the way it works?'

'Callum, I do hope you're going to be reasonable about this.'

'Should I empty my locker now or will the end of the day be soon enough?'

'That's entirely up to you.' Mr Costa folded his arms and sat back in his chair.

'You must be so thrilled,' I told him bitterly. 'Three down, only one more to go.'

'Meaning?'

'Meaning Colin has gone and you couldn't wait to get rid of Shania and now it's my turn.'

'Shania was expelled for gross misconduct,' Mr Costa said haughtily.

'Shania only slapped Gardner Wilson because he hit her

first,' I shouted at him. 'And everyone knows that, including you. How come Shania gets expelled and Gardner gets away with a telling off? Why isn't it gross misconduct when a Cross does it?'

It was the same story up and down the country. In the few schools into which us noughts had been allowed, we were dropping like flies. Expelled, or what the authorities euphemistically called 'excluded', for those things which would get Crosses detention or a severe telling off. The odd Cross or two may even have got suspended once in a while. But they certainly weren't being expelled with anything like the frequency we were.

'I have no intention of justifying school policy to you.' Mr Costa stood up. Our meeting was at an end. 'We'll be happy to review your situation once the dust from all this clears.'

But the dust was never going to clear, was it? And we both knew that.

'Good luck to you, Callum.' Mr Costa held out his hand.

'Yeah, right!' I looked at his hand with disdain.

Good luck to me, as long as it was somewhere else. The further away the better. As far as Mr Costa was concerned, I had already gone. I stood up and marched out of the room. I wanted to slam the door shut behind me, bring it off its hinges, but I wasn't going to give him the satisfaction of saying, 'See! I was right about him. Behaved just as I thought he would.'

And then I thought better of it. I turned back and slammed the door as hard as I could. I only just got my fingers out of the way in time but it was worth it. It was a futile gesture, but it made me feel good.

I strode down the corridor. Mr Costa came thundering out of his room.

'Callum, come here.'

I carried on walking.

'I said, come back here,' Mr Costa called after me, furiously.

I smiled – and carried on walking. I wasn't part of his school any more. I didn't have to do what he said. I wasn't part of the whole Cross way of life. Why should I do what any of them said? Only when I heard Mr Costa slam back into his office did I slow down. My throat had swollen up from the inside out. I was being gutted like a fish wriggling for its life on a slab. I was out of Heathcrofts.

And I was never coming back.

THE TRIAL . . .

sixty-five. Sephy

I hesitated for only a moment. Steeling myself, I knocked on my sister's bedroom door.

'Go away!'

I walked in, darting to my left as a pillow came hurtling towards me.

'Don't your ears work?' Minnie fumed. She was sitting up on her king-size bed, scowling like it was going out of fashion.

I wanted to giggle but I knew that might make her suspicious. Anyway, it would be a cider-induced giggle, not a real one. I wasn't so drunk that I didn't know that much.

'Minnie? I want to ask your advice about something.'

'Oh yes!' My sister raised a sceptical eyebrow. She's very good at that. She's going to be a Mother-clone when she grows up. Just like me, I guess – if I didn't do something about it.

'What would you say if I told you that I'm thinking of going away to school?'

I instantly had her full attention.

'Where?'

'Chivers.'

'The boarding school?'

I nodded.

Minnie looked me up and down until I began to feel really uncomfortable. She asked, 'What does Mother say about it?'

'She said no, but . . .'

'But then she would,' Minnie finished for me.

'So what d'you think?' I repeated.

'I think it's an excellent idea. Which is why I asked Mother the exact same thing a few weeks ago.' Minnie smiled dryly.

'You did!' I was astounded.

'You're not the only one who needs to get out of here.'

I sat down at the foot of Minnie's bed. 'Is it that obvious?'

'Sephy, you and I have never got on, and I'm sorry about that,' Minnie sighed. 'Maybe if we'd been able to count on each other, we'd have done better. Instead we've both tried to get through this on our own.'

'What d'you mean?'

'Come off it, Persephone. You drink to escape, I become more bitchy and spiteful. We each do what we have to do.'

Flames shot through my body. 'I don't drink . . .' I denied.

'Oh?' Minnie scoffed. 'Well, unless you've taken to wearing cider perfume, I'd say you're into booze big time.'

'Cider isn't alcohol.'

Minnie started laughing.

'Not like wine or whisky or something,' I said, furiously.

'And I just like the taste . . . That's the only reason. I'm not a lush.'

Minnie shuffled towards me as I spoke before she put her hand on my shoulder. 'Who're you trying to convince? Me or yourself?'

And then I did the last thing either of us expected. I burst into tears. My sister put her arm around me then, allowing my head to rest on her shoulder – which just made me feel worse.

'Minerva, I've got to get out of here. I've got to, before I explode.'

'Don't worry. I'm working on it with Dad.'

'Yeah, for yourself. But what about me?'

'No, I'm working on Dad for both of us,' said Minnie. 'I keep telling him that we both need to get away from the atmosphere in this house.'

I pulled away from Minnie to ask, 'Are you getting anywhere?'

'I think so. I'm wearing him down.'

'How come you didn't tackle Mother?' I had to ask.

'Because she cares too much,' Minnie replied.

'Whereas Dad doesn't care at all,' I said, bitterly.

'Not true. Dad does care in his own way.'

'Just not as much as he cares about his political career,' I added. 'He only moved back so it'd look good for the McGregor trial. And he's meant to be back but we hardly ever see him.'

'D'you want to see more of him then?' Minnie asked.

I considered. 'Not particularly.'

'Then be careful what you wish for,' Minnie told me.

'Don't worry, Sephy. Come September, you and I will both be out of this madhouse.'

'You're sure?'

'I promise.'

sixty-six. Callum

I sat up high in the packed public gallery. Far below me and to my right, I could see my father. Just the bruised left side of his face. It was only the second time I'd seen him since the police had crashed into our lives. The judge was droning on and on at the jury, telling them what the case was about and what it was not about. Twelve good men and women and true, hanging on the judge's every word. Twelve good Cross men and woman, of course. How else could justice be served? My stomach churned as the clerk of the court finally stood up and faced Dad.

'Ryan Callum McGregor, on the charge of Political Terrorism, how do you plead – Guilty or Not Guilty?'

'DAD, DON'T DO IT!' I couldn't help it. Even as the words left my mouth, I knew I was doing more harm than good but how could I just sit idly by and watch this . . . this farce of a trial.

'Any more outbursts from the public gallery and I will have all members of the public evicted from this court. I hope I've made myself understood,' Judge Anderson threatened.

He was glaring at me – as were all the members of the jury. Mum put a restraining hand over mine. Dad looked up and our eyes met. He looked away again, almost immediately. But not before the image of his battered face had burnt its way into my mind. His split lip and his bruised cheek and his black eye. But there was no condemnation on his face, just a sweeping, intense sadness. The clerk repeated his question.

'On the charge of Political Terrorism, how do you plead? Guilty or Not Guilty?'

Silence.

Silence that went on and on and on.

'The defendant will please answer the question,' Judge Anderson said brusquely.

Dad glanced up at Mum and me again.

'Not guilty!' he said at last.

A collective gasp broke out from every corner of the courtroom. Mum squeezed my hand. Whispers and inaudible comments flew around the room. Dad's lawyer turned around and smiled briefly at us. She was careful to wipe all trace of her smile off her face before she turned back to face the judge.

'You are charged, by means of the afore-mentioned state crime of political terrorism, with the murder of Aysha Pilling,' the clerk continued. 'How d'you plead? Guilty or Not Guilty?'

Dad's reply was stronger this time. 'Not guilty.'

And that was his reply to each of the separate charges read out to him. By the time the clerk had read the seventh murder charge, he had to shout to make himself heard.

So did Dad. 'NOT GUILTY!'

The courtroom erupted. The judge had everyone in the public gallery thrown out of the court, but I didn't care. It was one of the happiest moments of my life.

Not guilty! You tell 'em Dad!

sixty-seven. Sephy

I got the shock of my life. I received a subpoena saying I had to be in court on the following Monday. The subpoena was sent via Mother as I was underage, making her directly responsible for making sure that I turned up on the right day at the right time.

'Why do they want me there?' I said horrified, as I stared down at a whole load of legal jargon that I didn't really understand.

'That's what comes from hanging around noughts,' Minnie told me maliciously.

I was about to tell her where to go, when to my surprise, Mother jumped in before me.

'Minerva, if you kept quiet, you'd at least give the illusion that there's more in your head than just air!' Mother snapped.

Minnie flounced out at that – and good riddance. I turned to smile at Mother but her expression wasn't much better than Minnie's.

'This is exactly why I've always warned you to stay away from that boy – and his whole family,' Mother told me. 'Now our names are going to be dragged into court and through the mud and the newspapers are going to be ecstatic. Your father isn't going to like this one little bit.'

'It's hardly my fault,' I tried to defend myself.

'Then whose fault is it?' Mother snapped. 'Sephy, it's time you learnt that if you lie down with dogs, you're bound to get fleas.'

And she left the room, leaving me to stare after her.

sixty-eight. Callum

'Do you swear to tell the truth, the whole truth and nothing but the truth?'

I looked down at the Good Book under my hand. It was cool, almost cold beneath my fingers. The truth . . . Which version of the truth would this Cross court find acceptable?

'I do,' I replied. Although I spoke quietly, my voice rang out throughout the courtroom. They'd obviously turned my microphone up to maximum. They didn't want to miss a word. And I didn't want to say a word, afraid that one stray syllable would be the death of my dad. I looked around. The judge sat behind a raised platform. The witness box where I stood was next to the judge's platform from where we could both look out over the rest of the court. The prosecution lawyer, a hard-faced man called Shaun Pingule QC, sat glaring at me. Kelani Adams looked straight ahead, barely blinking. She looked like she was in a world of her own. Mind you, this was her world. It sure wasn't mine.

'You may be seated,' Judge Anderson told me.

'No,' I said, adding as an afterthought. 'Thank you. I'd rather stand.'

The judge turned away with just the slightest raising of one shoulder.

Shaun Pingule stood up. I held my breath.

'Could you state your full name for the record, please?'

Nothing to catch me out there. Or was there? Think. Keep your answers short, Callum.

'Callum Ryan McGregor.'

'Do you belong to the Liberation Militia?'

Kelani Adams jumped to her feet. 'I object, Your Honour. Callum McGregor is not on trial here.'

'It goes to witness credibility, Your Honour,' Pingule argued.

'I'll allow it,' the judge replied.

Pingule repeated his question. 'Do you belong to the Liberation Militia?'

'No, I don't,' I replied before the last word had died away.

'So you don't?'

'That's right. I don't.'

'Are you sure about that?'

'Your Honour . . .' Kelani was on her feet again.

'Move on, Mr Pingule,' Judge Anderson directed.

I stole a glance at the jury. Pingule had set me up and no mistake. By asking me the same question over and over, he'd made it out without saying explicitly that I was lying. I could see the suspicion in the faces of the jury already and I'd only been asked one question – admittedly three different ways, but only one question.

'Does your father belong to the Liberation Militia?'

I glanced across to where Dad sat. He was looking straight ahead, somewhere years ahead or years behind. 'No, he doesn't,' I replied.

Had I waited too long to answer? Had the jury been aware of the slight pause before I spoke? I glanced at them again. Two of them were writing something down in their notepads.

'How can you be so sure?'

'Because my father wouldn't hurt a fly.'

'Whereas the Liberation Militia would?' Pingule asked, dryly.

'Objection, Your Honour!'

'Sustained.'

'My dad doesn't belong to the L.M.,' I repeated.

'Callum, what's your opinion of the L.M.?'

'Your Honour, objection . . .'

'Overruled.' The judge didn't even look at Dad's lawyer this time. His eyes were on me.

My opinion of the L.M. . . . ? What should I say to that? I looked around. The noughts in the public gallery waited for me to answer. So did Dad's lawyer. So did the jury. So did Dad . . .

'I . . . any organization which promotes equality between noughts and Crosses is . . .' My mind went blank. I was starting to panic inside. What should I do now? 'Noughts and Crosses should be equal,' I tried again. 'I support anyone who tries to bring that about.'

'I see. And the end justifies the means does it?'

Kelani jumped to her feet again. A yo-yo had nothing on her. 'Your Honour ...'

'Withdrawn,' Pingule said with an airy wave of his hand.

I glanced at the jury. The statement may have been withdrawn but it'd done its work.

'Did your father ever mention belonging to or joining the L.M.?'

'No.'

'Did your brother Jude ever mention belonging to or joining the L.M.?'

'No.'

'So no-one in your family had anything to do with the planting of the bomb at the Dundale Shopping Centre?'

'That's right.'

'And you're sure that no-one in your family knew anything about it?'

'That's correct.' How many more times?

'Including you?'

'Including me,' I agreed, trying to keep the annoyance out of my voice. My sweaty palms told me that I was being led into a trap but I had no idea what it was. My shirt was beginning to stick to my sweaty body. I wanted to wipe my forehead but I thought that would make it look too much like I was lying, so I clenched my fists to keep them by my sides.

'Your Honour, my learned colleague has been asking the same question for the last ten minutes,' Kelani snapped. 'If he has a point, perhaps he could be instructed to get to it some time soon.'

'I have every intention of doing just that.' The prosecutor's smile was oily to say the least. 'Your Honour, I call into evidence exhibit D19.'

What on earth was D19? I watched as a TV with a massive screen and a VCR were wheeled into the court. As two men set up the equipment opposite the jury, I risked a glance at my dad. He was watching me. And the moment I caught his eye, he almost imperceptibly shook his head. At first I wondered if I'd imagined it, but he continued to look at me, his eyes burning into mine, and I knew I hadn't. I turned to Pingule, wondering what he was up to. And I swear he smirked back at me. One of the court clerks handed him a remote control handset. He turned to the TV. I did the same. If my heart was thumping before, it was dive-bombing now. The screen flickered to life. I don't know what I'd been expecting but the Dundale Shopping Centre wasn't it. The video had obviously been made from one of those closed-circuit TV cameras that were dotted all over the centre. And with a gasp of pure horror, it suddenly hit me what was coming.

'Your Honour, this tape has been put together by the police, my office and two independent witnesses from prominent nought groups, to ensure that what we see today is exactly what was taped on the day of the infamous bombing,' Pingule explained.

'Your Honour, I strenuously object,' Kelani began furiously. 'I haven't had a chance to preview these tapes and . . .'

'I only acquired them yesterday evening and I and my colleagues have been working through the night to assemble this footage . . .' Pingule didn't get very far.

'Your Honour, I must insist on being allowed to view the tapes first before they are entered into evidence so that I have a chance to prepare my defence . . .'

'Your Honour, there are precedents to presenting evidence in court not yet seen by the defence. If I can quote . . .'

'No, you may not,' Judge Anderson interrupted. 'I am well aware of the precedents, Mr Pingule. You're not the only one who went to law school.'

'My apologies.'

'Your Honour . . .' Kelani tried to bring the judge back to the subject in hand.

'No, Ms Adams. I'll allow it,' said Judge Anderson. 'I will however allow the court a recess after this witness has been questioned to give you time to prepare your response.'

As Kelani sat down she gave the judge a look that was pure ice. He didn't miss it either. I saw from the slight tightening of his lips that he was less than pleased. I glared at Kelani. How would antagonizing the judge help my father's case?

'Now then, Callum, please could you identify the person running out of Allan and Shepherds Fine Goods store?' asked the prosecutor.

I stared at the screen. Then blinked and swallowed hard. There was no mistake.

'It . . . it's me,' I whispered.

'Could you speak up please?' Pingule said.

'IT'S ME.' I didn't mean to shout, but that's how it came out.

'Can you tell me what you were doing in the Dundale at this time, approximately ten minutes before the bomb went off?'

'I can't remember.'

'Let's see if I can refresh your memory,' said Pingule.

He pointed the remote at the TV and pressed the fast forward button. The time code at the bottom of the video leapt ahead seven minutes before he stopped the tape.

'Is this still you entering the Cuckoo's Egg café?'

I nodded.

'We need a verbal response for the court audio tape,' the judge told me.

'Yes,' I said.

Pingule let the tape play. A few moments later I could be seen leaving the café and pulling Sephy behind me. Although you couldn't hear what was being said, it was obvious that all I wanted to do was get her out of there. The alarm at the shopping centre must've gone off then because Sephy started looking around, puzzled. I pulled her towards the nearest exit and then we both started running. Once we were out of the exit, Pingule fast forwarded for a couple of minutes and, without warning, there was a white flash from the café and the tape went dark.

The silence was damning.

'Do you still insist that neither you nor any member of your family knew anything about the Dundale bomb?' Pingule asked, scathingly.

'Yes.'

'I see. In this film, who are you pulling from the Cuckoo's Egg café?'

'Sephy . . .'

'Persephone Hadley? Kamal Hadley's daughter?'

'Yes.'

'What's your relationship with Persephone Hadley?'

'She . . . she's a friend . . .'

Someone up in the public gallery started to whisper at that.

'Could you tell this court why you were in such a hurry to get Persephone out of there?'

'I . . . er . . . I said I'd meet her and I was late.'

'Really?' Pingule raised a sceptical eyebrow. 'When you found her, why didn't you sit down in the café with her or go for a stroll around the shops? What was the hurry?'

'I was late and I was afraid her mum would appear at any second and . . . and I wanted to show her something.'

'What?' Pingule prompted.

'I can't remember.'

More murmurs from the public gallery.

'With everything that's happened, I can't remember. It was something silly – a car or a plane or something.'

'Indeed?'

'Yes.' I was sweating so much, I was going to have to swim away from the witness box.

'No further questions,' Pingule said, his voice ringing with contempt before he sat down.

I hung my head.

Forgive me, Dad.

I couldn't even look at him. I started to walk down the steps of the witness box.

'Just a moment, Callum.' Kelani's voice brought me back to the present. I looked up. She waved me back into the witness box. I did as directed.

'Could you describe your relationship with Mrs Hadley, Persephone Hadley's mother?' Kelani asked gently.

'Mrs Hadley doesn't like me . . . much.'

'Why d'you say that?'

'She told her secretary not to let me into her house.'

'I see. D'you know why?'

I coughed nervously. 'Sephy . . . Persephone was beaten up at school. Mrs Hadley blamed me.'

'Why? Did you do it?'

'No, of course not,' I said, appalled. 'Some girls from the year above her did it.'

Pingule rose to his feet. 'Your Honour, I fail to see the relevance of this line of questioning . . .'

'Ms Adams?' Judge Andersen prompted.

'I'll come directly to the point, Your Honour,' Kelani smiled. 'Callum, what would you have done if Persephone had been in the café with her mother?'

How should I answer that? Think! Think!

'I . . . would've waited until Sephy was alone before trying to speak to her.'

'But that might've taken a while.'

I faked a nonchalant shrug. 'I wanted to show Sephy what was outside but it wouldn't have been the end of the world if I hadn't. I would've waited until she was alone. I wasn't in a hurry.'

'Thank you, Callum,' Kelani smiled at me. 'That will be all.'

sixty-nine. Sephy

'Miss Hadley, could you tell us what happened when you were in the Cuckoo's Egg café on the day of the bombing?' Mr Pingule, the prosecutor, smiled at me encouragingly, which helped a little. A very little. I hadn't expected to be quite so nervous. I didn't want to be here. The courtroom was too warm and too big. They should've just painted huge eyes all over the floor and the walls and the ceiling and had done with it. And even that would've been far less intimidating than the judge, the lawyers and the jury.

'Take your time, Miss Hadley,' the judge smiled.

I smiled back at him, gratefully. Maybe I could do this. Maybe it wouldn't be so bad after all.

'I was having a drink in the café. Mother ... my mother had gone back to our car to put away our shopping.'

'Go on,' Mr Pingule prompted gently.

'Well, Callum came in and said we should leave ...'

'Why?'

I swallowed hard. I'd sworn on the Good Book not to lie. But the judge and the jury wouldn't understand the truth. The truth was more than just a spoken sentence. It was a combination of the thoughts and feelings and the history behind them. Was I making excuses? Dressing them up in reasons and justifications and deliberate evasions? Seven people died. No reasoning in the world would ever change that fact, or excuse it.

'Miss Hadley, did Callum give you a reason why you should leave the café?'

'He . . . he wanted to show me something . . . outside . . . I assumed he wanted to show me something outside. I mean . . .' Did I assume it? I must've done. Until the bomb went off.

'What?'

'Pardon?'

'What did he want to show you?' Mr Pingule's smile was wearing a little thin.

'I don't know. I can't remember. I don't think he said.'

'Come now, Miss Hadley . . .'

'He didn't say,' I insisted. 'It was going to be a surprise but . . . but the bomb went off before he could tell me.'

'And that's the truth?'

'Yes.' The truth. But not the whole truth and nothing but. I remembered a saying of my mother's. A wise person tells what she knows, but not *all* she knows. Did that apply in a court of law? Somehow I didn't think so. I watched as Mr Pingule regarded me, a strange look on his face. At last he spoke.

'Miss Hadley, Callum's your friend, isn't he?'

I nodded. 'Yes.'

'And you wouldn't want anything or anyone to hurt him and his family, would you?'

'No.'

'D'you understand that the only way you will hurt him

today is if you don't tell the truth?'

'I know that,' I replied.

'Good. So I'll ask you again,' An edge was beginning to creep into Mr Pingule's voice now. 'Why did Callum want you to leave the Dundale Shopping Centre so urgently?'

'He wanted to show me something outside.' My voice was stronger now.

'I see. Tell me something, Miss Hadley, how would you describe Callum McGregor?'

'Objection, Your Honour. What has Miss Hadley's opinion of her friend Callum have to do with my client, Ryan McGregor?' asked Kelani.

'I'm wondering that myself, Ms Adams,' Judge Anderson nodded. 'Objection sustained.'

'What is your relationship with Callum McGregor?'

'We're friends. Good friends.'

'Perhaps, more than . . . good friends?'

'He's my friend, that's all.'

'Your honour . . .' Kelani got no further

'Very well then,' Mr Pingule was well and truly annoyed now. 'Miss Hadley, do you know who is responsible for the bomb at the Dundale Shopping Centre. Yes or no?'

'Of course not. How could I?' I said, shocked that he'd even asked me.

'Indeed. No further questions.' Mr Pingule sat down.

I didn't know who'd planted that bomb. *I didn't want to know.* And that, more than anything else I'd said or even thought so far in court, was the truth.

seventy. Callum

Now that my evidence was out of the way, I was allowed to watch from the public gallery. I didn't sit with Mum, even though she wanted me to. But how could I? Between the two of us, Sephy and I had pretty much put the noose around Dad's neck. But then Kelani Adams showed why she was a red-hot lawyer. A man called Leo Stoll was called to the stand. I didn't recognize his name or his face when he entered the witness box. He was a middle-aged Cross who was obviously not short of a penny or two. I glanced across at Mum. She had a puzzled, quizzical look on her face. I shrugged. It was no good asking me who he was. I didn't have a clue.

I watched as Leo Stoll was sworn in, then waited with bated breath to see what he had to do with my father. Kelani Adams stood up, and faced the witness.

'Mr Stoll, could you tell the court what you do for a living.'

'I'm a police officer – now retired.' His voice was deep and melodious, like a baritone singer or something.

'You don't look old enough to retire.' I could hear the smile in Kelani's voice, although I couldn't see her face as she had her back to the public gallery.

'I was retired through ill health,' Mr Stoll replied.

'Oh?'

'I was knocked over by a nought joyrider. My hip was completely pulverised. I was offered a desk job but after years spent out in the field,' Mr Stoll shrugged, 'well, I just couldn't face it. So I took early retirement instead.'

'Do you recognize the defendant, Ryan McGregor?'

'Nope. Never seen him before in my life,' Mr Stoll said firmly.

Mr Pingule glanced at Kelani. I reckoned she had one more question before he jumped to his feet, bleating to the judge about the relevance of her questions.

'Mr Stoll, have you ever seen Callum McGregor before?'

'Who?'

My heart plunged down to my feet. Why was she asking him about me? Was that her strategy? To get Dad off by hanging me out to dry?

'Callum McGregor, could you stand up please?'

I hung on to the safety rail and pulled myself upwards. I was burning under the gaze of every eye in the court. This was just as bad as standing in the witness box.

'Oh yes, I've seen him before,' Mr Stoll said, with no hint of hesitation in his voice.

'Where?' Kelani asked.

'On the afternoon that the Dundale bomb went off,' Mr Stoll replied. 'I was having a cup of coffee in the Cuckoo's Egg café. That boy came in and started to drag out a girl who'd been sitting down minding her own business. As she was being dragged out, I asked if she was OK. I may have a dodgy hip but I still know a move or two!'

'Quite! So what happened then?' Kelani prompted.

'The girl said that the boy was a friend of hers and that he was just taking her out to show her something,' said Mr Stoll.

'You're sure that's what she said,' Kelani asked eagerly.

'Positive. Like I said, I used to be a police officer so I've been trained to observe and remember.'

Did Sephy say that? I couldn't even remember. I just remember my desperation to get her out of the Dundale before the whole place was blown to smithereens.

'Did the girl seem particularly scared or worried in any way?' Kelani asked.

'Not at all. She was treating the whole thing like it was a big joke.'

'And how come you survived the bomb blast?'

'I finished my coffee and left less than a minute after the boy up there and his friend.'

'Thank you, Mr Stoll. No more questions.' Kelani Adams sat down.

Spontaneous cheers erupted throughout the court-room. Judge Anderson tried to restore order but it wasn't going to happen. In the end he had to clear the court. But just like that, my story had been corroborated. And by a Cross police officer of all people. If it'd been funny, I would've busted a gut laughing.

seventy-one. Sephy

Every evening I sat glued to the early evening news for any information about Callum's dad's trial. I'd racked my brains to try and come up with some way of helping him. But I'd drawn a complete and utter blank. What could I do? What could just one person do? So I sat and watched like the rest of the country whilst a reporter told us in great detail what had happened that day in court. They occasionally showed Callum and his mum hiding their faces from the cameras as they came out of the court.

The night they showed Callum's house burnt to the ground I went to my bedroom and cried and cried. Luckily, Callum and his mum were staying with relatives but it still hurt to think of what my friend was going through. I wanted to phone but I didn't have Callum's new number. I wanted to visit him but I didn't have his new address. I still went down to the beach once in a while but Callum was never there. I pretended to myself that we just kept missing each other. I'd arrive at five, he'd arrive at six. I'd arrive at six, he'd arrive at seven. But deep down I knew that he'd stopped coming. He had more important things on his mind.

I don't know how Callum's mum managed to get Kelani Adams to defend Callum's dad but I was so glad she had. Even before I'd had to go into the courtroom, I'd heard of Kelani Adams QC and I wasn't really into politics or current affairs or anything like that. According to the reporters on the telly, Kelani was making sure that the trial was as fair as possible – and putting the judge's back up in the process. Good for her!

Ryan Mcgregor just had to be found not guilty. It was only right and proper.

It was only just.

It was only justice.

seventy-two. Callum

Dear Sephy,

This is a very hard letter for me to write. I keep putting it off and putting it off and this is about the tenth draft.

I scrunched up the paper and threw it in the already overflowing bin. Start again.

Dear Sephy,

I'm just going to come right out and say this. I don't know how you managed to get all that money together to help my dad but I love you for it. Our lawyer, Kelani Adams, is really on our side, to the extent that the judge has threatened twice to hold her in contempt of court.

I don't know how, but some day, some how, I'll make it up to you. I just want you to know that I'll be for ever . . .

Another sheet of paper scrunched up and thrown in the bin. I folded my arms on the table and rested my head on them. Good or bad, every aspect of my life lay in the hands of others. Kelani Adams, the jury, my so-called education at Heathcroft, even with Sephy. Maybe this was it. Maybe this was all there was or ever would be to my life. I was so sick and tired of being this helpless.

Over the last few months, I'd had a recurring nightmare about being in a cardboard box, no bigger than I was. A normal, simple cardboard box. But no matter how hard I pushed or punched, I just couldn't smash my way out. In fact the more I tried, the harder it became. And in my bad dreams, it was only when my hands were bloody and I was gasping frantically for breath that I realized I wasn't in a box at all. It was a coffin. And once I realized that, I stopped struggling and just waited to die. That's what terrified me the most.

I stopped struggling and waited to die.

seventy-three. Sephy

At last the trial was over. The jury was out, considering its verdict. I was actually flicking from TV station to TV station trying to find any news item that would bring me more up to date. I'd seen the so-called evidence weighed up by numerous experts on any number of news programmes as well as in the papers. And they all thought Callum's dad was guilty. No-one ever came right out and said so. There was a lot of useless talk about the 'balance of probabilities' and the 'pros and cons' of the case and discussions on the evidence. Funny, but I've never been the slightest bit interested in the news before. Now suddenly I couldn't stop watching it. When Minnie started moaning in my ear about watching something else, I went up to my room to watch it in peace and private.

Ryan McGregor wasn't guilty.

So why did I feel like I was the only person in the world – the only Cross in the world – to believe that?

seventy-four. Callum

Mum and I held hands as we waited for the foreman to speak. Hope and hopelessness churned in my stomach like oil and water.

'Foreman of the jury, have you reached a verdict upon which you are all agreed?'

'We have, Your Honour.'

'D'you find the defendant, Ryan Callum McGregor, Guilty or Not Guilty of the crime of Political Terrorism?'

Why was he taking so long to speak? Answer the question . . . What's your answer?

He opened his mouth and said something but I didn't hear. Why couldn't I hear? I shook my head and leaned forward, concentrating hard. Had he spoken? I'm sure he'd said something. I saw his mouth open and close. I licked my dry lips, feeling sick. I looked at Mum. Her expression was carved in granite. Next to Mum a blonde woman buried her face in her hands. The man next to her shook his head in disbelief. Why couldn't I hear anything? Maybe because I didn't want to hear.

'D'you find the defendant Ryan Callum McGregor, Guilty or Not Guilty of the murder of Aysha Pilling?' The clerk's voice rang out like a gunshot.

And I heard the verdict that time. God help me, I heard it.

THE WAY IT IS . . .

seventy-five. Sephy

I sat on our garden swing, twisting it this way and that. I
didn't actually swing any more – that was kid's stuff. I just
. . . twisted. It was hot. Too hot.

'Sephy, what're you doing?' Mother yelled across our
garden at me.

Uh-oh! Trouble! I'd come home and gone straight out
into the garden, when I knew Mother did her nut if she
saw me messing about in my school uniform.

'Come here please,' Mother hollered.

I was going to shout 'why' but I thought better of it.
For the last couple of weeks, Mother had got worse and
now I just did as I was told and kept my head down as far
as she was concerned. And for the most part it worked.
Jumping off the swing, I ran to the house.

'Go to your room and put on your navy-blue dress and
your blue shoes.'

'Which blue dress?' I frowned.

'Your Jackson Spacey one,' Mother told me as if it was
obvious.

My eyebrows went up at that. That dress had cost over
one thousand pounds and Mother told me I was not to
wear it without her express permission. The last time I'd

worn it was when I'd snuck out of the house to Callum's after Lynette had died. I and my dress had gone down like a lead balloon then. It kind of made me loath to put the thing on again.

It wasn't a special Saturday and it wasn't anyone's birthday. Or had I forgotten someone? No . . . Today was 24th July and the next birthday was my sister's and that wasn't until the middle of August.

'Why do I have to get dressed up?'

'Because I said so,' Mother snapped. 'Do as you're told. And tell your sister to hurry up as well.'

'Where're we going?'

'No more questions,' Mother said, edgily. 'Go!'

I headed for the kitchen door, turning in the doorway to ask Mum what was going on. She was pouring out a glass of Chardonnay, which she downed in a one-er. She poured out another one. I left the room and headed upstairs.

Minnie didn't know what was going on either – not that she would've volunteered to tell me if she had. Apart from the one time we'd confided in each other in Minnie's bedroom, my sister and I have never had much to say to each other. But I knew it was something very serious indeed when Mother opened our front door and Dad's official government Mercedes was parked on the driveway. And Dad was in the back. My face lit up like a Crossmas tree at the sight of him.

'Dad!' I ran over to the car and threw open the door before Karl had the chance to do it for me. I hadn't seen him in over a week.

'Sephy, get in this car and try to show that you've been brought up, not dragged up,' Dad ordered, his face as stiff a door.

It couldn't've hurt more if he'd slapped me across the face. One week apart – and that was all he had to say to me. Mother and my sister Minerva had reached us by this time. Karl held the door open for them. I hung back, waiting for them to get in first before I did. No way was I going to sit next to Dad. No way was I even going to say a word to him until he apologized. Mother sat next to him, very careful not to actually touch him. Next Minnie, then me. Less than a minute later, we were off – and I still had no idea where. I glanced down at my watch. Four-thirty. I looked at Mother and Dad and Minnie, hoping that someone would let me know what was going on without my having to ask. Nothing doing. I turned and looked out of the window. If everyone else wanted to be mysterious, then let them get on with it. I wasn't going to join in.

Our car drew up outside Hewmett Prison. Ten to six. There were cars ahead of us and cars behind and people walking in on foot. All the noughts walking through the pedestrian entrance were dressed in black and not one of them spoke. Every expression was a reflection of the one before it and the one after. When we reached the entrance of the prison, Dad flashed his ID card at the two security guards by the gates. We were waved straight through. What on earth were we doing in Hewmett Prison? Why did I have to put on my Jackson Spacey dress no less to go to a *prison*?

We were taken out into the prison courtyard. The early

evening air was humid and uncomfortable. Our car was air-conditioned so I hadn't realized how unpleasant it had become outside. Already my dress was beginning to stick to me. Half of the prison courtyard was taken up by seats placed in tiers, whilst most of the rest of the space was bare. At the far end of the courtyard was a scaffold. And still I didn't click. We were shown to our places right at the front of the seated area.

I looked around, puzzled. All the noughts were standing. Some were looking at the scaffold, a few were crying, some were looking at us Crosses on the seats, burning hatred on their faces. Without warning, my eyes caught and locked with Callum's. Shock, like a bucket of ice-water, flowed over me. What was going on? He stared at me. I hadn't seen him for so long that the jolt was all the greater for seeing him here.

'Ladies and gentlemen and noughts, we are here today to witness the execution of Ryan Callum McGregor of 15 Hugo Yard, Meadowview, having been found guilty of seven counts of murder and the charge of political terrorism. His appeal having been denied, the sentence of hanging by the neck until he is dead will now be carried out. Bring out the prisoner.'

And only then, when it'd been spelt out for me, did I finally realize what I was doing there. They were going to hang Callum's dad. I turned to the scaffold, appalled. A door opened to the left of the scaffold and Callum's dad was led out.

I turned to Mother and Dad. They were looking straight at the scaffold, their expressions grim, sombre. I tried Minnie. Her head was slightly bowed but she kept stealing glances at the scaffold. And still no-one spoke. We might've been in a graveyard.

We *were* in a graveyard.

I turned to Callum. He was watching me with a look on his face I'd never seen before. A look that cut right through me like the sharpest, keenest scalpel. I shook my head slowly.

I didn't know, I mouthed. I looked from the scaffold back to Callum, from Callum's dad to Callum, from my parents to Callum, from the crowds all around and back to Callum.

I swear I didn't know.

How to make my desperate thoughts reach him? I wouldn't have come if I'd known where we were going. Wild horses couldn't have dragged me through those gates. That's the truth. Callum, you must believe that.

' Mother, I want to leave,' I whispered furiously.

'Not now, Sephy.' Mother looked straight ahead.

'I want to leave – NOW!' I jumped to my feet, raising my voice.

Heads were turning in our direction but I didn't care.

'Sit down Persephone and stop making an exhibition of yourself,' Mother snapped.

'Nothing is going to make me sit here and watch this. I'm leaving,' I turned on my heels, trying to push past the other dignitaries in my row.

Mother stood up, spun me around and slapped my face. 'Now sit down and don't say another word.'

Cheek smarting, eyes stinging, I sat down. Some eyes were watching me. I didn't care about that. More eyes were watching the scaffold. Well, maybe I couldn't leave but they couldn't force me to watch. They couldn't force me to raise my head. And if they did, they couldn't force me to open my eyes. And if they did, they couldn't force me to *see*. But I couldn't keep my gaze lowered . . . Slowly, I raised my head, my eyes drawn to the sight, my heart disgusted by it. Angry with myself, I turned away, only to find myself looking straight at Callum. He wasn't watching his dad either. He was looking at me – and wishing me and every other Cross as dead as dead could be. I'd seen that look on other's faces – noughts looking at Crosses, Crosses looking at noughts. But I'd never seen it on Callum's face before.

And I knew in that moment that now I'd never ever stop seeing it. Flinching, I turned. Back to the scaffold. A choice of views. Hatred or hatred. They were putting a black hood over Callum's dad's head now. The prison clock began to strike the hour. When it struck six, it'd all be over.

One . . . All eyes on the scaffold.

Two . . . The noose around Callum's dad's neck.

Three . . . Someone begins to weep. Loud, heart-wrenching sobs.

Four . . . A man at the scaffold nods to someone behind him.

'Long live the Liberation Militia . . .' Callum's dad shouts at the top of his voice.

Five . . .

seventy-six. Callum

The clock struck five. One more . . .

'WAIT! WAIT!' A voice called out from beneath the scaffold.

'The governor . . .'

'That's the prison governor . . .'

I strained to see him, but part of the wooden scaffold structure was in the way. I wanted someone in the crowd around us to say what was happening, but now there was just silence. No-one spoke. No-one moved.

Six . . . The clock struck six times. I hardly dared to breathe, afraid the slightest motion would spring the trap beneath Dad's feet.

'Mum . . .' The merest whisper.

'Shush!'

'THE EXECUTION IS STAYED,' the same voice shouted out. I saw a Cross move from behind the lattice of wood-work and beckon to the guard up on the scaffold with my dad.

The peculiar thing was, there were no cheers, no shouts, no sounds at all. Maybe everyone was like me, unable to believe or understand what was going on. What did it mean? Were they going to let Dad go? Did they have new evidence to prove he was innocent? Maybe

Dad's lawyer had done it! From the moment Dad was found guilty, Kelani Adams had parcelled out all her other cases to her colleagues to concentrate solely on Dad's appeal. She'd told Mum and me that she wouldn't rest until Dad was a free man. I know that even as they were waiting to lead Dad out of the prison and up to the scaffold, Kelani had been busy making desperate phone call after desperate phone call. Obviously the phrase 'a lost cause' wasn't part of her vocabulary. Funny . . . it seemed to be a major part of mine.

The man who'd stopped the execution walked up the steps to the scaffold. He nodded to the guard who immediately took the hood off my dad's head. Dad blinked crazily for a few moments, his eyes wide like he was in the middle of a nightmare and even with his eyes open, he couldn't wake up. The governor walked up to Dad and said something to him. It looked like he had to repeat it, asking Dad if he understood. Dad shook his head. The governor put one hand on Dad's shoulder. Dad nodded. Murmurs sprang up through the audience. This not knowing was killing me. *What was going on?* The governor raised his hands for silence.

'Ladies and gentlemen and noughts, I am Governor Giustini. I have just this moment been informed that Ryan Callum McGregor has received a reprieve. His sentence has been commuted to life imprisonment. There will be no hanging today.'

'LONG LIVE TH . . .' Dad's knees buckled as if the ground had suddenly disappeared beneath him. The prison officer standing beside him only just managed to grab him in time to stop Dad from keeling over completely.

And then the whole place erupted. It was only because there were tall metal barriers between us and the scaffold that it remained in one piece. Our fury was so deep, we were all drowning in it. We wanted to get to Dad, to sweep him away, to get him out of there. But we couldn't get to him. Mum tried to pull me back but I was one of the first to push and shove my way forward.

'Dad! DAD!' I yelled until my throat hurt, but the tide of voices around me carried my words away.

Dad was hurried down the scaffold steps and back into the prison, along with the governor, but that didn't stop us. We could've torn down Hewmett Prison brick by brick. *We would've* – but we couldn't get past the barriers. I turned my head whilst being pushed forward. Turned to where *they* were sitting. I couldn't see her. Where was she? Watching all this and enjoying the free entertainment? The Crosses were all leaving in a hurry. We were penned in and had to stand up like cattle; they had seats. We were herded in through a side gate and ushered to our part of the courtyard. The Crosses got to drive in and sit down, like they were having a night out at the ballet or going to the cinema or something. Each one of us was scanned and searched. I bet not one single Cross was even stopped.

And then they wondered why we hated them so much.

People were beginning to get hurt. I saw a man in front of me fall, and whilst those around him tried to help him up, the ones behind still pushed forward. There were screams and shouts and shrieks and chaos. And I loved it. 'Cause it was just what I needed. A place to shout and kick out, where no-one could stop me because I was just one of many. At that precise moment I felt like I could rip the metal barriers out of the concrete beneath my feet with my bare hands. I was invincible because I was so filled with rage. It was a giddy feeling and I revelled in it. Someone grabbed my arm. I turned, ready to lash out. It was Mum.

'Callum!' she shouted. 'Let's get out of here. I want to see your dad.'

'Mum . . ?'

And just like that all my anger that was just about to break out subsided. I stood watching Mum, waiting for the pain inside to dampen down, waiting for the world around me to turn multi-coloured again instead of blood red.

'Come on.' Mum pulled me after her, in the opposite direction to the crowd. And with an overwhelming sense of regret and frustration, I let her.

seventy-seven. Sephy

'DON'T YOU EVER DO THAT TO ME AGAIN!'

'Don't talk to me like that,' Mother frowned.

But I was too far gone by now. Dad had gone straight back to his office in one of his colleague's cars, leaving me, Mother and Minerva to go home alone. And with each passing second, the fury in me had dug deeper and deeper. Mother had come home and gone straight to the kitchen. Minnie ran up to her room. I followed Mother.

'How dare you take me to that . . .that . . . thing? How *dare* you?'

'We had to go. It was our duty.' Mother took a half-empty bottle of Chardonnay out of the fridge.

'Our duty? To see a man get hanged?'

'Yes.' Mum poured out some wine into a tumbler. 'Because like it or not we have to support your dad, whether or not we agree with what he's doing.'

'But that was . . . barbaric. Taking us to watch a man die. Dad's sick. So are you.'

'I didn't like it any more than you did.' Mother downed her half pint of wine without even gasping.

'Liar. You couldn't take your eyes off it. I saw you.'

'I wasn't watching,' Mother said quietly, pouring herself another drink.

I'd had enough by then. I snatched the bottle out of her hand and threw it across the kitchen. It hit one of the cupboards and bounced off to spin around on the floor. But it didn't break. What little wine there was left, trickled out in a silent puddle.

'Go to your room,' Mother stormed at me.

Finally, a reaction. And it left me cold. 'You really don't care, do you?' I said, making no attempt to hide my disgust. 'You would've cared more if they were hanging a wine bottle instead of a person.'

Mother slapped me hard – but I was ready for it this time. I turned back to face her almost immediately.

'There's wine spilling out over there. Go and lick it up then. You wouldn't want to waste any, would you?'

Mother gasped, a sound she tried to smother at once, but she was too late. I heard it.

'Waiting for me to leave before you get on your hands and knees?' I sneered. 'OK then. I'll leave you to it.'

Mother grabbed my arm and swung me around to face her. 'You don't know every damn thing, Persephone,' she hissed at me. 'You think you're the only one hurting here? Ryan McGregor was my friend. So was Meggie McGregor. D'you think I wanted to see him hang?'

'Why did you go then?' I shouted at her.

'One day you'll realize that you can't always do what you want to do in this life. And when you realize that, maybe you'll think of me,' Mother told me.

'I want to think of you as little as possible,' I said bluntly. 'You say they were your friends? Nothing would make me go to the hanging of one of my friends. Nothing. Not even Dad.'

'I tried to help . . .' Mother whispered.

'How? By getting blind drunk before and afterwards?'

'You stupid girl. Who d'you think paid for their lawyer and all their legal fees?' Mother took hold of my shoulders and shook me. 'I prayed and paid and did everything I could to make sure that Ryan wouldn't hang. What more could I've done? You tell me?'

'*You* paid for their lawyer?'

Mother turned away from me. 'Yes, and that's not to leave this room. And not for the reason you think either.'

'That was just your guilty conscience,' I told Mother. 'You've never done anything for anyone other than yourself in your life. So go back to your bottle. You've earned it.'

And I ran out of the room, knowing that Mother was

watching. I bolted up the stairs like the devil himself was chasing me.

Strange how much you can cry, don't you think? Strange how many tears you can hold inside. I lay on my bed and cried until my whole body shook and my head pounded like a pneumatic drill, and even then I couldn't stop. And I knew no-one would hear me cry either. Minnie's room was next to mine but our rooms were practically soundproofed. So I didn't need to bury my head under my pillow, or choke back my sobs. I just cried. For Callum, for his dad, for the day – and for myself, I admit it.

seventy-eight. Callum

Two hours and a lot of arguing from our solicitor later, we were finally allowed in to see Dad. Mr Stanhope, our solicitor, said he'd wait for us outside as we were shown into the visitors' hall. Mum and I sat in silence, our eyes trained on the door. At last the door opened – and I almost wished it hadn't. Another anonymous prison officer entered, followed by Dad. And he looked terrible, half-deflated and pale as a ghost. On the scaffold, he'd been tall and straight and in a funny way I'd felt so proud of him. But now he looked . . . old. Stooped and shrunken into himself. Mum stood up. I did the same.

Dad saw us, but he didn't smile. Mum opened her arms. Dad walked into them and they hugged silently for a long, long time.

'I hear I'm being blamed for the riot outside,' said Dad, his voice almost a monotone.

He pulled away and sat down. All of us, except the prison officer, did the same. I glared at him. Was he going to just stand there, listening to our private conversation? Obviously he was.

'How are you, Ryan?' Mum couldn't care less what was happening outside.

'How d'you think?' Dad said bitterness modulating his voice slightly.

'At least you're still alive. I'm grateful for that . . .'

'I'm not. I was ready to die,' said Dad sombrely.

'Ryan . . .'

'I mean it, Meggie. D'you really think I want to stay here, rotting away in a prison cell. They should've hanged me. It would've been kinder.'

'Don't say that!' Mum cried.

'Why not? It's the truth, isn't it?'

Mum glanced down, struggling for something to say. The click of the door had us turning around. Kelani Adams swept in, her arms out, her expression triumphant. We all stood up. Kelani hugged each of us in turn, even hugging me for good measure.

'Well, we've won the first battle. On to the next one,' Kelani nodded. 'I've already launched an appeal and . . .'

'With all due respect, Miss Adams, this is as far as you'll get,' Dad interrupted.

'Oh no it's not,' Kelani denied. 'I'm calling in every

favour I'm owed – and then some. You're innocent of these charges and I'm going to prove it.'

Mum grasped Kelani by the hand, her smile sincere. 'I want to thank you for your help in all this, Miss Adams. If it wasn't for you . . .'

'Your thanks are a tad premature.' Kelani returned Mum's smile. 'But that's OK.' She turned to Dad. 'What we need to do now is . . .'

'Kelani, it's over,' said Dad. 'They didn't kill me quickly. They just decided to draw it out instead. I'll never see the outside of this prison and we both know it.'

The conviction in Dad's voice silenced us all – but only momentarily.

'You may know it, but I certainly don't,' said Kelani firmly.

But I don't think Dad heard her.

'Ryan, please don't give up,' Mum begged. 'There's still hope. We can appeal. There are lots of things we can do . . .'

'I don't want you to do anything. There has to be a way out of here and *I'll* find it . . .' said Dad.

'Ryan . . .' Mum was worried.

'It's OK, love. I've got it all figured out,' said Dad.

I shook my head slowly as I watched Dad, before stopping abruptly when I realized what I was doing. I glanced up at the officer. He was still looking straight ahead but now his expression was troubled rather than neutral. He glanced down at Dad, then turned to Mum and shook his head.

'I don't wish to interfere,' he began softly. 'But please tell your husband there is no way to escape from this prison. He's been talking about nothing else since his reprieve. Tell him the security gates are guarded at all times and the fence is electrified twenty-four hours a day, seven days a week.'

Mum looked from the guard to Dad. 'Ryan, you're not going to do anything stupid, are you? Promise me . . .'

Dad smiled, a slow, frightening smile, and opened his mouth to answer but at that moment a buzzer sounded.

'Ryan, please, *please* trust me to do my job,' Kelani said to Dad. 'I *will* get you out of here. You have to believe it.'

'I'm afraid visiting time is over,' the officer said.

Dad headed for the door.

'Ryan . . ?' Mum called after him.

'Meggie, don't worry about me. I'm getting out of here,' said Dad. 'You just see if I don't.'

And he carried on walking away from us, towards the exit. The prison officer nodded politely to my mother and Kelani. Kelani nodded back. But Mum didn't even see him. She was watching my father leave. The prison officer followed Dad out of the room. Mum muttered something to herself, utterly desolate.

'What did you say?' I asked her as gently as I could.

Mum turned to me, tears in her eyes. 'He didn't even say goodbye.'

seventy-nine. Sephy

It took a while before I heard the strange tip-tapping at
my window. And once I was conscious of it, I instinctively knew that it'd been going on for a while. Not
bothering to wipe my face, I headed for my window and
opened it. Tiny stones lay at my feet.

Callum . . .

Callum in our back garden. I leaned over my balcony
and saw him at once.

'What . . ?' I lowered my voice. 'What're you doing
here?'

'I need to see you.'

'I'll come down.'

'No. I'll come up.'

I looked around anxiously. 'OK. But be quick.'

'How do I get up there?'

'Just a sec. Er . . . can you climb up the drainpipe and
use the ivy for footholds?'

'I'll break my neck.'

'Hang on, I'll tie some sheets together then.'

'No, don't bother.'

Without another word, Callum clambered up the
drainpipes and the ivy, reaching my balcony in about ten
seconds flat. My heart leapt up into my throat as I watched

him. If he fell now ... The moment he reached my balcony, I hauled him over, terrified he'd plummet to his death.

'Did you phone me? I didn't hear your signal,' I told Callum, confused.

'I didn't phone. I came straight here,' Callum replied. 'I hid in the rose garden until the coast was clear.'

We stood in the middle of my room. He looked at me and I looked at him and all the events of our lifetimes finally caught up with us. I wanted to say sorry for everything that'd happened to his dad, sorry for everything that was still happening, but even in my head the words sounded trite and totally inadequate. Better to say nothing. Safer. And I couldn't forget the way he'd looked at me as the prison clock struck. I was the first to look away. I'd known Callum all my life and yet I felt as if we'd only just met.

'Is there anything I can do?'

Or maybe I'd done enough. Me and my kind ... I risked a glance at Callum. He didn't answer. He just watched me.

'How's your mum ..?' Stupid question. 'Is she still staying with relatives or friends? Is she ..?'

'She's at my aunt's house,' Callum replied.

I looked around my room. Should I sit or stand? What should I say? What should I do? Inside, I was beginning to panic.

I ran to lock the door. The last thing either of us needed was to have my mother or sister enter the room. Sighing with relief at the click of the key in the lock, I turned, only to bump straight into Callum. Dazed, I looked up at him.

'I . . . I thought you were going to get help,' Callum told me.

I shook my head, shocked. Why would he think such a thing? 'Listen, if I wanted to get help, you wouldn't have made it to my bedroom window,' I told him.

But he was hardly listening. He just kept staring at me, his expression freezing by degrees.

'Callum . . ?'

'Your father must be so proud of himself,' Callum's eyes narrowed. 'An innocent man is going to rot in prison and just like that his political reputation is restored.'

'No . . .' I whispered. 'It wasn't like that . . .'

But it was – and we both knew it.

'Is this the way it's going to be from now on? Whenever a politician is in trouble in the polls, if they can't start a war, they'll just search out the nearest nought to imprison or hang – or both?'

I didn't take my eyes off Callum's face. Out of the corner of my eye I saw him slowly clenching and unclenching his fists. I didn't move. I didn't blink. I hardly dared to breathe. Callum was hurting so much, it was tearing him up inside. And he wanted to hurt someone.

'And what about you, Sephy?' he asked.

'W-what about me?' I whispered.

'No more you and me, I take it,' Callum said with contempt. 'After all you wouldn't want to ruin your future career prospects by being spotted with the son of the Dundale bomber.'

'I know your dad didn't do it.'

'Oh yes? Well, so did the jury – for all the difference it

made. D'you know how long they deliberated? One hour. One lousy, stinking hour.' His head slumped in despair.

'Callum, I'm so sorry . . .' I touched his cheek.

His head shot up. He glared at me with white-hot, burning hatred. My hand fell quickly to my side.

'I don't want your ruddy pity,' he shouted.

'Shush . . .' I pleaded, glancing at my bedroom door.

'Why should I?' Callum challenged. 'Don't you want anyone to know you've got a blanker in your room?'

'Callum, don't . . .' I didn't even realize I was crying until a salt tear ran into the corner of my mouth.

'I want to smash you and every other dagger who crosses my path. I hate you so much it scares me,' he told me.

'I . . . I know you do.' I whispered. 'You've hated me ever since you joined Heathcroft and I called you a blanker.' I realized it as I said it. And in that moment I realized a lot of things, including why I'd started knocking back wine.

'And you've hated me for turning my back on you at school and not being there when you needed me,' said Callum.

I didn't deny it.

'So why're we still together?' Callum spoke softly to himself, almost forgetting that I was right in front of him. 'Why do I still think of you as . . ?'

'As your best friend?' I supplied. 'Because you know that's how I think of you. Because . . . because I love you. And you love me, I think . . .'

My words snapped Callum out of his reverie with a

vengeance. A hard, mocking look flashed over his face. I waited for him to do something; laugh, lash out, deny it, leave – anything. But he didn't.

'Did you hear what I said?' I tried again. 'I love you.'

'Love doesn't exist. Friendship doesn't exist – not between a nought and a Cross. There's no such thing,' Callum replied.

And he meant every word.

'Then what're you doing in my room?' I asked, choking inside. 'Why did you come?'

Callum shrugged. 'I'm damned if I know.'

With a sigh I moved over to the bed and sat down. After a moment's hesitation, Callum came and sat down beside me. I can't remember either of us ever feeling more awkward. I struggled desperately to find something to say. Risking a glance in Callum's direction, I saw at once from the look on his face that he was having exactly the same problem.

I had so many things I wanted to tell him. The words tumbled and jumbled around in my head, making me dizzy. But nothing would come out. I turned to Callum and slowly held my arms out towards him. He looked puzzled, then his expression cleared. He watched me intently. My gaze dropped. Another of my stupid ideas. I started to lower my arms. Taking hold of my hands, he shuffled along the bed towards me.

Wrapping his arms around me, he lay down on the duvet cover, taking me with him. We faced each other, our eyes locked. I licked my lips nervously. Now what? Callum kissed me. And I kissed him back. We were comfort kissing, that's all. We wrapped our arms around each other for solace. Bear hugging. Squeezing the life out of each other as if we were trying to merge together. When at last we loosened our grip, in a strange way we were both more . . . calm. Physically, at least. Not mentally.

'Turn around,' Callum whispered.

I was about to argue but then I thought better of it. I did as I was asked. He wrapped his arms around me. We were cuddled up like a couple of spoons in a cutlery drawer. I toyed with the idea of suggesting that we get under the covers but I decided not to push it. I didn't want to give Callum a reason to panic and leave. Maybe there was some way to suggest it . . . gently? I raised an eyebrow. Gently? Yeah, right! But it would've been wonderful. Just Callum and me locked together, locking out the whole world. Bliss. But one step at a time. And besides, what we were doing now wasn't too shabby! Better to settle for this than his hatred. Better this than nothing at all.

Callum sighed. I shuffled back to get closer to him. I felt him relax, his body warm against mine. My sigh echoed his.

'Are you OK?' His breath was warm and soft in my ear.

'Uh-hm!' I mumbled.

'I'm not squashing you'

'Uh-uh!'

'You're sure?'

'Callum, shut up.'

I felt rather than saw him smile. His first smile in a long while, I think.

'Don't leave without giving me your new address and phone number,' I murmured. 'I don't want to lose you again.'

I don't even know if he heard me and I was too comfy to find out. Then I thought of something else. Something which struggled through my lethargic haze. Something that'd been troubling me for a while now.

'Callum,' I whispered. 'I'm sorry I sat at your table.'

'What're you talking about?'

'Your table. At school,' I said, sleepily. 'And I'm sorry for what happened at Lynette's funeral.'

And sorry for all the million and one other well-meant but badly thought out things I'd done in my life. Acts to make me feel better. Actions that had hurt Callum rather than helped him. Sorry, Callum. Sorry. Sorry.

'Forget it. I have,' Callum's warm breath whispered across my cheek, before he kissed it.

I closed my eyes and allowed my mind to drift away. I was cuddled up with Callum and for once this time was ours and no-one else's. With that thought in my mind, I drifted off to sleep, with Callum still holding me.

eighty. Callum

Sephy was out like a light. Lucky her. I lay on her bed with my arms wrapped around her, wondering how on earth we'd managed to end up like this. I'm not sure what'd been on my mind when I came to see her, but this wasn't it! Strange the way things turn out. When I'd come into her room, I'd been burning up with the desire to smash her and everything else around her. Sephy was a Cross I could actually hurt. And yet here she was, asleep and still holding on to my arms like I was a life-raft or something. There's not a single millimetre of space between her body and mine. I could move my hands and . . . And. Anything I liked. Caress or strangle. Kill or cure. Her or me. Me or her.

I lifted my head, to make sure she was really asleep. Eyes closed, regularly breathing, in-out, in-out. Dead to the world. Lucky her.

She turned in her sleep to face me, her arms instinctively reaching out to hug and hold me close to her. I lowered my head back down to the pillow. Each time Sephy exhaled, her breath tickled my cheek. I moved my head down slightly so that our noses were almost touching. So that when she breathed, she'd have to breathe my breath and I'd have to breathe hers. And then I kissed her. Her eyes opened almost immediately, sleepy but smiling. Her hands crept up to frame my face and, closing her eyes again, she returned my kiss, her mouth open, her tongue dancing against mine. Fireworks were shooting through my body. I was finding it hard to breathe. So was she. I pulled away abruptly.

'Why are you kissing me?' I asked, frustrated anger creeping into my voice. 'Passion or guilt?'

Sephy looked so sad, so hurt, that I instantly regretted my words. She went to roll away from me, but I held her arm and wouldn't let her.

'Sorry,' I murmured.

'Maybe you should go . . .' Sephy whispered, still not looking at me.

'Not yet. Please. I'm sorry.' I placed my hand under Sephy's chin and raised her head so that she could look at me and know I meant it. She tried to smile. I tried to smile back.

I opened my arms for her. 'Let's just get some sleep – OK?'

Sephy nodded. I lay on my back and Sephy settled down to lie with her head on my shoulder. She was asleep again in less than a minute. Lucky, lucky, lucky. Ten minutes must've passed. Then fifteen. I couldn't stand it any longer.

'Sephy, d'you want to know a secret,' I mouthed against her ear.

She moved her ear slightly away from my mouth. My breath must've tickled her. But she was still fast asleep.

'Here is my confession,' I whispered. And I told her what I'd never told anyone else. What I hadn't even admitted to myself. The biggest secret of all.

God, if you are up there – somewhere – you've got a very peculiar sense of humour.

eighty-one. Sephy

'Miss Sephy? Are you all right in there?'

'Persephone, open this door. At once.'

The dream I was having was so warm and comfortable,

apart from that incessant calling somewhere in the background. I opened my eyes slowly, only to have them fly right open when I saw whose shoulder I was perched upon. Callum's. His arm was around my shoulders and he was fast asleep.

'Persephone, open this door right this second or I'll get someone to break it down,' Mother yelled.

'Miss Sephy, are you OK. Please.' Sarah pulled at the door handle.

I sat bolt upright. 'Just . . . just a minute,' I yelled, shaking Callum awake.

'What . . . what's the . . ?' Callum began sleepily.

Putting one hand over his mouth, I pointed to the bedroom door. He got it at once. I pointed to my bathroom door. Callum jumped off the bed and ran towards it.

'Look, why don't I just let them in,' I whispered. 'I want Mother to know about us. Besides, we haven't done anything wrong.' The look Callum gave me instantly changed my mind. 'Bad idea?'

'Duh!!' Callum replied.

I looked down at my clothes. I still had my Jackson Spacey dress on – although by now it had so many creases in it that it looked like the skin on a day-old macaroni cheese. If Mother saw it, she'd kill me.

'Just a minute, Sarah. I'm just putting on my dressing-gown,' I called out.

After pulling the belt tight and making sure none of my dress could be seen, I ran to the door, waiting until Callum had scooted into my bathroom before I turned the key in the lock.

'What's the matter? Is the house on fire?' I asked as

Sarah and Mother bustled past me.

'D'you know what time it is?' Mother asked.

'So I overslept a few minutes. Big deal,' I said, annoyed.

'Ten minutes? It's almost noon and your door is locked. You never lock your door,' Sarah said suspiciously.

'Maybe I decided to bring a little excitement into your lives,' I yawned.

And then I saw them. Callum's trainers, right by my bed in plain, full, multi-colour view. My heart dropped to my ankles then bounced right up to my mouth.

'I'll be down as soon as I've had my shower,' I smiled brightly. 'I promise.'

'There's nothing wrong?'

''Course not. What could be wrong?' I said, a little too emphatically judging by the deepening look of suspicion on Sarah's face. She looked around slowly, stopping abruptly when she caught sight of the men's trainers on the floor. She gave me a profoundly shocked look and I knew at once what was going on in her head. Pursing my lips, I fought hard to stop myself from looking guilty. I hadn't done anything wrong. And if Callum and I had been at it all night like bunny rabbits instead of fast asleep, it still wouldn't have been any of her business.

'There's something strange going on around here,' Mother said slowly.

'Just 'cause I overslept?' I asked, more to focus her attention on me than for any other reason.

Sarah walked towards Callum's shoes as Mother scrutinized my face. Although my eyes were on Mother, I was aware of Sarah's every movement. She was going to hold up Callum's trainers with a flourish for Mother to feast on.

'Sarah, what . . ?'

As Mother turned around, Sarah kicked the trainers under my bed. All Mother saw was Sarah tidying up my bedclothes as if she was making my bed.

'Don't do that, Sarah,' Mother admonished. 'My daughter is quite capable of making up her own bed. That's not your job.'

Sarah dropped my duvet with a prim 'Yes, Mrs Hadley.'

Mother marched out in high dudgeon, followed by Sarah trotting behind her.

'Get Callum dressed and out of here!' Sarah whispered urgently as she passed me.

'How did you . . ?' My mouth snapped shut. I shut the door behind them, carefully locking it so neither of them would be alerted by the noise.

'OK, Callum. You can come out now.'

Callum popped his head around my bathroom door and had a look around before he came back into my bedroom. We looked at each other and burst out laughing. And it felt so good.

'How am I going to get out of here?' Callum asked.

I had a long, hard think. 'We'll have to sneak out of the house and across the grounds to the beach. If we see anyone, I'll distract them whilst you sneak past.'

'Just your ordinary average Sunday-morning activity!' Callum said dryly.

'Never a dull moment,' I agreed.

'Fancy another cuddle in the bed first?' asked Callum.

I smiled. 'You betcha!'

eighty-two. Callum

'Ryan Callum McGregor, the convicted bomber of the Dundale Shopping Centre, was killed this morning whilst trying to escape from Hewmett Prison. He was electrocuted whilst trying to scale the electrified fence surrounding the prison. Ryan McGregor, who was due to hang four days ago, received a dramatic last-minute reprieve from the Home Office. His family are said to be devastated at the news and were unavailable for comment. Officials have launched an immediate enquiry.'

eighty-three. Sephy

Dear God,
    Please leave Callum's family alone. But it's not you, is it? My mistake. This has nothing to do with you. This is more like the devil's work. Another mistake? Maybe hatred has nothing to do with the devil either. Maybe it's something we've invented. And then we just blame it on you, God, or on the devil, because it's easier than blaming ourselves. I'm not thinking straight. I can't think. Dear God, look after Callum and his family. Help them. Help us all.

eighty-four. Callum

I entered the burger bar and waited my turn in the long queue. This Friday was just like the Friday before and would probably be exactly like the Friday to follow. My days stretched out before me like some kind of galactic desert. Funny how the days could go so slowly and time could pass so fast. They'd killed . . . they'd murdered my dad in July and when he died, I think something inside me had died as well. And although since then the weeks had come and gone, it still cut like a knife every time I thought of my dad – which was all the time. Officially, the authorities might call it suicide, but I and every other nought knew differently.

And I hadn't seen Sephy since the Saturday night-Sunday morning I'd spent with her. Sarah hadn't given us away but she'd made sure it was practically impossible for me to slip back into the house again. A guard was now on permanent patrol.

I'd visited the beach a few times but to be honest I never stayed very long. Going to the beach felt like trying to recapture the past – an impossible task. Too much had happened over the last year. I never saw Sephy anyway, which was probably just as well. At least the memory of that night in her bed was beginning to fade a little. Not much. But a very little. If I tried very hard to think about something else – and rubbed my stomach and patted my head at the same time! I forced myself to think of Dad. What were the thoughts running through his head as he stood before the fence? What was the last thing he thought of before he died? I'd never know. Something else to hate the Crosses for.

I gave my order to the cashier, ignoring the plastic smile on her face as she served me, and waited for my food. When I'd received my burger, french fries and milk, I sought out the darkest corner of the burger bar. I finally sat down with my back to the throng and slowly chewed on a chip. I wasn't even hungry. It was just something to do to pass the time until the afternoon had passed. Now that I wasn't at school, I never knew what to do with myself. Totally aimless, I had nothing to do and nowhere to go. Since Dad's death, Mum was lost somewhere deep inside herself where I couldn't reach her. No-one could. I had tried, but it was hopeless. Maybe if I'd been Lynette, her favourite child, or Jude, her first-born son, but . . . I chewed on another chip. I was sixteen and a half, and already it felt as if my life was over. The good times, the *best* times, were over.

'Hi, little brother.'

I looked up and my eyes began to hurt I was staring so hard. Jude . . . *Jude!* I leapt up and, leaning across the table, I hugged him – hard!

'I've missed you,' I told him.

'Get off. Are you mad, or what?' Jude glanced around

before sitting opposite me. I sat back down, beaming at him.

'Stop grinning like an idiot!' Jude told me sourly.

'It's great to see you too!' I replied. 'Where've you been? I really have missed you.'

Jude took another look around. 'I've been keeping my head down for a while.'

My smile disappeared. 'You ... you know what happened to Dad?'

'Oh yes, I know,' Jude said grimly. 'I know all about it. And it's payback time.'

'What d'you mean?'

Jude sat back in his chair. His eyes darted here, there and everywhere and although he sat perfectly still, he reminded me of a nervous cat, ready to leap off at a nanosecond's notice.

'I hear they booted you out of Heathcroft,' Jude said at last.

'I wasn't booted. I walked,' I told him huffily.

'Good for you. That wasn't the place for you, little brother.'

'I know that now.'

'It's a shame you didn't listen to me when I told you months ago. It would've saved you a lot of grief.'

I shrugged. What else was there to say?

'So what're you up to now?' Jude asked.

'I eat chips.' I pointed at my polystyrene tray.

'Would you like to do something more worthwhile?'

'Like what?'

Jude stood up. 'I have to go now. Someone will be in touch.'

'Jude, don't do your "Man of Mystery" routine on me.' I frowned. 'What am I meant to tell Mum?'

'Don't tell her anything,' Jude said vehemently. 'Where we're going, she can't follow.'

'And where are we going?'

'I think you know, little brother.'

'Stop calling me that,' I protested. 'What're you up to, Jude?'

'Just tell me one thing,' Jude said. 'Are you in or out?'

He was deliberately being enigmatic, answering each of my questions with a question of his own. And it was really cheesing me off. But I knew what he was asking. This was my chance to link up with the Liberation Militia. And I knew in my gut that if I turned Jude down now, I'd never be asked again.

'Well?' Jude prompted.

I licked my lips, trying to delay the moment of decision.

'This is your chance to make a difference,' Jude told me.

And just like that, I felt a calmness, a *purpose* I hadn't felt in a long, long time. I looked at Jude and said, 'I'm in.'

Jude nodded, satisfied. 'Then go home, pack your bags and make your peace with Mum. You'll be contacted tomorrow some time. After that you won't be seeing Mum or anyone else we know for that matter for a while. Are you still in?'

I nodded.

'Welcome to the lifeboat party, little brother,' Jude said adding, 'I hope I can trust you.'

And a moment later, he was gone.

eighty-five. Sephy

Dear Callum,

I was going to phone you but I knew I'd bottle out and never say what I wanted to say. So I've decided to write it all down. I've thought and thought about it and I think I've found a way for both of us to get away from all this madness. You're sixteen, nearly seventeen and I'm almost fifteen so don't say I'm too young or anything stupid like that. Just read this letter with an open mind, that's all I ask.

I think you and I should go away together. Somewhere. Anywhere. Just the two of us. For good. Before you throw this letter in the bin, my brain hasn't dropped out of my ear. I know what I'm saying is right. I want to be with you and I think you want to be with me. I'm not going to swear undying love or any of that other stuff you despise so much, but if we don't leave now and together, then something tells me we never will. I'm not talking about the two of us becoming lovers or anything like that. I don't think either of us is ready for that. Besides, I know that's the last thing you'd want. But the two of us could set off together. Set up together. Stay together. Save each other – if that doesn't sound too melodramatic. I think it probably does. But I mean it. And if you think about it, you'll realize deep down that I'm right.

So let's just do it before we get too old and scared. Let's do this before we turn into <u>them</u>. *I've got plenty of money saved in my own personal bank account, plus there's my regular monthly allowance from both Dad and my grandmother's trust fund. And we can both work. Just as long as we're together. All you have to do is say yes. I thought we could move right away from here. Maybe rent a place up north somewhere. Maybe in the country.*

If you say yes.

Mother has finally agreed to my going to Chivers Boarding School and I'm leaving at two o'clock on Sunday afternoon. If I don't hear from you by then I'll know what your answer is. I'll wait for you right up until the moment I have to leave. But either way I'm going to get out of here.

Take me away from all this, Callum. Don't let me leave for Chivers. I want to be with you. Please don't let me down.

~~*All my love*~~

Yours for ever,
  Sephy

I stuffed the letter back into its envelope as I heard footsteps approach the kitchen. I was in luck. It was Sarah.

'Sarah, I . . . could you do me a favour? A really big one.' I chewed on my lip nervously, trying to read her expression.

'Oh yes? What's that then?'

'Could you deliver this letter to Callum McGregor? He's staying with his aunt. I've written the address on the front.'

'I don't think so!' Sarah scoffed. 'I need this job.'

'Please, Sarah. I'm begging you. It's really important.'

'What is it?' Sarah asked.

'A letter.'

'I can see that. What does it say?'

I chewed on my lip some more. A horrified look appeared on Sarah's face.

'You . . . you're not pregnant, are you?'

I stared at her, then burst out laughing.

'I guess not,' Sarah said dryly.

'Please,' I pleaded, my smile fading. 'I wouldn't ask you if it wasn't really, *really* important.'

Sarah regarded me thoughtfully. 'OK,' she said at last. 'I'll deliver it on my way home tonight. But only on one condition.'

'What's that?'

'That you don't do anything . . . hasty.'

'It's a deal!' I wrapped my arms around her and hugged her tight. 'Thank you. Oh, thank you.'

'Hhmm!' Sarah didn't sound convinced that she was doing the right thing at all.

I licked the envelope and sealed it before pressing it into her hand before she could change her mind.

'Thanks, Sarah. I owe you one.' I grinned at her as I skipped off.

'You owe me several, Miss Sephy,' Sarah called after me.

'I know.' I twirled around before heading up the stairs.

Hasty! This wasn't hasty at all. I'd thought and considered and planned this for days, weeks, months, all my life. Everything Callum and I had ever done had been leading up to this moment.

Callum would read my letter and come for me and together we were going to *escape*.

Wasn't life glorious?!!

eighty-six. Callum

'Callum, there's someone downstairs to see you ... What're you doing?'

I closed my eyes briefly, my back towards Mum. I'd hoped to escape any kind of explanation.

'I'm going away, Mum.'

'Where?'

'Away,' I replied. 'Somewhere where I can make a difference.'

Silence. When I could bear it no longer, I turned to see what Mum was doing. She stood in the doorway, watching me.

'I see,' she said at last.

And she did see. That was the trouble.

'When will you be back?'

'I don't know,' I answered truthfully.

Pause. 'Will you see your brother?'

'I don't know. Probably.'

'Tell him ... Give him my love,' Mum said at last, adding, 'Do one thing for me, will you?'

'What's that?'

'Keep your head down. And tell your brother to do the same.' Mum turned to walk out of the door, her whole body slumped and drawn in on itself. She turned her head.

'What about Sarah downstairs?'

'Sarah?'

'Sarah Pike who works for Mrs Hadley. She's downstairs.'

'Tell her I'm busy at the moment. I don't want to see her.' I shook my head. The last thing I needed right now was a stale morality lecture from Mrs Hadley's dogsbody. 'I can't take all my stuff,' I decided. 'I'll be back tomorrow afternoon for the rest.'

Mum carried on downstairs. I flung a clean T-shirt into my rucksack and closed it, waiting for the sound of the front door to close downstairs. My leaving would please Aunt Charlotte at any rate. I'd already received my orders. Go to the bus garage just outside town, sit on the bench outside the bus garage and wait. All very hush-hush, cloak-and-dagger. It was a big waste of time and effort if anyone were to ask me, which no-one did. But if it kept my brother happy then fair enough.

I felt quite upbeat about what was going to happen actually. I was going to join the Liberation Militia. It wasn't what I'd planned for myself a couple of years ago, but at least I'd stopped drifting. At last, I belonged.

The moment I heard the front door shut, I headed downstairs.

'Sarah left this for you,' Mum pointed to a letter on the hall-table.

'I'll pick it up tomorrow with the rest of my stuff,' I said, impatiently, without even looking at it. What Sarah couldn't say to my face she'd written down, eh? Well, it could wait. I was off to spend my Saturday evening outside a bus garage.

'I'm off now, Mum.'

Mum nodded. 'Take care of yourself.'

'You too.'

We stood in the hall like two lemons on display.

'See you, Mum.'

'Bye, son.'

I skirted round Mum trying to make sure I didn't knock her with my rucksack. And then I was out of the door. Mum closed it quietly behind me as I walked off towards the other end of town.

eighty-seven. Sephy

He's coming. He's not going to come. He's coming. He's not going to come. He's . . .

'Persephone, move it!' Mother snapped. 'D'you want to go to Chivers or not?'

'I'm coming,' I called out. I took one more look around, searching the grounds, the path, towards the gate.

Nothing.

He wasn't going to come. The desire to cry came and died. Dry-eyed I moved towards the car. Karl, the chauffeur, stood by the passenger door, holding it open for me.

'Sephy!'

I turned as Minnie came hurtling out of the door. She

stopped right in front of me.

'Enjoy yourself at Chivers,' she said at last.

'I wish you could come with me,' I told her.

'Do you?'

I nodded.

'Well, Mother can't do without both of us and as I'm the oldest and my exams are only just around the corner, and going to a new school would be too disruptive, so I might as well stay here . . .'

Mother's arguments, not Minnie's.

'I'm sorry, Minerva.'

Minnie shrugged. 'Yeah, so am I.'

'Couldn't you have another word with Mother? Maybe she'll . . ?'

'It wouldn't do any good,' Minnie interrupted. 'She's determined that I should stay.'

'You worry too much about pleasing everyone,' I told her.

'Unlike you. You couldn't give two hoots for anyone else's opinion,' Minnie smiled.

If only that was true. I sometimes acted first and thought about it afterwards but I did care what other people thought. That was the trouble.

'Don't . . . don't get too . . . like Mother – OK?' I said.

'I'll do my best.' Minnie winked conspiratorially. 'And you lay off the booze. Agreed?'

'I'll try,' I told her.

'I thought you stopped for a while?'

'I did.'

'What made you stop?'

I shrugged. How to answer that? Feeling wanted. Being

cuddled. Not feeling sorry for myself any more. Any number of answers. Lots of reasons.

'Well, what made you start again?'

I shrugged again. Being lonely. *Missing him.* The absence of hope until I'd written my letter.

'Sephy, you're not Mother. Stop trying to be,' Minnie said.

I started at Minnie's words, staring at her. Is that what I was doing?

'Sephy, please come on,' Mother called out from behind us.

'Bye then.' Minnie bent forward awkwardly and kissed me on the cheek. I couldn't remember the last time she'd done that. I couldn't remember the first time come to that! I headed for the car, still looking around.

He wasn't coming.

Wave goodbye to Dreamland, Sephy. I sat down next to Mother.

'At last!' she said, annoyed.

Oh Callum . . . Why didn't you come? Didn't you believe me? Or maybe you didn't believe in me? Or maybe you were the one who had to have sense enough for both of us. Or maybe you were just scared enough for both of us.

Karl walked around the car to the driver's seat – and we were off.

Callum, why didn't you come?

eighty-eight. Callum

Faster. Move. I have to do it. I just have to. Wait. Please wait.

I race like the wind towards Sephy's house. Faster than I've ever run before. As fast as if my life depends on it.

Please God, if you're really up there . . .

I clamber up the rise to the rose garden, just in time to see a car turn out of the security gates. Sephy is in the back, next to her mum. But she's looking down, not at me, not anywhere near me.

Please God . . .

'WAIT! SEPHY, IT'S ME. WAIT!'

Run. Move. I sprint after the car. I stop breathing so drawing breath won't slow me down. Run. Race. Sprint.

'SEPHY . . .'

The car is several metres ahead of me now. The driver's eyes meet mine in the driver's mirror. Sephy's Mercedes accelerates smoothly but noticeably away from me.

'SEPHY . . .' I speed after the car. My lungs are about to implode and every muscle, every bone in my body is on fire. But I'll follow that car to hell and back, if I have to. If I can.

Please, please God . . .

I trip over my feet and hit the ground face first. Dazed,

I look up, but the car is almost out of sight. I grip Sephy's letter in my hand, lying on the ground, listening to the sound of all my hopes and dreams moving further and further away. Like listening to the sound of a door being slammed in my face.

THE HOSTAGE . . .

eighty-nine. Sephy

Funny the way things work out. When I first arrived at Chivers, I thought I'd made the biggest mistake of my life. I'd cry myself to sleep over what had been and what might've been, over Callum not wanting to leave with me, live with me. He didn't even bother to say goodbye. It took a long time to stop crying.

And shaking.

I didn't really believe I was drinking that much and I certainly wasn't an alcoholic, but after the second day of feeling wretched and wrung out, I finally realized I was suffering from alcohol withdrawal pains. The school nurse reckoned I had the flu and was very sympathetic, but I knew differently. It took three weeks before I could call my body my own again – and even then, I had to fight hard against the sudden cravings I got for a glass or two or three of wine or cider. So I buried myself in schoolwork and activities, the more physical the better. And it had slowly but surely begun to pay off.

Chivers is definitely the best move I could've made – under the circumstances. It gave me a chance to remake myself, start from scratch. I stopped hanging on to my childhood and started moving forward. I made new friends like Jacquelina and Robyn, who saved my sanity because they liked me for who I was, not for what my father did, or the money my mother had.

The schoolwork was harder than it'd been at Heathcroft, because at Chivers no-one pushed me, so I had to push myself. And I was terribly homesick for the first few months. I still get homesick if I allow myself to think about home for too long, but I don't allow that to happen any more – much. I spent the whole Crossmas holiday with Jacquelina and the Easter holiday skiing with Robyn. It was great. I talk to Mother on the phone of course, and she'd been up to see me a few times, but so far, I'd managed to stay away from home.

And I joined a dissident group. We were Crosses fighting for change in the system. But we had to be careful. We each made a pledge to do what we could – now and in the future – to further the cause of true integration between noughts and Crosses. I think we all felt that the only way we'd achieve real progress was to wait for all the old dogs to die so that us new dogs could replace them and their thinking. Old dogs like my father who couldn't see beyond the fact that noughts used to be our slaves. As far as he was concerned, they'd never be much good for anything else. The dissident group was the one thing that kept me focused when I was at Chivers. It was my reason for doing well, for succeeding. Our group kept me sane. It was a shame my sister didn't have something similar to believe in.

I used to comfort myself with the belief that it was only certain individuals and their peculiar notions that spoilt things for the rest of us. But how many individuals does it take before it's not the individuals who are prejudiced but society itself? And it wasn't even that most Crosses were prejudiced against noughts. I still didn't believe that. But everyone seemed to be too afraid to stand up in public and say 'this is wrong'. And, by everyone, I meant me included. No-one wanted to raise their head above the parapet. At least our group knew that the way things were was wrong. At least we were trying to do something about it – albeit from behind the scenes. We moved quietly but irrevocably, like a relentless army of tiny termites eating away at the rotten fabric of a house. And we would succeed. Each of us believed that, for the simple reason that we had to.

A few months after joining our group, I thought long and hard about asking Minnie to join us, but in the end I decided against it. Minnie's only got one more year at school and judging from the twice I've spoken to her, she's finding being at home difficult to say the least. She's determined to go to a university as far away from our home as she can get, but Mother cries or throws a tantrum or both if she even so much as mentions it. I'm glad I got out before her. Selfish but true.

According to Minnie, Mother's still drinking. I'm not. Even when some of the girls sneak the odd bottle or two into the dorm at night, I don't touch the stuff. I don't trust myself. It's very easy to hide away in a wine bottle, but very hard to come out again. Besides, that's part of my past too. I'm designing my future.

A future without Callum.

I've decided to be a lawyer. But I'm only going to work on those cases that I believe in. I'm going to be another

Kelani Adams. I'm going to stand up and speak out and I'll be so famous and popular that no one will be able to touch me. Not the government, not the P.E.C., no-one. It's great to finally have some direction to my life.

I admit that I think about Callum. Often. But I've stopped brooding and I've stopped yearning for the impossible. Maybe in another lifetime or in a parallel universe somewhere Callum and I could be together the way we should be. But not here. Not now.

And that's OK too. He's moved on with his life, and now so have I.

I wonder if he ever thinks of me? I doubt it, but just occasionally, when I'm doing my homework or washing my hair or cutting my toenails, I pause for a second or two and wonder.

But only for a second.

Or two.

ninety. Callum

My dad said something once about the Liberation Militia. He said that once they had you, they never let you go. I learnt exactly what he meant over the next couple of years. I started off as little more than the tea boy, but I was eager and keen. I soon worked my way up the ranks. I moved on from tea boy to grunt, following the orders of anyone and everyone in my cell of six men and three women. From grunt I moved on to private and on up the ranks until I earned the rank of sergeant and joined a new cell. Sergeant at nineteen – I was proud of that.

And whilst I was working my way up the L.M. ranks, I took the time to take care of some personal business. Namely, Dionne Fernandez, Lola Jordan and Joanne Longshadow – the ones at Heathcroft who'd beaten up Sephy for sitting with me, for being with me, for not knowing her place – which was kilometres above mine. With the contacts and resources now at my disposal it wasn't difficult to find out where they lived. I made it my business to find out all about them: their home lives, their family circumstances, their likes and dislikes – everything. If there's one thing that being in the L.M. taught me, it was that everyone had a weakness. You just had to know where and how to look for it.

I dealt with each of them in turn. Lola first, then Joanne. Dionne last, but by no means least. I took particular trouble to make sure that Dionne suffered – just as she'd made Sephy suffer. They say that revenge is a dish best served cold – and they're right. I served it icy-cold. And I lost more of myself as I did so. But that was OK. Because the Callum Ryan McGregor who loved to sit on the beach and watch the sun go down didn't exist any more. He'd been taken and I'd been left in his place. A poor trade, but an inevitable one.

In the new cell, there were four of us altogether. Pete, Morgan, Leila and me. Pete was in charge. We called him the quiet one. He didn't say much, but he smiled a lot. I was careful to watch my back around him. He was deadly with a knife and had at least four that I knew about always stashed on him somewhere. Morgan was twenty and the joker of the pack. He was our computer expert and the best driver in any L.M. cell for kilometres around. Leila was my age and knew everything there was to know about breaking into buildings and blowing stuff up. She'd been my call.

One evening, just a couple of months after my eighteenth birthday, I'd been sitting sipping a coffee outside a café in the city and surreptitiously timing the guards' movements in the glass-fronted office block opposite when I first spotted her.

It was one of those cafés which likes to pretend it's *très chic* by serving croissants at night and coffee that's all foam and no flavour − or liquid for that matter. The evening was quite chilly so apart from me, there were only three other men huddled at another table about two metres away from me.

Leila came over to me first.

'Spare some change for a coffee?'

I looked at her and shook my head. She moved on to the only other occupied table outside the café.

'Spare some change please?'

'Here's five quid.' One of the morons at the table waved it under her nose. 'What will you do for it?'

I turned to watch, interested to see what she'd do next.

'Well?' The man winked at his friends and continued to wave the money under Leila's nose.

I could tell from her tense stance that she was furiously angry, but the guy who was showing off to his mates was too thick-skinned to realize it. Or maybe he just didn't care? Leila lurched forward to try and snatch the money from the moron's hand, but he snatched it back.

'Come on, you tart! You can do better than that.'

'What did you call me?' Leila asked softly.

I moved my coffee to the other side of my table.

'If the shoe fits . . .' The moron laughed and his friends joined in.

'Stand up and I'll show you what I'll do for that fiver,' Leila said silkily.

And like a jackass the man stood up. Seconds later he was doubled over after Leila's foot made painful contact with his goodies.

'You were right. The shoe does fit!' Leila hissed at him, snatching the five pounds out of his unresisting fingers.

Moron number one collapsed to the floor, coughing his guts out. Morons two and three should've remained seated but they decided to go for it. Big mistake! It took less than fifteen seconds for Leila to sort out those two. By the time she'd finished, they were all rolling on the ground like human skittles.

I waved to one of the waiters inside the café who was watching the proceedings with horror.

He edged out, giving Leila a wide berth.

'My bill, please,' I told him. I turned to Leila. 'Would you like to have dinner with me?'

Leila spun around, belligerence all over her face. 'Are you talking to me?'

'Yes. Would you like a dinner – somewhere away from here though. The police will be here in about five minutes.'

She looked me up and down – and more than once

before she answered. 'Yeah, OK then.'

I glanced into the café but my waiter was taking his time. So guessing at the price then doubling it, I put my money down on the table. We strolled off down the road towards a good meat restaurant I knew. I'd been poor for too long to be a vegetarian. And as we walked along, Leila never said a word. When we got to the restaurant, she sat down on her chair poised to leap straight on to her feet if the situation demanded it.

'Two menus please,' I said to the waitress. 'I'm Callum,' I told my new companion, holding out my hand.

'Leila,' she replied, digging her hands deeper into her pockets.

And that was the beginning of our friendship. It'd taken me a while to get to know her but it was well worth the effort. She and I had a similar sense of humour – which always helps. I was the one who recommended that she be taken under our wing. She'd been on her own for a long time before she joined our cell, so she was ridiculously grateful at belonging to the L.M. So grateful that she suggested becoming my lover. It was a couple of months later when we were held up in one of our safe houses, waiting for Pete and Morgan to return from a reconnaissance trip.

'Thanks for the offer,' I told her. 'And I'm very, very flattered but I've only got room for one thing in my life now – and that's my work.'

'You're sure?' she asked.

I nodded. To my surprise, Leila put her hands on my shoulders and kissed me. It was nice too, but that's all it was.

'You're sure you won't change your mind?'

'I'm sure,' I smiled.

'Well, the offer is always open,' she shrugged.

'I'll remember that.'

And we'd both carried on cleaning our field guns. I didn't want to get involved. In fact, I didn't want any distractions, no matter how lovely they were – and Leila was lovely. She was as tall as me and super-fit with dark brown, short-cropped hair, cat-green eyes and a ready smile in spite of all the crap that'd happened to her. Of course, Morgan and Pete couldn't believe the fact that I'd turned her down. I heard the two of them discussing whether or not I batted for the other side. That made me laugh wryly, but I left them to wonder. Sometimes I felt lonely enough to take Leila up on her offer, but I never did. The last thing any of us needed were lovers' quarrels taking our minds off what we were meant to be doing.

So in a short space of time, I made quite a name for myself. I was known as the crazy one – the first one into danger and the last one out. Everyone in my cell was convinced I had nerves of steel. So much so that Pete had to take me to one side and tell me to take it a bit easier or I'd wind up dead. No-one realized that that was the whole point.

By the time I was nineteen, I'd gained my stripes – and lost my soul. But a soul was unnecessary in my line of work. To make it as a grunt I had to beat up a dagger. I ambushed one on his way home from work and knocked seven bells out of him. To prove myself as a private I had to take on three of them, but for that I was allowed to be armed. I had a knife and I'd been taught how to use it. I won that fight as well. And one of the daggers died later from his wounds. I waited for days to feel something, anything, but I never did. Confirmation, if I needed any, that I was dead inside.

And to become a sergeant . . . Well, it doesn't make any sense to dwell on it. I did what I had to do. I did the only thing I could do. I became one of the youngest sergeants in the whole of the Liberation Militia. Second-in-command of our well respected cell. One of the most respected. And one of the most wanted.

I missed my mum. I sent money to her whenever I could, but I never made any attempt to see her. It would've been too dangerous, for both of us. And I never posted the money from the same place twice either. In my line of work, there was no such thing as being too careful. Poor Mum! One way or another, she'd lost us all – through no fault of her own.

I never once saw my brother. I heard he was in charge of a cell further north. We never had any contact with each other. I was told not to expect any favours because I was Jude McGregor's brother and Ryan McGregor's son – and I didn't. I didn't expect anything. I didn't want anything. I didn't ask for anything – except complete loyalty from those in my cell. And absolute obedience the couple of times I had to take charge. And I got it too.

The police didn't know my identity, my real name. They didn't even know what I looked like, I was careful that way. They just had the codename of our cell – *Stiletto* – like the very sharp, very deadly dagger. Isn't that ironic?

My cell was never given anything too onerous to do, or too dangerous for that matter. We were more of an acquisitions cell than otherwise. Money, explosives, guns – you name it, we did what we had to do to get it. I was on my way up and nothing was going to get in my way. Nothing.

Our cause was just.

Our aim was true.

A couple of months after my nineteenth birthday, Pete received a direct order from L.M. command. They were sending a lieutenant to assess his cell's 'efficiency'.

'Efficiency, my left buttock!' Pete fumed. 'There's nothing wrong with my cell's efficiency.'

The rest of us could see the strop the message had put Pete in, from over five kilometres away and wisely kept our distance for the rest of the day. There was no word as to when we could expect this lieutenant and Pete was determined he or she wouldn't be able to fault any of our work or procedures. He made Leila go through our inventory with a fine-tooth comb to make sure that everything was accounted for. Pete went through our accounts himself, whilst Morgan and I grumbled like hell about having to clean our main headquarters in the tunnel complex beneath Celebration Park from top to bottom. We were holed up in the old access tunnels which were no longer used by anyone but the rats. We received reasonably fresh air from the ventilation grills still scattered throughout the park, but nothing we did got rid of the permanent sewer stench. To be honest, after a couple of weeks in the tunnels, I didn't even notice the smell any more. We weren't going to be in the tunnels for longer than a month or two, so there was no point in belly-aching about it. We all just got on with it. Morgan and I made sure each tunnel was secure and our warning devices on the grills were in place and working.

At last, when Pete was reasonably satisfied, we all sat down for our dinner – a take-away meal of burger and chips.

'Why isn't there anyone outside guarding the main entrance?'

I recognized that voice at once. I leapt up, shocked. 'What the hell are you doing here?'

'Unless you're in charge here, I'd sit down and shut up if I were you,' came the reply.

'I'm in charge,' Pete stood up slowly.

'You should've been expecting me. I'm your new lieutenant,' said my brother, Jude. 'And I asked you a question. Why is no-one outside guarding the main entrance?'

I sat down slowly, never taking my eyes off my brother. He turned and looked at me, his eyes burning into mine and I knew right then and there that he still didn't quite trust me. And that everyone in our cell was in danger because of it.

ninety-one. Sephy

It was time to go back home. I'd finished my end-of-year exams and the summer holidays had already started. And I didn't have to wait for the results to know that I'd passed all my subjects. So, as Mother had tersely pointed out, there was no reason for me not to go home. Except that I really didn't want to go back. Over two and a half years away from home and to be honest, I had no desire whatsoever to return. I'd dragged my feet for two weeks but August had started and Mother wasn't taking no for an answer. I'd run out of excuses. Mother and Minnie had been up to see me a few times – sometimes together, a few times apart, but somehow I'd always managed to avoid reciprocating. There was always something stopping me – a holiday with this friend, a long visit to that friend, the excuses had been trotted out one after another. Backpacking, camping, overseas expeditions, you name it, I went on them. Anything to keep me away from home. And I'd got away with it.

But not this time. Mother was putting her foot down and insisting. So I had no choice. If I'd had my way, I'd've been seventy not seventeen-going-on-eighteen when I returned home. I hated that place. So many bad memories. Too many.

Karl was sent to pick me up at Chivers. On the long drive home, we barely exchanged a word once the platitudes were over. He was fine, everyone in his family was fine, I was fine, school was fine – end of conversation! It was a long drive home!

Getting home was a bit of an anti-climax too. Minnie was spending the week with one of her friends and Mother was out on one of her rare visits to her Aunt Paulina and had left a message on our answering-machine saying that her car had broken down on the motorway so she'd be late getting home. To be honest, not meeting up with Mother immediately was a bit of relief. I still hadn't worked out how I was going to handle her. Should I be all sunshine and flowers and smile and take nothing seriously? Or should I be morose and sombre and take everything she said too seriously? Either way, there was no way I was going to stay put for more than a few days. I'd lined up a summer job with a law practice near to Chivers school and I had one week before I was due to start. One week. The new term didn't start until October and Mother was expecting me to stay for the rest of the summer break. Some hope.

'Welcome home, Miss Sephy,' Sarah hugged me as she emerged from the study. I hugged her back.

'It's good to see you, Sarah,' I smiled.

Sarah looked around quickly. 'A certain someone found out that you were due home today and he left a message for you.'

She whipped out a folded brown envelope from her pocket and stuffed it into my hand. Without another word, Sarah disappeared back into the study. No need to ask who it was from. I recognized the handwriting on the envelope at once. My heart bounced about at the mere sight of it. What did he want, after all this time? I should just put the letter in the bin. Yeah, right! In another lifetime maybe. I tore open the carefully sealed letter and began to read.

Dear Sephy,

I know it's been a long time since we last met and you probably don't even remember me any more. But if you do, please could we meet tonight around nine o'clock at our special place. It's very important. But I'll understand if you can't make it. Two, almost three years is a long time. A lifetime.

C.

Why did he want to see me? Why was it important? All the feelings I thought I'd bundled up and thrown away years ago suddenly came rushing through me again. Did I really want to see him again? It didn't take much intuition to realize that Callum was the one person who could upset my carefully constructed plans for what I wanted to do with the rest of my life. Look at this! One letter and I was already confused and uncertain about what I should do next.

No! I wouldn't do it. Callum had his life now and I had mine and they were worlds apart. But I hadn't seen him in such a long time. And what harm could a short ten-minute meeting do? I was a big girl now! Not a child any more. I'd go and say hello and we'd pass the time by catching up with each other's lives and then we'd part on better terms than happened years ago. Where was the harm in that?

Don't go, Sephy . . .

Where's the harm in that?

Don't go . . .

Where's the harm?

Don't . . .

ninety-two. Callum

'Is everyone clear about what they're supposed to do?' Jude asked.

Nods and grunts and a low-pitched, grumbled 'Yeah! How many more times?'

'She might not even come,' I warned.

'If she got your message, she'll come,' Jude announced. He gave me an assessing look. 'What about you, little brother? You up for this?'

'Why wouldn't I be?' I asked, pulling on my black leather jacket.

'We need to know we can count on you, on your loyalty,' said Jude.

Everyone stopped what they were doing. The room grew very still. I regarded my brother, not attempting to disguise my hostility.

'Meaning?'

Jude looked at me, but he didn't say anything.

I looked around. 'Which one of you doubts my loyalty then?'

Silence.

'I'm glad to hear it,' I said.

'You let us down, and I'm going to forget you're my brother. Understand?' said Jude.

I didn't deign to answer. My brother could go rivet himself.

'This is going to make us famous,' said Morgan as he and Pete slapped hands in gleeful anticipation.

'And rich!' Jude grinned. 'Just think about all that lovely money we're going to be able to add to the Liberation Militia's coffers.'

'Come to Papa!' Morgan laughed, rubbing his hands together.

'And if this comes off,' Jude said to Pete, 'you'll be able to write your own ticket. You'll be able to set up your own L.M. division anywhere in the country.'

'Sounds good to me,' Pete smiled.

It was the first smile he'd directed at my brother. The promise of a bigger and better army to lead had sweetened him up no end and all his resentment about being usurped by Jude seemed to have melted away.

'Let's not count our chickens,' I said brusquely.

'Ever the voice of doom, eh?' Jude smiled. 'If you do your part, nothing will go wrong. Nothing.'

ninety-three. Sephy

I took off my sandals and headed for the moonlit water. I couldn't remember when I'd felt more at peace with myself. I'd finally got a lot of things straight in my head.

Like Dad. For him, his political career came first, last and every number in between. Dad was never going to have any time for me and my sister and my mother. The only reason we'd been around at all was because a 'stable' family was a necessary, compulsory adjunct for a politician. And that was OK. That was the life Dad had chosen for himself and my days of pining about it were over.

I shifted my heels, then toes, to stop my feet from sinking into the wet sand. I kicked up the water lapping over my feet and ankles, watching it fly up and out in an arc of silvery droplets. Laughing, I did it again and again, alternating kicking feet, delighting in my childish game. And then I thought of my mother, and the game stopped.

Mother. I'd always be a disappointment to her. That was never going to change. I was simply not enough. Not ladylike enough, not smart enough, not pretty enough. Not enough. And that was OK too. Her life was her major disappointment, her mistakes carved into every premature line in her face, but I wasn't going to let her use my life as her second chance. I had plans. In September I'd be eighteen years old and I had my whole life and the whole world in front of me. A world full of choices and decisions and opportunities – and they were all mine for the taking.

And as for Callum and me? Well, I didn't want the moon. I was prepared to settle for friendship between us. It would never be the way it was years ago and it'd never be the way I wanted it to be, but maybe we could find something new to take the place of what we had before. Maybe.

I glanced at my watch, wondering where Callum had

got to. I turned, almost as if thinking about Callum would conjure him up. I gasped. Callum was standing right behind me, his appearance so sudden that he might've been a ghost, able to appear and disappear at will. And he looked so different. He'd shot up like a beanstalk. He was lean now, rather than skinny. He'd definitely sprouted muscles! And his dark cords and leather jacket made him look . . . mysterious somehow. His hair was longer too, almost shoulder-length. It suited him. Everything about him seemed different. Callum the boy had disappeared and in his place . . . I smiled, chiding myself. It was as if I'd expected time to stand still for him. I'm glad it hadn't though! Had I changed as much? I guess I must've.

'Good sneaking!' I congratulated him with a wry smile.

Slipping on my sandals, I stepped forward, my arms outstretched for a hug. I expected a similar jovial reply in greeting, but he didn't even smile. And even in this light, I could tell something was wrong. My arms dropped to my sides.

'Callum?'

Callum stepped forward and kissed me. A brief, icy-cold kiss on the lips. He stepped away from me, his eyes filled with regret. And then I saw them behind him. Four of them. Four noughts. Walking towards us. Towards me. A quick glance at Callum. Shock on my face. Confirmation, resignation on his. And I didn't wait to see any more. I turned and ran. Ran along the shore. Away from them. Away from Callum. Ran for my life. I could hear them yelling behind me. Not the words. I didn't try to decipher the words.

Run, Sephy. Don't stop . . .

No sounds of footsteps on the sand. Just shouts and curses and laboured breathing. No lights to guide my way. Even the moonlight was fading as a cloud hid the moon's face from me. Salty, damp air caught in the back of my throat. Run. *Run*. RUN.

Don't look back . . . They'll catch you if you do . . . Don't look . . .

And most of all, don't think. Don't think about *him*. Don't think about anything. JUST RUN.

And then I realized my mistake. I was kilometres from anywhere. And I was running away from the cliff steps, not towards them. And I had four noughts after me . . . Five.

Head for the sea . . .

I turned on my heels and sprinted towards the darkness. Before my third step, I was grabbed by the waist and swung around. I kicked back with my heels and swung my head back at the same time.

'Oof!'

He dropped me and I hit the ground running.

'Bloody dagger bitch!'

I ran straight into a crucifying punch to my stomach that had me instantly doubled over and retching onto the sand.

'That's for my sister,' a voice above me said. At least I think it did. My stomach was on fire and all I wanted to do was curl up in a ball. Arms clamped around my waist from behind and lifted me up, tightening until I could hardly breathe. The man who held me shook me hard then banged me down onto my feet. Without giving me a chance to catch my scattered breath, he immediately began to drag me backwards, his hands under my arms.

My bare heels dragged over sharp rocks and stones. I raised my arms to try and slide out of the man's grasp. But he was ready for that one. My arms slid down his but he grabbed my hands before I could free myself and now I was being pulled backwards by my hands. My legs and my back were being punctured by the rocks and stones. The man holding me jumped up onto a boulder, almost pulling my arms out of their sockets as he dragged me after him. My whole body was pain now. Closing my eyes, I whimpered.

Don't pass out! Open your eyes . . .

I opened my eyes to see the moon almost directly above me and just for one split second my body no longer hurt. Then a dark bag was shoved over my head and the world turned to blackest ink.

ninety-four. Callum

'We did it!' Jude was jubilant. 'We ruddy DID it!'

Pete and Morgan danced an impromptu jig around each other. Yes, we had done it. We had Persephone Hadley, Kamal Hadley's daughter. And she wouldn't see the light of day again if Kamal didn't agree to our demands. As simple as that. We'd bundled the unconscious Sephy into the boot of our car and now we had her stashed away where no-one would ever find her – or us. We were in the middle of nowhere – the perfect location. Weren't we clever?

'I'm proud of you, little brother.' Jude slapped me on the back.

I spun, grabbed his jacket and shoved him against the wall, all in one movement.

'Don't you ever doubt my loyalty again. D'you understand me?' I hissed, my face only centimetres away from Jude's.

Out of the corner of my eye I saw Morgan step forward, only to be pulled back by Pete. I didn't care. I'd take on all of them to get to Jude if I had to. My brother and I watched each other for silent moments.

'D'you understand?' I repeated, slamming him against the wall again.

'I understand,' Jude said.

I released him at once. We regarded each other.

'So the mouse can roar, can he?' Jude smiled.

I took a step forward, my fists clenched.

'Peace, brother. Peace.' Jude held up his hands, laughing at the expression on my face.

I clenched my fists even harder at that. Never before had I wanted to hurt him as much as I did now. I wanted to *destroy* him. Hatred churned inside me, feeding on itself and growing bigger.

'You did a good job,' Jude told me softly.

I turned away from the approbation on his face. Morgan, Pete and even Leila had the same look of praise and admiration all over their stupid faces too.

'What's our next move?' Pete asked Jude, all past resentments forgotten.

'We deliver the ransom note with proof we have her to the girl's father,' Jude replied.

'What kind of proof?' I asked more sharply than I intended.

'What would you suggest, little brother?'

Another test. 'I'll sort that out. I'll cut off some of her hair and film her holding today's paper.'

'Maybe we need something more convincing than just her hair?' Jude suggested.

Another test.

'What did you have in mind?'

'You tell me, little brother.'

I made my mind go blank. It wasn't Sephy in there. It was just some Cross female who we needed to get what we wanted. It wasn't Sephy . . .

'Something of hers that's bloodstained might be more effective,' I suggested.

'Good idea.' Jude nodded. 'What would you suggest?'

'Leave it to me. I'll sort that out too.' I took the camcorder down from the shelf and put a fresh disc inside it. A strange silence filled the room. I looked up to find all eyes upon me.

'Yes?' I said through gritted teeth.

Everyone made a big display of going about their business at that. I took some scissors and a sharp knife out of the drawer and, tucking today's paper under my arm, I headed for Sephy's prison cell. I walked along the short corridor of our three-room brick cabin. It wasn't much. The kitchen was disgusting, with years of neglected grease and grime over practically every surface. Jude had suggested that someone clean it, looking pointedly at Leila as he said so. In response, she'd let her fingers do the talking. Apart from the kitchen there was the living room, full of rolled-up sleeping bags, a small oak table and all the equipment we might need in a hurry: tins of food, weapons, a few explosives, a small TV, a radio, that sort of thing. The third room had been turned into a cell. Not by us. That was just what this place was used for, a place to hold a prisoner or two and their wardens.

Ever since the information had filtered down over two weeks ago now that Sephy could be on her way home, Jude and Pete had been plotting and planning for this moment. They'd got permission from the General himself to go ahead. And the General's second-in-command was due to come and see us the day after it happened. So much scheming and calculating to bring us to this moment. We were pretty safe in this cabin; it was known to a select few on a need to know basis only. But we weren't going to take any chances. Two of us would be on guard at all times, one out front and one out back. And as the cabin was in a clearing in some woods, anyone coming towards us would find themselves without cover of any kind before they reached us.

Everything was taken care of.

And we'd succeeded. We had Sephy. NO! Not Sephy . . . Just a Cross girl – who deserved everything she got, who'd get us everything we needed. I paused outside the cell door. I could do this. I had to do this.

Be what you have to be, Callum, not what you are . . .

I repeated that phrase over and over in my head, the way I used to do when I first joined the L.M. The way I had to whenever there was something . . . distasteful that needed to be done.

Be what you have to be, Callum, not what you are.

I unlocked the cell door and went inside.

ninety-five. Sephy

At the sound of the door being unlocked, I struggled to sit up. My bed was just a wire spring base with a mattress as thin as a carrier bag. I groaned and winced, wrapping my arms around my painful stomach. It ached like nothing I'd ever felt before. My whole body hurt, from my heels to my nape. Had they tried to strangle me? My throat certainly hurt as if someone had done exactly that. The door opened. I moved my hands away from my abdomen. I wasn't going to show any of my captors how badly hurt I was.

Callum . . .

The sight of him standing in the doorway was like an arrow whizzing straight through my body. He wasn't the Callum I'd grown up with and I'd been an idiot to think he would be. It had all been a trick. A trap. And like the biggest fool in the universe, I'd fallen for it. He took a step towards me. Afraid, I drew back. For a briefest of seconds, I thought he flinched. But I was just imagining things. He couldn't care less how I thought of him.

He came over to me. I drew back even further. What

was he going to do? It was only when he was leaning over me that I noticed the scissors in his hands. I trembled, terrified, then clamped my teeth together hard in an effort to stop myself from shaking.

Whatever happens, don't cry. Don't beg.

As Callum's hands touched my hair, I froze. I looked up at him without even blinking. I couldn't even wonder what he was doing. My mind was shutting down. Then I heard the clip of the scissors and Callum moved away. Only then did I look away, my body slumping with such relief that I felt sick with it. My hand flew to my head. He'd cut off some of my hair. That was all. Just some of my hair.

'I want you to hold this newspaper,' Callum told me.

His voice was different. Deeper. Gruffer. And I'd missed it. I'd missed a lot of things.

'Why?' I asked.

'I need to film you holding today's paper.'

That wasn't what I was asking.

'I'm not going to help you.' I folded my arms across my chest. No way was I going to hold that paper or do anything else he told me to do.

Two other noughts appeared behind Callum in the doorway. With a start, I saw that one of them was a woman, not the man I'd thought her on the beach.

'Hold that paper or we'll break your arms and arrange them in such a way that you'll have no choice,' the man behind Callum hissed at me.

Callum turned to look at him. I'd seen him somewhere before, if I could just figure out . . .

'I don't need you standing over me, supervising,' Callum fumed.

'Not supervising. Just observing, little brother.'

And only then did I recognize him. Jude, Callum's brother.

'Nothing like keeping kidnapping in the family, is there?' I told them.

'Hold the newspaper, Sephy,' Callum held it out for me.

Reluctantly I took it. Callum lifted up his camcorder, only to lower it again immediately.

'Look, I don't need an audience,' Callum told the spectators.

'I've come to see the daughter of the famous Kamal Hadley,' the woman replied. 'Let's see the silver spoon then.'

I regarded her, trying not to cringe at the venom in her voice. Without knowing a single thing about me, she hated my guts. I was a Cross and that was all she wanted or needed to know.

'I bet you've never had more to worry about in your life than chipping the odd fingernail,' the woman hissed at me.

'Leila, go and do your job. Guard the front,' Jude told her.

Casting one last poisonous look at me, Leila did as directed. I'd have to be careful of that one. She wouldn't spit on me if I was on fire. None of them would.

'I want you to read out that message for your father,' Callum told me, handing me a piece of paper with my lines on it. He held up the camcorder to watch the preview screen. I glanced down at the sheet. If he thought I was going to say any of this then he was crazy. I scrunched it up and threw it across the room.

'Dad, don't give them a penny,' I shouted.

Callum lowered the camcorder but before he could say a word, Jude flew across the room, grabbed hold of both my jacket lapels with just one hand and slapped my face, before shaking me viciously.

'You're not in control here. We are. And you will do as you're told or you won't leave this place alive. D'you understand?'

I rubbed my cheek, fighting to hold back the tears.

'You will do *exactly* as you are told or I will make this place your hell on earth. None of us are going to take any of your crap,' Jude said softly.

He let go of me so suddenly I fell backwards onto the bed, hitting my head against the brick wall behind me. Jude straightened up and headed out of the room, pausing briefly as he reached Callum.

'Make sure she does as she's told,' he said, making sure I could hear.

Moments later he was gone.

I wondered about making a break for it but Callum was between me and the door, plus from the sound of it the front door was guarded by that girl, Leila. And Jude wouldn't hesitate to take me down if he reckoned it was required. I had to bide my time. If only my head would stop ringing so that I could think straight. If only my stomach would stop hurting so I could at least sit up without pain. If only . . . if only . . .

I had to get him talking. I had to get him to remember me, remember us as we used to be. I had to get him to think of me again as a fellow human being with a name and thoughts and feelings, instead of the nothing I obviously was to him now.

'Callum, I understand why you feel you have to do this,' I began. 'I really do. But this isn't the way.'

Nothing.

But I wasn't going to give up. 'Callum, listen to me. At Chivers I became involved in protests and debates and sit-ins. If you try to change the world using violence, you'll just swap one form of injustice for another. This isn't right. There are other ways . . .'

'Like what? Like being educated to fight the system from within?' Callum challenged. 'I tried that – remember?'

'I know, but if you'd just give it another try . . . I could help you . . .'

'I don't want to hear it. And I don't want your ruddy help. I'm sick of your charity and your handouts,' he interrupted. 'You're just like all the others. You think we noughts can't do a damned thing unless you Crosses are there to help or supervise.' And his body shook with such rage that I had to force myself to continue.

'Don't hate me for wanting to change the way things are. I believe in you, Callum. You can change the world, I know you can. But not like this,' I said. 'I'm not trying to be magnanimous or patronizing. I genuinely want to help but . . .'

'Enough! Hold up the newspaper and read the words on this,' Callum ordered, handing me the now smoothed-out sheet of paper again. I looked up at Callum.

'Read it,' he said, his attention on the camcorder and nothing else.

'Callum, please . . .'

'READ IT.'

After a moment's pause, I began to read.

ninety-six. Callum

'Dad,

I've been ordered to read what's on this sheet. I've been kid-napped and the kidnappers say you'll never see me again unless you do exactly as instructed. Your instructions will be in the envelope along with this video disc. You have twenty-four hours to follow their instructions to the letter. If you don't, I'll . . . I'll be k-killed. If you go to the police or tell anyone, I'll be killed. The kidnappers will know every move you make and every person you talk to. If you ever want to see me alive again, please do as they say.'

Sephy looked up from her sheet of paper, tears trickling down her cheeks. I moved my hand up to indicate that she should lift up the newspaper. She did so at once. I zoomed into the paper so there could be no doubt about the date, then I moved to zoom into Sephy's face. She quickly wiped her eyes with the back of her hand. She wasn't looking at the camcorder. She was looking at me. I switched off the camcorder.

'That ought to do it.' I took the newspaper from

Sephy's unresisting hand. I looked her up and down critically. 'What're you wearing?'

'Pardon?'

'You heard me.'

Puzzled, Sephy said, 'Trousers, a jacket, a jumper.'

'Tell me everything you're wearing,' I ordered.

Silence.

'I can always find out for myself,' I threatened.

'Sandals, jeans, knickers, watch, bra, T-shirt, jumper, necklace, jacket, earrings. Satisfied?'

'Take off your T-shirt.'

'No way.'

'Take off your T-shirt or I'll do it for you.'

Sephy gave me a long, hard, fearful look. She obviously decided I was serious, which I was, because she started to take off her jacket.

'Are you going to kill me, Callum?'

'Don't be ridiculous!' I closed my eyes and turned away so Sephy couldn't see my face. Why couldn't she just shut up? Why did it have to be her? I thought I could do this . . .

'I never realized just how much you and your family hate us,' Sephy whispered. 'Jude looked at me like he wanted to kill me just now. Why does he hate me so much? Is it me personally or just what I am?'

I didn't answer. I squatted down to pack the camcorder back into its holdall as she carried on undressing.

'I'm not stupid, you know,' Sephy said wearily, taking off her jumper. 'None of you are wearing masks or disguising your voices. I could identify each and every one of you, but you don't care. Which means only one thing.

You have no intention of letting me go, even if my father gives in to all your demands.'

My head shot up at that.

We regarded each other as Sephy continued. 'One of you is going to kill me. It's just a question of when . . . and who.' She pulled her T-shirt over her head and threw it down on the floor. 'W–what now?' she asked.

'You can put the rest of your clothes back on,' I told her, picking up the T-shirt.

As she pulled on her jumper, I tried not to stare, I really did. But her body had changed so much in the years we'd been apart. She had breasts now! Her purple lace bra just emphasised them rather than hid them. And her waist went in, instead of straight down, and her stomach was flatter and her legs were longer and her face had lost its baby fat – and she was so very, very beautiful. I turned away as Sephy pushed her head through the neck of her jumper. I didn't want her to catch me staring.

'If your father does as he's told, you'll be OK . . .'

'OK? Like I'm OK now?' Sephy scoffed. 'Come on, Callum, this is your chance to really take your revenge. Don't you want to get your own back for all those times you had to put up with me on the beach? And all those years pretending to be my friend, just praying for this moment.'

Shut up! Shut up . . . Ignore her, Callum. Just ignore her. Put a strait-jacket on your feelings. Don't let her see how much she's getting to you . . .

'What about the night we spent together in my room?' she asked. 'Didn't that mean anything to you?'

'You mean, the couple of days before you murdered my father?' I asked, harshly.

'Your father died trying to escape . . .'

'My father chose to die because he didn't want to spend the rest of his life in prison for something he didn't do.'

Sephy's gaze lowered briefly. She looked up again and said, 'I didn't murder your father, Callum. I didn't want him to die.'

'You and your kind killed him,' I told her, zipping up the camcorder case.

'So you *are* going to kill me. But not you personally, I bet,' Sephy's voice trembled. 'That's not your style, is it? You set me up so your friends could capture me. You're real good at letting others do your dirty work for you.'

I spun around at that. 'You wouldn't be the first dagger I've killed. Not by a long shot.'

'And I'd be easy to kill, wouldn't I?' Sephy said quietly. ''Cause I don't count. I'm nothing. Just a black dagger bitch. Just like you're a white blanker bastard.'

And now I was furiously angry. Just like I'd wanted to be before I could do what I had to do next. I grabbed her left hand and before she could pull away, I drew my knife across her index finger. Sephy gasped, tears instantly springing to her eyes. And my anger died with such a suddenness that I knew it hadn't been real to begin with. Manufactured to get me through the moment. The day. My life.

'Sorry . . .' I mumbled, wrapping her T-shirt around her finger. I concentrated on getting her blood on to the T-shirt. I didn't look at her. I couldn't. The white cotton of her shirt soaked up the blood like blotting paper. I unwrapped the shirt and dragged her still bleeding finger up and down it. The final proof for her father that we were deadly serious. The final proof that we were deadly. Sephy kept trying to pull her hand back but I wouldn't let her.

'I bet you enjoyed that,' Sephy hissed at me.

'No, I didn't,' I snapped back, letting go of her wrist at last.

Sephy put her finger into her mouth, wincing as the wound stung anew. She took her finger out of her mouth to look at it. It was still bleeding. The cut was deep – for both of us. Deeper than I'd intended. A scratch would've been deeper than I intended. She went to put her finger back in her mouth but I grabbed her hand again. She struggled, trying to pull her hand away. Maybe she thought I was going to cut her again. I put her finger in my mouth. And she was instantly still. I don't know how long we sat there, watching each other. A second? An hour? Sephy moved first. She slowly pulled back her finger.

'When you all decide you don't need me any more,' Sephy whispered, 'I want *you* to . . . do it. One favour though. It's the last thing I'll ever ask you. J–just make it quick. OK?' And she turned around and lay down on her side of the bed, her back towards me.

I stared at her back, my fists clenched, reining myself in so tightly, I thought my back would snap. Only when I could trust myself to stand without falling to the floor did I get up. I left the room, carefully locking the door behind me. I leaned against the door, my eyes closed. I had to do this, make it through this. And I would. I turned to walk back to the living room, only to find my brother further down the corridor, watching my every move.

'Yes?' I asked, annoyed.

Everywhere I turned at the moment, Jude seemed to be watching me.

'Give me the disc.'

I handed over the T-shirt and Sephy's hair before taking out the camcorder. I opened it up, took out the video disc and put it in its case before handing it over.

Jude held it up carefully, before slipping it into his pocket. He looked long and hard at the T-shirt. When at last he looked at me, his grin was full of admiration and relief. 'Now I know for sure whose side you're on. Well done, little brother. Pete and I are going to deliver all this as well as our demands. Leila and Morgan will guard the house. Sephy Hadley is your responsibility. Understand?'

I didn't answer. It was unheard of for the first- and second-in-command to go off on a joint mission together like this. Why wasn't Jude going with Morgan? Or Pete going with me? Why did Jude want to be with Pete? There was something going on here . . .

'We should be back by morning,' Jude continued. 'If the General's second-in-command arrives before we get back, make him welcome – after he's given you the password.'

'Which is?'

'Golden Man.'

Jude went to move past me. I stood back against the wall to let him go. Jude was my brother but I trusted him less far than an elephant could jump. More than ever I sensed the need to watch my back, my front, my sides and every other part of me – if I wanted to keep them in one piece, that is.

ninety-seven. Sephy

The door opened again. I didn't even bother turning around this time. I lay on my side facing the wall. Rubbing my sore hand over my aching stomach, I fervently wished the pain away.

'Dinner,' came Callum's rough voice.

I ignored him and carried on rubbing my stomach, waiting for the sound of the door closing. It didn't come. Callum's footsteps echoed across the hard cement floor. I stopped rubbing my stomach at once, but I still didn't turn around. Callum put his hand on my shoulder and pulled me round to face him.

'Dinner.'

He thrust the plastic plate into my hands. I sat up and after firing a lasering look in his direction, I threw the plate across the room. It hit the wall with a thud and the plate fell first, followed by a brown sticky mess trickling its way down the wall towards the floor.

'You shouldn't've done that.'

I deliberately turned away from him and lay down again. Silence. But I wasn't going to turn around to see what he was doing. After a short while, I heard him cross the room and leave, locking the door behind him.

He never forgot to lock the door.

ninety-eight. Callum

If I could just stop thinking for five seconds then I could get some shut-eye. But it wasn't happening. And the sleeping bag seemed to twist in the opposite direction to whichever way I turned. I couldn't get Sephy's words out of my head.

One of you is going to kill me . . .

But we didn't have to do that. OK so she'd seen us, but once her dad met our demands we could be long gone. But even as I thought it, I knew I was just deluding myself.

One of you is going to kill me . . .

'You look like you could use some company.' Leila's voice above me was the last straw. I opened my eyes, giving up all pretence of trying to sleep.

'Who's guarding the front?'

'I came in for a loo break – if that's all right with you.'

I unzipped my bag and sat up. 'No, it's not OK with me. You want to take a leak, do it in the woods, but don't leave the front of the cabin unmonitored.'

'I'm not a man,' Leila protested. 'I can't wee standing up.'

'That's no excuse.'

'Callum, you're mad as hell at something, but don't take it out on me.'

I pulled on my T-shirt. 'I don't know what you're talking about.'

'You don't have to get dressed on my account,' Leila said silkily, running her hands lightly over my chest.

'Go and guard the front like you're supposed to,' I told her.

Leila stood up. 'Suit yourself. D'you know, I think that's why I like you.' At my puzzled look she explained. 'You're the only man I know who hasn't tried to get on my good side in five seconds flat!'

I smiled. 'Nothing personal, Leila.'

'Thanks!' She raised an eyebrow. 'That makes it worse!'

I got to my feet as she left the room. Pulling on my boots, I decided to hunt down a beer and join Morgan out back. Without warning, there was a sudden commotion out front. I ran towards the front door when it burst open. For one split second, I thought we'd been rumbled, that the police had somehow tracked us down. But it wasn't the police. It was Leila and a stranger. He was as tall as me, with blond hair tied back in a pony-tail. He wore a dark polo shirt and expensive brown trousers tucked into fancy boots. His long, dark trenchcoat had the collar turned up and flapped open like a cloak or a cape. The peculiar thing was, the stranger had Leila in an armlock, not the other way round. Morgan came running up behind me.

'Who's in charge here?' the stranger asked.

Morgan looked at me. I didn't take my eyes off the intruder. The stranger turned to me. 'I see that you are. I believe you've been expecting me.'

'Let me go!' Leila hissed, trying to twist away from the man who held her.

The man pushed her forward – hard. She only just kept her balance. She spun around, arms raised, ready to take him out. The man raised one hand.

'I wouldn't if I were you,' was all he said. But it was enough.

A second or two later, Leila dropped her hands.

'So this is the famous *Stiletto* unit, is it?' The man looked at each of us in turn. 'So far, I'm not very impressed.'

'We've been expecting you, have we?' Morgan said.

'That's right.'

'What's the password then?' I asked.

'You first,' the man ordered.

I regarded him. 'I don't think so. You're the guest here, not us.'

I signalled to Morgan behind my back to get ready. We'd been caught on the hop but there were three of us and only one of him.

'How about Gold Man?' said the stranger.

'Not even close.' Morgan and I started forward.

'Then how about Golden Man,' the stranger laughed.

I regarded the man with undisguised venom. I didn't like to be made a fool of and that was precisely what he was doing.

'Hi. I'm Andrew Dorn.' He held out his hand.

After a moment's pause I took it, still on my guard.

'You're the General's second-in-command?' Morgan said sceptically.

'Yeah. D'you want to make something of it?' asked Andrew.

'Only asking,' Morgan shrugged. 'Excuse me. I'm on guard duty.'

With a brief nod of his head, Morgan turned and headed for the back door. Leila followed his cue by heading out the front, still rubbing her upper arm where Andrew had twisted it behind her back.

'Congratulations on the success of the first part of your mission,' Andrew told me when the others had gone. 'Let's hope the rest runs as smoothly.'

'No reason why it shouldn't.'

'No reason at all,' Andrew agreed.

'Want some coffee?'

'Wouldn't say no. Can I see the prisoner first?'

I opened my mouth to say that she was probably asleep, but I managed to snap it shut in time. We moved along the hall to the door. I dug into my trouser pocket for the key and unlocked it. Sephy was sitting up on her bed, facing the door. She regarded both Andrew and me without saying a word.

'I hope for your sake that your father loves you very, very much,' Andrew told her.

Sephy stared at him, frowning. I saw her glance down at Andrew's boots, then start. I glanced down at Andrew's boots myself. They were brown with silver chains just above the heel of each one. A bit too ostentatious for my taste but nothing special. So what was it about them that had caused such a reaction?

'Be a good girl and you'll soon be out of here,' Andrew told her.

And still Sephy didn't speak. If anything, her frown deepened. Andrew left without another word. I followed him out, locking the door behind me.

'Make sure she doesn't leave that room alive,' Andrew said quietly. 'Orders from the General himself. Understood?'

The ground started rocking beneath my feet. 'Understood, sir. I'll take care of it myself.'

'Good man. Make sure you do.' Andrew headed towards the kitchen.

I stood totally still, waiting for the earth to stop moving.

ninety-nine. Sephy

The moment Callum locked me in again, I carried on exploring my room. A forty-watt bulb gave the only light in the room. There were no windows and the locked door could've been reinforced steel for all the good it did me. The floor was cement and the walls were bricks and plaster. I thought again about shouting for help but logic told me that we had to be kilometres away from anyone who could help me, otherwise they would've tied me up and put a gag in my mouth. I tapped my way around the walls, not really sure what I was listening for, but listening for some change of note, a hollow sound that could re-kindle some hope within me.

But there was nothing.

That man who'd come in with Callum . . . I'd seen him

somewhere before. I knew I had and yet I couldn't quite place him. It was frustrating the hell out of me. I pulled the bed away from the wall. It dragged across the floor with enough noise to wake the dead. I stopped at once and listened. I couldn't hear anyone coming. I moved the bed more slowly. Was there anything behind it that could help me?

What was that scratched into the plaster behind the bed?

To my fellow Crosses, keep the faith.

The writing was jagged and uneven. From the look of it, it could've been written with a fingernail. *Keep the faith* . . . God knows there was little else to do in this hell-hole.

There was nothing in the room, apart from the bed with its one blanket and a bucket in the opposite corner. And short of standing behind the door and using the bucket to brain the first person who came in, there was nothing in the room I could use as a weapon of any kind.

Keep the faith . . .

I pushed the bed back and lay down again. I wondered what my family were doing at that moment – Minnie and Mother and Dad. Did Dad know that I'd been kidnapped yet? I hadn't seen him in almost six months. How would he take the news? How much money did the kidnappers want anyway? How much was I worth to them? Maybe they didn't want money. Maybe they were after something else, like the release of L.M. prisoners or something like that. I didn't even know. How long ago was it that I hadn't wanted to go home? A day? Two? It was hard to tell how long I'd been in this place.

A strange joke. I hadn't wanted to be at home and now

I'd got my wish. I would've given my right arm to see my family one more time. Just once more. And with that thought I knew that I'd given up on any chance of seeing any of them, ever again.

one hundred. Callum

'We interrupt this programme to bring you a newsflash.'

We sat forward, all eyes on the telly. The atmosphere in the room was edgy as we waited to hear. I glanced at my watch. Kamal Hadley appeared at seven o'clock precisely, just as he'd been instructed.

'I am here to announce that I shall be temporarily with-drawing from public office for personal family reasons,' Kamal announced. 'I don't wish to say anything further at this time. Thank you.'

And then he was out of the press office like a rat up a drainpipe. Jude punched the air.

'Yes! He's agreed to our demands.'

'I don't trust him,' I said, still watching the telly as the newsreader discussed Kamal Hadley's surprise announce-ment with the channel's political correspondent.

'I don't trust any of them,' Jude replied. 'But we've got him over a barrel – and he knows it.'

It was a crisp early autumn evening: the perfect evening to pick up our ransom money and let Kamal Hadley know we had further demands before he could see his daughter. At least, that's how Jude had described it. The money would fund future L.M. activities but Sephy wouldn't see her dad again until five L.M. members had been released from prison. The authorities didn't realize that three of the five we wanted released were key members, not just the underlings they thought they were.

'You're all ready for the telephone relay?' Andrew asked.

'Of course,' Jude frowned. 'We've been through it a dozen times. Leila will stay here with the girl. Pete, Morgan and I make our relay phone calls from three different locations around town to stop them tracing the calls. Callum will drop off the second set of instructions, pick up our money and head straight back here. It's all arranged.'

'And you'll each be in your proper places at the right times?' asked Andrew.

'Of course.' Jude was getting annoyed now and not doing a very good job of hiding it. 'This isn't amateur hour, you know. We know what we're doing.'

'Good! Good! But I think it'd be better if Leila makes the pick-up,' said Andrew. 'That's always the most dangerous part of a kidnapping and as a girl she's more likely to go unnoticed.'

'Then I'll go in Pete's place and make one of the phone calls,' I volunteered.

'No. Of all of us, you're the one Hadley knows the best. We can't take any chances of him recognizing your voice,' Andrew said at once.

'I'm not staying here,' I said furiously. 'I'm not a ruddy babysitter.'

'You're needed here,' Jude told me.

'Why can't Andrew stay behind and look after her?' I asked.

'Because I'm off to another part of the country,' Andrew replied. 'And I'm here as an observer, not to do your dirty work for you.'

'You'll have to forgive my brother,' Jude smiled uneasily. 'He's still very young.'

'I'm not staying here,' I protested.

'You'll do as you're told,' Jude rounded on me.

I was embarrassing Jude in front of the General's second-in-command. I'd get it in the neck for that when they all got back.

'You're staying here and that's final.'

Reluctantly I kept quiet, but my outraged scowl told them all what I thought of that idea.

'Let's go, people. And remember to keep your eyes and ears open at all times,' said Andrew. 'Never underestimate the daggers. A lot of our members made that mistake and they're either languishing in prison or swinging at the end of a rope because of it. I'll be keeping a close eye on your situation. A very close eye.'

They all headed out of the door with me trailing miserably behind them.

Andrew turned to me. 'If the police or anyone suspicious arrives, you shoot the girl first and ask questions afterwards. Get it?'

'Got it.'

'Good.'

Jude was the first one to the front door but the last one out of it. 'Don't let us down, brother – OK?' he whispered to me.

'I won't,' I replied.

'I know you won't.' He slapped me on the back and then they went off. I shut the door behind them, and stood in the hallway. I didn't want to be here. I didn't want to be anywhere near here where I could hear Sephy's voice, or see her face.

Let me leave, before I forget why I'm here.

Get me out of here, before I break down or lose my mind at all the things I've done since we've been apart.

I didn't even have to close my eyes to remember the sight of Sephy's car driving away from me that day. My life might've been very different if I'd read her letter in time, if I'd managed to reach her car before it sped away from me.

I might've been very much alive, instead of ice-cold inside.

At least I thought I was – until I saw her again.

Get me out of here, before I do something I'll regret.

one hundred and one.
Sephy

Lying on my back, I concentrated on breathing regularly. In. Out. In. Out. The pain in my lower abdomen was less than it had been but it was still sharp. My eyes closed and, still forcing myself to breathe in a slow, regular pattern, I moved my hand in a circular motion over my abdomen below my navel.

'What's the matter?'

My hand slowed for a moment but did not stop. I turned to lie on my side, my face averted, my eyes now open and wary.

'Sephy, what's the matter?' Callum moved further into the room to stand beside my bed.

'It's nothing. Go away.'

I kept my back towards him. Even if I'd been ordered and chastised, I couldn't have looked at Callum. To look at him would be to weep and scream and beg. And I wasn't going to do any of those things. Ever. I'd never give him the satisfaction. He was one of them now. My Callum was dead. The mattress sank where Callum sat down. Neither of us spoke. I continued to rub my abdomen. Slow, circular strokes. If only this pain in my stomach would ease – just for a second. Callum's brother must've really enjoyed that thump he gave me. From the continuing feel of it, he'd put his whole heart and soul into it. And my finger was as sore as blazes. Every time I stretched it out, the wound opened up again. Between them, the McGregor boys had really sorted me out.

Without warning, my hand was moved away from my body and moments later, Callum's hand replaced it. I turned to Callum, eyes wide with shock. I tried to push his hand away. Gently but firmly, Callum placed my hand at my side and continued rubbing my abdomen. I couldn't breathe. My heart slammed against my ribs as I stared at my captor.

'What're you doing?' I whispered.

'You're hurting.'

'Like you care.'

At first I thought that Callum wasn't going to reply.

'I care,' he said at last.

'Then let me go. *Please*.'

'I can't.'

Ashamed of myself for having asked, I tried to turn my head away, but Callum's restraining hand on my cheek stopped me. He carried on rubbing my stomach. We watched each other in a silence that surrounded us like a bubble of barbed wire. There was no outside, no sight, no sound. The world was reduced to the room we were in. Time was condensed to the moments that passed between us.

'I love you,' Callum said softly.

'Then let me go. Please . . .'

Callum's finger on my lips stilled the words. 'I love you,' he repeated. 'I told you once before – when you were asleep and couldn't hear me. I was afraid for you to hear me. But I'm not any more.'

Callum *loved* me . . .

My heart began to rocket against my ribs again. Yesterday those words would've enabled me to fly. But that was yesterday.

'You don't. You can't love me. It doesn't exist. You told me so.'

'If it didn't exist, I wouldn't've cared when I saw you drive off for Chivers. I came after you, you know. But I was too late.'

'Y-you . . . came after me?'

Callum smiled sadly. 'I didn't read your letter until

about twenty minutes before you were due to leave. I ran and ran all the way, but I was too late . . .'

I closed my eyes to stop my tears from escaping, but they did anyway. They trickled slowly down my face like solitary raindrops on a window pane. What might've been . . .

'Ignore me,' I said, wiping my eyes. 'Just go away, please.'

'Do you hate me?' asked Callum.

I was finding it hard to think straight. *Callum had come after me* . . . He had wanted us to be together. His hand was still stroking my abdomen but it was no longer soothing. Instead it seemed to burn through my clothes and straight down into my insides.

'Do you?' Callum prompted.

I shook my head. 'Another place . . . another time . . . you and I . . .'

'I don't know anything about another place and another time,' Callum interrupted. 'All I know is here and now.'

And he bent his head to kiss me. He moved so quickly, I had no time to even be surprised. Before I could make a sound, his lips were on mine and I could see nothing but his face, his eyes. His lips were so soft. Even softer than I'd remembered. I'd daydreamed so many times of doing this, until I'd realized that I was dreaming about something that was never, ever going to happen. And then the dream had been, not exactly abandoned, but buried deep where not even I could reach it easily. But now the world had turned upside down and Callum was kissing me. His lips coaxed open my mouth, but there was very little coaxing to be done. I closed my eyes.

This wasn't real.

None of it was real.

It couldn't be.

It was forbidden.

Against the law.

Against nature.

So I was dreaming again. Lost in my own world where there were no noughts and Crosses. Just me and Callum, as Callum and I should be, whilst the rest of the world smiled kindly at us or turned their backs on us – but either way, we were left alone. Callum's hand moved from my abdomen to my waist and higher. I pushed at his hand but it didn't move. His kiss became gentler.

'Callum . . .'

'Shush! I won't hurt you. I'd never hurt you. I love you,' Callum whispered against my mouth. His breath was hot and made my insides melt. Uncertain, confused, I tried to pull away, but his kiss grew more urgent and all at once I didn't want to move away any more. I pulled him closer to me, wrapping my arms around him, kissing him just as desperately as he was kissing me. Like if we could just love long enough and hard enough and deep enough, then the world outside would never, could never hurt us again. And then, it was as if we'd both caught fire. Sort of like spontaneous combustion and we were burning up together.

'I love you,' Callum whispered again.

But I could hardly hear him over the sound of my blood roaring in my ears. His hands were everywhere, moving over my arms, my breasts, my waist, my thighs.

And every caress, every stroke robbed me of my breath and burnt through my skin. I pulled him closer and closer, my hands moving over his back and his bum and his legs. He sat up, pulling me with him. He raised my hands to pull off my jumper. I unbuttoned his shirt. He unfastened my bra. I unzipped his trousers. We stripped each other until we were both naked. And I was shaking. But not from the cold. I was melting inside. Never had I felt so scared and exhilarated and *alive* all at once. We both knelt on the bed, facing each other. Callum's gaze moved down over my body. I'd never realized before just how physical a mere look could be. Callum reached out with both hands and touched my cheeks. He ran his hands over my lips and my nose and my forehead. I closed my eyes, just before his fingers softly touched my eyelids. And then moments later, his lips were exploring my face the way his hands had done. He lay me down gently, his hands and lips still exploring my body. I wanted to do the same to him. I was going to do the same to him. We were going to make this time last for ever. Callum was right. We had here and now. And that was all that mattered. I let myself drift away, following wherever Callum led. Beside him all the way as he led me into a real, unreal world. Not quite heaven. Not quite hell.

I sat up, scrambling for my jeans and my jumper. I couldn't stop sobbing. My head was pounding and my nose was running and my throat was hurting, but I couldn't stop.

'Sephy . . .' Callum began.

Did I look like him? So miserably unhappy after what had just happened to us? If I did, then I wouldn't look at him again. His expression was my reflection. I pulled on my jeans and my jumper and hunted frantically for my sandals. I was aware of Callum getting dressed even though I couldn't bring myself to look at him.

Stop weeping . . . Just stop . . .

But I couldn't. More tears for the impossible. My sandals were on the wrong feet. I didn't know what I was doing. I kicked them off and tried again, still weeping.

'*Sephy, please . . .*'

Callum tried to put his arms around me. I pushed him away. He pulled me toward him again, which just made me cry harder and push against him more frantically.

The door of my prison cell was flung open and in ran Jude and Morgan, only to stop abruptly when they saw Callum and me together on the bed. Callum leapt up, but it was too late.

Stop crying . . . If only I could stop crying . . .

one hundred and two.
Callum

It's not what you're thinking . . . It's exactly what you're thinking . . . Someone say something. Anything.

Nothing.

'What's happened?' I asked at last.

'You tell us,' Jude said with quiet menace.

He kept looking from me to Sephy and back again. 'Where's Leila?'

'Arrested,' Morgan replied.

'Where's Pete?'

'Dead,' said Jude. 'They had undercover police everywhere. They must've been monitoring every phone box in town. Either that or they knew exactly where we'd be. Morgan and I changed our locations at the last moment otherwise they might've captured us too. We were lucky to escape in one piece.' Jude looked at Sephy, his face sombre. 'I thought we could take the girl and move out of this town to somewhere safer, but now . . .'

He turned to me, the rest of his sentence clearly spoken but unsaid.

What have I done? Sephy, forgive me. I've killed us both.

'I'll pack up all our equipment . . .' I said.

'I don't think so,' Jude replied. 'Morgan, go and pack up everything essential. Leave the rest. We've got to get out of here.'

Morgan left without a word.

'Why is she crying?' Jude indicated Sephy.

My face began to burn. I kept my mouth shut.

'And her jumper is inside out.'

Jude and I glared at each other. What was I meant to say to that? Nothing. Jude had already made up his mind what had happened in his absence.

'You stupid, stupid berk. You've put a noose around all our necks.' Jude grabbed me by my T-shirt. 'We could've got what we wanted and let her go, in spite of what Andrew Dorn said. They'd never have found us.' He punctuated each half-sentence by backhanding me around the face. 'But not now. You raped her and now it's her or us. You stupid, stupid . . .'

I clenched my fists and the next thing I knew Jude was flat on his back with blood trickling down from his nose.

'Don't you ever hit me again as long as you live,' I hissed at him.

He sprang up and swung at me. I blocked his arm easily and hit him again. And then we were at it. A vicious, scrappy brawl, with each of us determined to hurt the other more than we were hurting. Something rushed by me but I barely noticed.

'Stop her! Stop!' Jude pushed me away. 'She's escaping. Get her.'

We both sprung to our feet. I looked around, confused. Where was Sephy? I looked towards the open door and realized. Jude and I both took off after her. We raced out of the front door.

'Morgan! Round here!' Jude yelled. 'She's escaped.'

I looked around but I couldn't see her. It was night-time now, almost midnight, but we had a full moon on our side and there were no clouds, so that was something.

'There she is!' Morgan pointed over to the left towards the trees.

I turned, just in time to see Sephy disappear into the darkness of the wood. All three of us chased after her. I had to find her before the others. I needed to find her.

God help me if I didn't.

one hundred and three.
Sephy

Run, Sephy. Just keep running.

The shadows were long and ominously silent all around me. I ran round tree-trunk after tree-trunk, the moonlight dappling through the branches and leaves above me.

And still I ran. Whatever happened I couldn't let them catch me. Something sharp dug into my right foot. I cried out, biting my lip a moment later – but too late.

'Over there!' A voice cried out from behind me. Too close behind me.

I darted to the right. Where was I? I couldn't tell. I couldn't see where I was going. It was just – away.

I could hear leaves and bracken crunching behind me. Getting closer.

Hide, Sephy!

I made out the outline of some undergrowth between a clump of trees. For a second, I considered hiding in it but I didn't want to have to lie down. If I did that and I was discovered, I'd never get away in time. Footsteps approaching. I made for the nearest, darkest tree and hid behind its trunk. I leaned back against it, trying to merge with it, desperate to disappear.

Please, God . . .

The footsteps slowed then stopped. And they were so close. I stopped breathing. I couldn't breathe. I didn't dare. *Please, God . . .*

'Persephone, I know you can hear me . . .' Jude's voice. 'We're kilometres from anywhere here. You'll wander around this forest for days without seeing another soul. With no food. No water. Come out now and we won't harm you – I promise.'

Silence. Moments later, a muffled curse fractured the silence. I drew a hasty breath before my lungs could burst and held it. The night wind rustled through the leaves all around, making them sound like they were whispering, commenting on what was happening on the ground below them. I opened my mouth and exhaled softly, feeling the warm air dance across my lips, terrified that what I could feel the others would hear. I closed my eyes.

Please, please God . . .

'Sephy, come out now and nothing will happen to you.' Jude's voice seemed further away.

Or was that just wishful thinking.

'But if you don't show yourself and we find you . . .' The threat hung in the air like the very darkness around me.

Footsteps sounded, getting further away. I opened my eyes, my feet already moving to head in the opposite direction only to stop abruptly. I gasped. Callum stood right in front of me, less than a metre away. And the fear I felt then was like a moment spent dying.

'Callum . . .' I breathed.

'What was that?' A voice I hadn't heard before asked.

Callum put his finger to his lips.

'It's only me,' he called out. 'I tripped.'

'We've got to find her.' The other man's voice was getting closer.

'I SEE HER!' Callum yelled suddenly.

I shook my head, my eyes pleading with him, my heart about to crack.

'She's trying to double back on us. She must be heading back for the cabin,' Callum shouted out.

'Blast!'

The immediate sound of running. Away from me. Away from us. Callum stepped towards me. He took my unresisting hands in his. He looked up.

'D'you see Orion's Belt?' he said softly.

I looked up and nodded.

'Always keep it immediately behind you. When you reach the road, turn left on to it and keep going.'

'Callum . . .'

'Just go, Sephy.' He let go of my hands and turned away.

'Callum, we have to talk . . .'

'No. Just go.' He turned away again.

'Callum . . .' And then I remembered what had been bothering me about the stranger since I'd first seen him. I grabbed Callum's hand. 'Wait. That man with the blond pony-tail, the one who came in with you to see me?'

'What about him?'

'He works for my father. I saw him a couple of years ago at our house.'

'You're sure?' Callum frowned.

'Yes. I'm positive. It was him. He works for Dad. He wore the same boots with the silver chains. I recognized them. It's definitely him.'

'Thanks.' He pulled away from me and a moment later he'd melted into the shadows. I tried to train my eyes to see him but he'd gone. I turned and ran.

THE CONFESSION . . .

one hundred and four.
Callum

Reporters surrounded Kamal Hadley. And there were so many cameras flashing around him that it looked like a firework display. Kamal Hadley raised his hands and immediately the clamour around him died down. The firework display didn't.

'I . . . I will make a short statement and t-that's it.' Kamal Hadley wiped the back of his hand across his cheeks before continuing. 'My daughter is still unconscious after being found this morning. Her doctors describe her condition as critical but stable. The police are present and will interview her the moment she regains consciousness. Acting on information received, we captured one of the kidnappers and another opened fire on the police and was killed as a result. No ransom was paid. That's all I'd like to say at this moment.'

'How many kidnappers were there?'

'Where was your daughter held during her ordeal?'

'What are the extent of her injuries?'

Kamal Hadley turned without another word and headed back inside the hospital. Jude pressed the mute button on the TV remote control just as the newsreader's face appeared on screen. I slumped back in my chair, dog-tired. We were hundreds of kilometres away from the cabin in the woods, having got out of there in a hurry once it became clear that we'd lost Sephy. We were holed up in one room in a seedy bed-and-breakfast hotel, with twin beds for Jude and Morgan and a sleeping bag for me. The walls looked like they hadn't seen a lick of paint in at least three generations and the windows and fittings were caked with grease and grime. There was a carpet on the floor which I think had a pattern once, a long time ago, but it was so worn it was impossible to tell what the pattern might've been or even its original colour. Not that I had much time to dwell on our surroundings. Morgan and Jude were all too ready to beat the crap out of me – at the very least – until I told them what I'd learnt about Andrew Dorn.

'Where did you get this information from?' Jude asked.

'Sephy,' I replied.

'And it never occurred to you that she could be lying.'

'She wasn't.'

'How can you be so sure?'

'Because I know her. If she says she saw Andrew Dorn with her dad then she did. Besides, she volunteered the information.'

'Because she wanted us to be paranoid about each other,' Morgan said scornfully. 'Andrew Dorn isn't a traitor. He's the General's second-in-command for God's sake!'

'Then tell me this. How did the police know where each of you was going to be when you went to set up the telephone relay and pick up the ransom? We set up different locations for everyone precisely so that wouldn't happen. Only five people knew our plans apart from Andrew. One is dead. One is captured and us three are here up to our armpits in alligators. So you explain that then?'

Jude and Morgan exchanged a long look. At least I had them thinking.

'You said you changed your positions at the last minute?' I carried on. 'So you didn't have a chance to tell Andrew what you were doing and I bet that's the only reason you're both still here to talk about it now. He betrayed us. Sephy was right.'

'But she can't be . . .' Morgan couldn't believe it.

I remembered something else. 'He kept whispering to me that Sephy wasn't to leave the cabin alive. I think that's because he knew she'd recognized him. He ordered me to kill her first and ask questions later if anyone came to the cabin. But if I'd done that, I wouldn't've stood a chance of getting out alive.'

Jude and Morgan were silent as they considered what I said.

It took a while to convince them but, in a way, Leila being captured and Pete being killed finally did it for me. The police must've known our plans to be able to round up two of us. And Andrew must've told them. No-one else could've.

'I'll find him if it takes the rest of my life.' Morgan was spitting mad by now. 'And when I do, my hands and his throat are going to make long and painful contact.'

We discussed various ways of stopping Andrew from betraying us or anyone else in the future but the problem was, we had no proof. And you didn't go round accusing the General's second-in-command of being a traitor without proof, not if you wanted to live to a reasonable age.

'Besides,' said Jude, looking directly at me, 'we have a more pressing problem.'

'We'll never be able to settle in one place long enough to figure out what we're going to do next.' Morgan said grimly. 'They are never going to stop looking for us.'

'I didn't rape her,' I said through gritted teeth.

'So you say,' Morgan sneered. 'But here's some free advice. If you can't keep your trousers on, don't leave any witnesses next time.'

'I didn't rape her.' I turned to Jude. From his expression, he obviously didn't believe me either.

'You shouldn't've done it,' he said at last.

I closed my eyes briefly and looked away. Talking to those two was like banging my head off a brick wall.

And the worst thing of all was, Jude was right. I shouldn't have done it.

'Morgan, I think it'd be better if we all went our separate ways for a while,' Jude said carefully. 'Together we'll be much easier to track down. We should each fend for ourselves for say, six months and then meet at a pre-arranged time and place.'

'That's a good idea,' Morgan agreed.

'We'll meet up on Callum's birthday. And no-one is to go blabbing about Andrew Dorn in the meantime,' Jude warned. 'If he suspects we're on to him, he could have other cells pick us off one by one before we could do anything about him.'

'But we can't just let him carry on betraying the L.M.

to the Crosses,' Morgan protested.

'None of us has the ear of the General. We don't even know who the General is. And if we tried to get a message to him, it's bound to go through Andrew first. So we're going to have to bide our time.'

'So in the meantime more of our people will go to jail or swing from the scaffold at Hewmett Prison?' said Morgan.

'If that's the way it's got to be until we can expose him – yes.' Jude replied fiercely. 'We have to lose this battle to win the war.'

'That sucks!'

'Tough,' Jude snapped. 'I don't like it any more than you do, but we have no choice. Morgan, could you go out and get us a meal?'

'What kind of meal?'

'I don't know.' Jude frowned impatiently. 'Get a curry or a chicken wrap or some burgers or something.'

Grumbling, Morgan left the room.

'You do know we'll be lucky if we survive a month without being wiped out by either our own side or the police, don't you?' Jude said quietly. 'Andrew has probably already got the word out that we're to be . . . eliminated.'

I'd figured that out for myself.

Jude sat back on his single bed and rubbed his eyes wearily. 'D'you want to hear something bust-a-gut funny, little brother?'

The last thing in the world I felt like doing was laughing.

'D'you remember when Mum had to go to hospital

because she broke a finger slapping Dad's face?'

I nodded.

'Remember when she asked you to disappear because she had something to tell me?'

'Yeah, I do.' I frowned.

'You see her?' Jude pointed to the photo of a smiling Sephy now being shown on the TV screen.

I looked away, unable to look at her for longer than a microsecond. Just that quick sight of her had my heart drumming.

'She and her whole family have ruined our lives. It's as if they've made it their business to mix up their lives with ours,' said Jude. 'They've always believed they were better than us and they weren't.'

I frowned at him. 'What're you talking about?'

'Mum's grandfather, our great-grandfather was a Cross. That's what Mum told me that day. We've got Cross blood in our veins.'

'I . . . I don't believe it,' I whispered.

'It's true. Mum only told me because I joined the L.M. She said I was part Cross, so killing them would be like killing my own. Poor Mum! That backfired on her.'

'What d'you mean?'

'None of them ever wanted us. What has any Cross ever done for me except look down at me? I hated all of them even more after Mum told me the truth. Poor Mum.'

I was drowning in Jude's words, trying to find something of sense to hold on to.

'I had no idea . . .'

'There's no reason why you should.' Jude shrugged.

'We're going to split up soon and I don't even know if I'll see you again. But I've got some free advice for you, Callum. Stay away from Persephone Hadley.'

'I . . . of course I . . .'

'Stay away from her, Callum,' Jude interrupted. 'Or she's going to be the death of you.'

one hundred and five.
Sephy

Not again! I only just made it to the bathroom, collapsing with my head over the toilet bowl before I brought up what felt like most of the acid in my stomach. It was seven o'clock in the morning and I'd only just woken up, so my stomach was totally empty. And retching on an empty stomach was far worse than vomiting with a full one. My stomach acid stung my nose and made my mouth taste bitter and nasty. And this was about the fifth morning in a row that I'd woken up feeling like last Crossmas's left-over turkey.

Only when I was reasonably sure that I could get to my feet without keeling over did I stand up. I cleaned my teeth and gargled for at least a minute with mouthwash. But I still felt wretched. I made my way out of my bedroom and headed downstairs, feeling very sorry for myself. As if everything that'd happened to me in the last five weeks wasn't enough, now I'd caught a tummy bug.

The last five weeks . . .

After I'd regained consciousness, it seemed like every doctor in the northern hemisphere had prodded and poked me and given me test after humiliating test until I felt more like a specimen in a lab than a human being. And the police had asked me question after embarrassing question.

Especially about what my kidnappers had done to me.

'Whatever happened, you mustn't feel it was your fault. You were powerless. You can tell us *everything* that happened, we'll understand . . .' The policewoman had smiled and hugged and tried to get me to confide in her until all I wanted to do was slap her senseless. She interviewed me in a room with a huge mirror on one wall and kept stealing quick glances at it when I wouldn't answer her questions. I mean, did she really think I was that stupid? Jeez! I knew a one-way mirror when I saw one.

I had nothing to say to them. I had nothing to say to anyone about my ordeal in the cabin in the woods. I didn't even want to think about it. It hurt my head and stung my eyes and broke my heart to think about it. Not the kidnapping so much, although that'd been bad enough. But Callum . . . I couldn't bear to think about Callum. And yet every thought seemed to find its own way back to him. He was never out of my mind. And it was driving me crazy.

I entered the kitchen and made myself some dry toast and a cup of weak blackcurrant tea. It helped. A bit. A very little bit.

'Oh, there you are,' Minnie entered the kitchen to sit

opposite me at the breakfast bar. 'You OK?'

'Yes. Apart from this tummy bug?'

'You've been sick for the last couple of mornings, haven't you?' Minnie frowned.

'How d'you know?'

'I've heard you calling on the porcelain telephone!'

I raised an eyebrow and carried on eating my toast. I wasn't in the mood for any of my sister's so-called jokes.

'When're you going to talk about what happened to you when you were kidnapped?' Minnie asked.

'Never.'

'You shouldn't bottle it up inside . . .'

'Back off, Minnie. OK?' I snapped. 'My being kidnapped won't reflect badly on you in any manner, shape or form so you can leave me alone now.'

'What're you talking about? I'm concerned about you.'

'Yeah, right!' I took another bite of toast.

'What happened to you out there?' Minnie asked softly.

'I was kidnapped. I escaped. Now you know as much as I do.' I chewed my last piece of toast and swallowed it down with a sip of rapidly cooling fruit tea.

'Sephy, are . . . are you pregnant?'

'What're you talking about? Of course I'm . . . not . . .' The words trailed away to nothing. I stared at my sister, in a daze.

'So you could be?' Minnie said grimly. 'Who was it? One of the kidnappers?'

'I can't be . . . I can't be pregnant . . .' I whispered, aghast.

'Who was it, Sephy? You can tell me. I won't tell anyone, I promise.'

I sprang up and raced from the room, like if I could only run fast enough I could leave my sister's words far behind me.

Come on, Sephy! Just do it. The pregnancy test doesn't work unless you actually use it! Just do it. And one minute later, you'll know. If it stays white you're not pregnant. You'll have ducked a bullet and no one need ever know. And if it turns blue . . .

For heaven's sake, do it. Anything's better than this not knowing.

I picked up the leaflet and read the instructions again. It seemed straightforward enough. One indicator stick included. Just add urine. Nothing to it. So get on with it. I took a deep breath and followed the instructions. Which was silly of me, because I knew I wasn't pregnant.

I couldn't be. Not now. Not like this.

I placed the now-wet indicator stick on top of the toilet cistern whilst I washed my hands.

All I had to do now was wait. Just one minute to go.

The longest minute of my life. I sat down on the closed toilet lid, my back to the indicator stick as I counted up to sixty. I stopped at fifty-nine, unable to even think the next number, never mind say it.

I'm *not* pregnant. Just because I've been a bit sick in the mornings . . . That doesn't mean anything. It's just a delayed reaction to everything that's happened to me over the last few weeks. That's all. Steeling myself, I turned around, my eyes closed. I opened my eyes slowly. I didn't even have to pick it up. I could see its colour very clearly.

What am I going to do? God help me, what am I going to do?

one hundred and six.
Callum

Now I don't have anything. Not even the Liberation Militia. And there's still three months to go before I meet up with Morgan and my brother again. I miss them. When you work with people for so long, your life in their hands and their lives in yours, they almost become family. Sometimes even closer than real family. I thought about going to see Mum. I even got so far as to stand outside my aunt's house. I had so many questions I wanted to ask her. But then I changed my mind. Some things are best left unsaid. And seeing me would hurt Mum even more than not seeing me, especially as there was no way I could stay.

Sometimes when it's late at night and I'm all alone in a room or sleeping rough on the streets, I look up at the moon or one of the stars and imagine that at that precise moment, *she* is looking at the very same thing.

Why did she cry?

I guess I'll never know. I doubt if I'll ever see her again.

I've finally figured it out. I'm dead. I died a long time ago, woke up in hell and didn't even realize. Thinking about it, I must've died just before I started at Heathcroft school. That's what happened.

I know I'm right.

one hundred and seven.
Sephy

There came the lightest of taps at the door. I quickly wiped my eyes and jumped off the bed to sit at my dressing-table. I picked up the first thing to hand, a comb, and began to comb my hair.

'Come in.'

Minnie entered my room, closing the door quietly behind her. I watched her via my dressing-table mirror. She'd been watching me very strangely for the last few days. Or was it the last few weeks?

'Sephy, are you OK?'

'Is that what you came in here to ask me?' I frowned. Minnie nodded.

'Yes, I'm fine. Now stop asking me that,' I snapped.

'I'm concerned about you.'

'Well, you're wasting your time. I've already told you, I'm brilliant, wonderful, marvellous. I've never felt better in my life. So back off.'

Minnie gave me a deeply sceptical look. 'Then why haven't you gone back to school?'

' 'Cause I don't want everyone pointing their fingers at me and whispering behind my back and feeling sorry for me.'

'And why do you always look like you've just stopped crying or you're just about to start?'

'You need to get your eyes tested.'

'And why have you taken to wearing leggings and baggy T-shirts and jumpers?'

I was really beginning to lose it now. 'Minerva, what's the matter with you? Since when have you been the least bit interested in what I wear?'

'You *are* pregnant, aren't you? The T-shirts and jumpers are just to hide the fact that your pregnancy is beginning to show.'

'No, they're not. I'm only wearing them because . . . because . . .' And like a moron, I burst into tears, burying my head in my hands.

Minnie was immediately at my side, her arm around my shoulders.

'Oh, Sephy, you idiot! Why didn't you just come right out and say so? I could've helped you. We all could've helped you. Why d'you always insist on doing everything the hard way?'

'Minnie, I don't know what to do,' I sniffed. 'I've thought and thought and there's no way out.'

'Ignoring your growing stomach isn't going to alter the fact that you're pregnant,' Minnie said, exasperated. 'What were you thinking?'

'It's all right for you. You're not the one who's pregnant. I am,' I said angrily.

'You're going to have to tell Mother . . .'

I pulled away from Minnie and stared at her. 'Have you lost your mind?'

'Sephy, sooner or later she's going to find out for

herself. Even if you manage to hide your entire pregnancy, how d'you expect to hide a baby?'

'I don't know. I haven't thought that far ahead.'

'Well, you'd better start.'

'Minnie, promise me you won't say a word to anyone,' I begged.

'But Sephy . . .'

'Please. Promise me. I'll tell Mother but it has to be in my own time and in my own way. OK?'

'OK, I promise. But don't leave it much longer or I may change my mind.'

I nodded gratefully. I'd bought myself a few more days, possibly a few more weeks.

'D'you want to talk about what happened with the kidnappers?'

I shook my head.

'I take it the father is one of your kidnappers?'

I didn't answer.

Minnie stood up. 'Well, just remember, if you do want to talk, my bedroom is right next door to yours. OK?'

'OK.'

The moment Minnie left my room, I flung myself down on my bed, weeping like I'd only just discovered how to do it. All my plans had turned to ashes and dust. All my dreams and schemes for the future had turned into . . . a baby.

one hundred and eight.
Callum

'What about you, Callum? What would you do with all the money in the world?'

Gordy must've seen from my face what I thought of the question.

'Oh, come on. It's just a bit a fun,' Gordy teased.

Four months had passed since ... since the kidnapping. I was working as a car mechanic three hundred kilometres away from home in a place called Sturham. The December afternoon was already getting dark. The heating in the garage was supposedly turned right up, but it was still chilly, and the work was mind-numbingly boring but I was glad of it. It stopped me from brooding all day, every day. And the guys I worked with weren't bad. Gordy was a nought who'd worked as a car mechanic since he was thirteen. He was now fifty-seven and he was still a car mechanic. Nothing had changed for him. Tomorrow was going to be the same as yesterday as far as he was concerned. He was just punching time until he died. I looked at him and saw my uncles and Old Man Tony and even my dad – until Lynette had died. I looked at him and was so afraid I was seeing myself in ten, twenty, thirty years time.

Rob was a couple of years older than me. He was a talker. He was going to change the world by using the only means at his disposal, by grumbling about it. I'd only been working here for three weeks and already I'd had to hide my fists behind my back and go and sit in the toilets for a good ten minutes to stop myself from swinging for him. He drove me nuts.

'Well? Don't you have any dreams – or are you too good to share them with the likes of us?' Gordy teased.

I forced myself to smile. 'I don't like to dwell on what I'll never have,' I shrugged.

'You never know,' Rob said, inanely.

'So what *would* you do?' Gordy urged.

'Build a rocket and leave this planet. Live on the moon or some place else. Any place else,' I answered.

'If you had all the money in the world, you wouldn't have to live on the moon. You could do whatever you liked right here,' said Rob.

'D'you know what they call a nought with all the money in the world?' I asked.

Rob and Gordy shook their heads.

'A blanker,' I told them.

They didn't laugh. They weren't supposed to.

'Things would change if we had a ton of money,' Rob tried to tell me.

I tried – and failed – to keep the pitying look off my face. 'It takes more than money, Rob. It takes determination and sacrifice and . . . and . . .'

Rob and Gordy were both looking at me like I'd lost my mind. I shut up.

'Just ignore me,' I told them ruefully.

'We'll have to call you the deep one,' Gordy said. 'Or better yet, the *profound* one.'

'Don't you dare,' I warned him.

'We will come to you for spiritual guidance!' Gordy bowed low, his hands together as if in prayer. 'Oh, profound one, share your mystical insights with us. Enlighten us . . .'

'If you three can't be bothered to get on with your work, there are hundreds of others out there who'd be only too happy to take your jobs,' Snakeskin emerged from his office to holler at us.

Without a word we got back to work, waiting until Snakeskin had slammed his way back into his office before adopting our previous positions.

'What a horse's ass!' Rob sniffed.

'There's a lot of it about,' I said.

'Amen to that,' Gordy agreed.

'What I want to know is, how does . . ?' Rob began.

'Shush! *Shush!*' I hissed at him. I moved over to the workbench to turn up the volume on the radio. Something on the news had caught my attention.

'. . . *has refused to confirm or deny that Persephone Mira Hadley, his daughter, is pregnant, and that this is the result of her ordeal a few months ago at the hands of her kidnappers. We can only speculate as to what this poor girl has been subjected to at the hands of the nought men who abducted her. Persephone herself has so far refused to speak of her two terrifying days in captivity, the memories being obviously too painful, too shocking . . .*'

'Hey!' Gordy was staring at me and I had no idea why, until I saw the radio lying on the floor, smashed to smithereens where I'd thrown it against the wall.

'I've got to get out of here.' I headed for the exit.

'Er . . . Callum, where d'you think you're going?' Snakeskin called after me.

'I've got to leave.'

'Oh no you don't.'

'Watch me!'

'If you go out that door, don't bother to come back.'

I carried on walking.

one hundred and nine.
Sephy

Mother sat down beside me in the family room. Dad paced up and down in front of me. I turned to glare at Minnie.

'So much for your promises,' I said bitterly.

At least she had the grace to be embarrassed and look away, unable to meet my stare. I should've known she wouldn't be able to keep her mouth shut. Some secrets are obviously too juicy to keep. And no doubt this was her chance to get back at me for all those years of 'Minnie' instead of 'Minerva'. As well as telling Mother and Dad, she'd probably told one person, who'd told someone else, who'd told someone else and before you knew it, it was the world's best-kept shared secret. It was inevitably only a matter of time before the press found out. Maybe that's what Minnie wanted all along. Whatever else happened, I'd never forgive her for this, never if I lived to be five hundred.

'What we have to do,' Dad began, 'is deal with this situation as quickly and discreetly as possible.'

'It's for the best, darling,' Mother took one of my hands in hers and patted it gently.

'We've already booked you into a clinic for tomorrow morning,' said Dad. 'By tomorrow evening it will all be over. You won't be pregnant any more and we can all put this whole thing behind us.'

'I know it's hard, love, but it's definitely for the best,' Mother agreed.

'You want me to have an abortion?' I asked.

'Well, you don't want to keep it, do you?' Mother said, puzzlement in her voice. 'A child of your kidnapper? The bastard child of a raping blanker?'

'Of course she doesn't,' Dad said brusquely. He turned to me. 'You should've told us, princess. You should've told us what they did to you. We could've sorted all this out so much sooner and avoided all this press speculation.'

'I'll take you to the clinic myself,' said Mother, trying to dredge up a smile from nowhere.

'We'll both go,' said Dad. 'This time tomorrow, it will all be over.'

'Leave everything to us,' said Mum.

'You can hardly be expected to make decisions for yourself or even think straight at a time like this,' Dad said.

Mother and Dad – together at last. Reunited. Acting, moving, thinking as one. And I'd done that. I couldn't help but wonder. The thoughts going through my head, were they the result of straight thinking or crooked thinking? How could I tell which was which?

'We're all behind you on this, love,' said Dad. 'And once it's over we'll all go away somewhere on a holiday. You can put it behind you and get on with the rest of your life. We all can.'

Put it behind me . . . Is that what he thought? A quick operation and just like that, my baby would be gone and forgotten? Looking at Dad was like looking at a stranger. He didn't know me at all. And I couldn't even feel sad about it.

'I'm not going to the clinic tomorrow,' I said softly.

'You won't be alone. We'll be with you . . .'

'You'll be on your own then, because I'm not going.'

'Pardon?' Dad stared at me.

I stood up to face him directly.

'I'm going to keep my baby.'

'Don't be ridiculous,' Dad wasn't shouting. He was merely incredulous. He didn't believe I meant it.

'I'm going to keep my baby,' I repeated.

'No, you are not.'

'It's my body and my baby, and I'm keeping it.'

'Persephone, be reasonable. You're not being sensible. You're only just eighteen. How can you keep the baby? Everyone will know how it was conceived. You'll be pointed at and scorned and pitied. Is that what you want?'

He really didn't know me at all.

'I'm keeping it.'

'You'll change your mind tomorrow,' Dad decided.

'No, I won't,' I told him. 'I'm keeping it.'

one hundred and ten.
Callum

All the way down to the coast, I phoned Sephy's house using our signal from years ago. I had no idea if she was at the house by the coast or even if she heard my signals but I wasn't going to let that stop me. I had to see her. I had to *know*.

It took me a whole day to get back to our home town and then I had to wait until nightfall to sneak up from the coastal cave to the rose garden outside her bedroom window. It was the longest, hardest wait I've ever had to endure. I was so close to her, just a couple of kilometres but she might not be there or she might not want to talk to me. A world of doubts and fears stretched between us. And planning to go to her house had to be one of the stupidest things I'd ever attempted. And yet I wasn't even close to reconsidering my actions.

I had to see her.

I was going to see her.

one hundred and eleven.
Sephy

He's out there. I don't have to see him to know he's out there. He's down there in the rose garden, just below my window. I can sense it. I can sense *him*. My whole body is tingling and my mouth is dry and my stomach keeps flipping over like a pancake. What should I do? What will I do if he says the same as Mother and Dad?

Go and see him, Sephy. You owe yourself that much. You owe him that much.

Go and see him.

one hundred and twelve.
Callum

The entire rose garden was now under glass in what had to be the biggest greenhouse I'd ever seen. I'd snuck into it past the guard, only to be knocked back by the overpowering scent of the roses. They'd grown since the last time I was here – a lifetime ago. The arches and trestle woodwork were now completely covered with rose stems and thorns and flowers. It was hard to make out all the colours in the dark. Each flower melted into the next and the next.

Was she up at the house now?

Would she come?

'Callum?' The merest whisper behind me but it was enough. I spun around, my heart racing, my palms sweating. She stood less than a metre away. How had she managed to get so close without me hearing her? My mind had been pre-occupied, remembering . . . But seeing her again was like . . . was like a lightning bolt hitting my heart. She was wearing a dark-coloured dress, burgundy or maybe blue. It was hard to tell. And her hair was shorter. But her eyes were the same as they always were.

I opened my mouth to speak but the words wouldn't come. Instead I gaped pathetically like a drowning fish.

'You shouldn't've come here,' Sephy whispered, her gaze never moving from my face. 'It isn't safe.'

'I had to,' Was that really my voice, so hoarse and strange? 'I had to.' I tried again. 'Is it true?'

'Yes.'

We watched each other. And then she stepped forward and put her arms around my waist and rested her head on my shoulder. I immediately pulled her closer. She was having a baby. *Our baby.* I could hardly breathe for the wonder of it. I placed a finger under her chin to raise her head, and I kissed her. She hugged me tighter, returning my kiss, our tongues dancing together. And in that moment, the ice inside me shattered into a trillion pieces.

We shared a world of hope and regret and pleasure and pain in that one kiss, until we were both breathless and dizzy. I moved away slightly to rest my hands on her abdomen. Her hands covered mine. Her stomach was only sightly rounded but the moment I touched her, a frisson of electricity passed right through me. Like my child inside her was trying to connect with me somehow. She was carrying our child. I looked into Sephy's face but I could hardly see her for the tears in my eyes.

'If it's a boy, I'm going to call him Ryan after your dad.'

'If it's a girl, call her . . . call her Rose,' I said, looking around.

'Callie Rose.'

'Hell, no!'

'Hell, yes!'

We both started to laugh. It felt so strange. Unusual. Peculiar. One look at her face and I knew Sephy wasn't going to give in on this. 'OK. Callie Rose, it is.'

Sephy moved to hold me once more. 'I thought I'd never see you again.'

'Sephy . . .' I had to ask. 'A-about that night . . .'

'Yes?'

'Why did you cry?'

Sephy stepped away from me, her gaze dropping. 'Don't ask me that.'

'Did I hurt you? If I did, I'm sorry. I . . .'

'Of course you didn't. You know you didn't.'

'Then why?'

At first I thought she wasn't going to answer, but then she looked straight at me and I held my breath as she began to speak. 'When we made love, I knew I loved you. That I always have and that I always will. But I also realized what you'd been trying to tell me all these years. You're a Nought and I'm a Cross and there's nowhere for us to be, nowhere for us to go where we'd be left in peace. Even if we had gone away together when I wanted us to, we would've been together for a year, maybe two. But sooner or later, other people would've found a way to wedge us apart. That's why I started crying. That's why I couldn't stop. For all the things we might've had and all the things we're never going to have.'

'I understand.' And I did. I'd been hurting inside over the same thing for most of my life.

'When you said...' Sephy paused, looking embarrassed. 'When you said you loved me ... Did you mean it? I don't mind if you didn't...' She rushed on. 'Well, I do but ... I mean ...'

I held out my hands and she put hers in mine, looking at me ruefully. Love was like an avalanche, with Sephy and I hand-in-hand racing like hell to get out of its way – only, instead of running away from it, we kept running straight towards it.

'Let's get out of here,' I smiled. 'Let's go away. We can be together, even if it's just for a little while, we could tr ...'

Light after light after light clicked on around us, dazzling and blinding.

'Callum, run. *RUN!*'

I put one hand up to my eyes but I couldn't see. And then something hit my head and I was knocked to the ground and all the lights in the world went out.

one hundred and thirteen.
Sephy

'I thought one of the kidnappers might try again, or maybe try to get to you so that you wouldn't be able to identify them, so I had extra security installed throughout the premises when you were in hospital.'

'You've got the wrong man,' I screamed at him again. 'Why won't you listen to me. Callum hasn't done anything wrong.'

No-one was listening to me. I'd screamed at the police to let him go as they carried Callum away, but they'd ignored me. I'd tried to hold on to Callum, to pull him back but Dad had dragged me inside the house with an angry demand that I stop making such a spectacle of myself.

'Callum hasn't done anything. We were just talking,' I lowered my voice. Maybe if I stopped shouting, he'd listen to me . . .

'You're lying,' Dad replied at once. 'I know for a fact that Callum McGregor was one of your kidnappers.'

'Then you should also know for a fact that he saved my life. When I escaped from my prison cell into the woods, Callum found me. He could've told the others where I was but he didn't . . .'

'No, he just raped you and made you pregnant instead,' Dad said bitterly.

'Kamal, please . . .' Mother began.

'Callum didn't rape me. He didn't.'

'But you're pregnant so he must've done,' Mother frowned.

'I'm pregnant because we made love to each other,' I shouted angrily. 'And it was the most magical, wonderful night of my life. My only regret is Callum and I can't do it again . . .'

Dad slapped me so hard he knocked me off my feet. Mother tried to rush to my side but Dad pulled her back. He drew himself up to his full height, looking down on me with an expression on his face I'd never seen before.

'You are no longer my daughter. You are a blanker's slut,' Dad said with quiet venom. 'But I'll tell you this, you *will* go to the clinic and you *will* have an abortion. I will not allow you to embarrass me any further. D'you hear me? D'YOU HEAR ME?'

'I hear you . . .' I rubbed my cheek, ignoring the tears streaming down my face. Dad turned and marched out of the room.

Mother looked down at me, anguish filling every curve and line of her face. 'Oh, Sephy . . . Sephy . . .' she whispered. And then she turned around and left me. Alone.

That's what I was now. That's all I was now, according to my dad. A blanker's slut. I buried my face in my hands and cried.

DECISIONS . . .

one hundred and fourteen.
Callum

I lay on the bunk bed in my prison cell, reading the news-paper. I was still in the newspapers but now that my trial was over I was no longer front-page news. I'd been rele-gated to the third or fourth pages. And they were no more accurate than the front page. I was only reading it to pass the time. After all, I had nothing better to do. One article did catch my attention though.

SUSPECTED 'MOLE' WITHIN THE LIBERATION MILITIA
Sources from within the Liberation Militia stated that the whole movement is in turmoil over a suspected mole who, it is believed, is actually working for the government. The mole is rumoured to be someone high up in the party echelons. Our sources have revealed that all LM activity has been suspended until the mole is found.
The editor says . . . See page 7

'Well done, Jude,' I thought. That's if it was Jude. If he wasn't dead yet.

There was no way to get to the General so a few

rumours in the right places, a couple of discreet interviews, and the General would become aware of our suspicions. I could only hope that the General would catch Andrew Dorn before he had a chance to cover his tracks or disappear. I scrunched up the newspaper and dropped it in the bin beside my narrow bed. What was the point of reading the news? No point at all. My thoughts turned to my sister, Lynette. Funny, but I thought of her more and more often these days. She'd always been there for me. She made our home bearable. Each time I thought I couldn't take it any more, she'd smile or put her hand over mine and I'd calm down inside. When she'd died, part of me had despised her for being a coward. Part of me had hated her for leaving me. It'd all been about me. Now I thought about all the things Lynny had been through. I'd allowed all the things that'd happened to me to rob me of my humanity. Do unto others before they did unto you, that'd been my philosophy. That's how I'd coped with the world. Lynny's solution was better. Just fade out, until you were ready to fade back in. Only she hadn't been ready. Maybe that's why she'd died. She'd been pulled out of her unreal world too soon.

'Cal, you have a visitor,' Jack told me.

'A visitor?'

Jack nodded, his expression sombre. Jack was a Cross prison guard but in the short length of time I'd been at Hewmett Prison, we'd become friends. I'd even say good friends. Something I'm sure was against the rules. But if Jack didn't mind, why should I? I looked at him now. Judging from his expression, this visitor was obviously someone I wouldn't particularly welcome. I had no idea who it could be. I hadn't been allowed any visitors at all since I'd been brought to Hewmett Prison, so I was curious – to say the least.

'Man or woman?' I asked.

'Man.'

'And I take it I have to see him?'

Jack nodded again.

'OK,' I said, picking up my T-shirt. 'I'll just put on . . .'

'Don't bother. You're not going to the visitors' hall. He's coming to see you.'

'Here?'

'Yep!'

I put my T-shirt back on anyway. The prison cells were like ovens during the day and although we were meant to keep our clothes on, most of the guards turned a blind eye if we took off our shirts. I'd taken mine off when it'd started to stick to my sweaty body like clingfilm. Heels clicked along the corridor. A man's heavy, determined footfall. And angry too by the sound of it. I stood up and waited. Then the man appeared before my cell bars. My mouth fell open. Kamal Hadley. He was the very last person I'd been expecting.

He entered my cell. Jack stood outside. Kamal wore a dark charcoal-grey suit and a royal-blue shirt with matching tie. His black shoes were so highly polished I could see the light strip above reflected in them.

'You can leave us now,' Kamal ordered, his eyes never leaving my face.

'But . . .' Jack began.

Kamal turned to him with a look that brooked no disagreement. Jack set off down the corridor. I considered knocking out Kamal and taking off down the corridor. But how far would I get? I considered knocking out Kamal just for the hell of it. It was definitely tempting.

'I'm sure you can guess why I'm here,' said Kamal.

I couldn't actually, so I kept my mouth shut.

'I'm here to offer you a deal,' Kamal went on.

'What kind of deal?'

'If you do as I say, I'll make sure you don't hang. You'll be sentenced to life imprisonment and I'll make sure you serve no more than eight to ten years. You'll come out of prison still a young man with your whole life ahead of you.'

I studied Kamal as he spoke. He hated being here, he despised having to ask me for anything and he was having trouble hiding just how much he loathed it. It made me smile inside. I had something he wanted very, *very* badly. But I had no idea what.

'And what exactly do I have to do for this . . . largesse?'

'I want you to state publicly that you kidnapped and . . . raped my daughter. I want you to freely admit to the crimes you're charged with. No more denials.'

'Why?'

At first I thought Kamal wasn't going to answer. I waited. I had all the time in the world. I wasn't going anywhere.

'My daughter won't be able to put this whole business behind her and get on with her life if you don't,' he said at last. 'She feels she owes you something because you saved her life in the woods. If she knew you weren't going to die, then she'd be only too willing to get rid of your child. A child she never wanted. A child she still doesn't.'

Every word he spoke was well rehearsed and deliberately wielded to cause the maximum amount of pain. And it worked too. I half-sat, half-collapsed down onto my bed, looking up at him. My guts were being shredded and he knew it.

'And she told you this, did she?'

'Of course.'

I didn't believe him. I almost didn't believe him. He was lying. But suppose he wasn't?

My life or my child's?

Was that really the only reason Sephy was still carrying it? Because of misplaced guilt over me? I didn't want to believe it. I didn't know what to believe.

My life. Or my child's?

'Is it just the thought of Sephy and I having a child together that you can't stand, or is it all mixed-race children in general?' I asked.

'We're not here to discuss my feelings.' Kamal waved aside my words like he was swotting flies. 'What's your answer?'

My life? Or my baby's?

Oh Sephy, what should I do? What would *you* do?

'I need to think about it.'

'I want your answer here and now,' Kamal demanded.

I stood up slowly.

'Well?' he prompted, impatiently.

Time to choose. A choice to live with or die with. I looked Kamal Hadley straight in the eye – and told him my decision. I knew it would damn me to hell, but I knew it was the right one.

one hundred and fifteen.
Sephy

Dad barged into my room without even knocking on the door first. It was very late, almost midnight, but I wasn't the least bit sleepy. I couldn't even remember the last time I'd had a good night's sleep. I sat at my table, writing in my diary when Dad came in. I shut the book and swivelled round in my chair. Dad stopped in the middle of the room. We regarded each other. We hadn't exchanged a word since he'd slapped me. Dad sat down on the corner of my bed, suddenly looking very weary.

'I'm not going to beat about the bush, Persephone,' he told me. 'Callum McGregor is going to hang for what he did to you.'

I swallowed hard but still didn't speak.

'And you're the only one who can stop it,' Dad continued.

Every cell in my body was put on full alert at Dad's words. I sat very still and watchful, waiting for him to carry on.

'It's within my power to ensure that he doesn't hang. I'll make sure he only goes to prison. He'll get a long sentence but at least he'll be alive.'

And where there's life . . . there's a price. I kept my

mouth shut, waiting for the other shoe to drop.

'And all you have to do is agree to have an abortion,' said Dad.

Like all I had to do was agree to eat my greens or go to bed early – that's what he made it sound like.

'Why?' I whispered.

'Why!' The incredulous word exploded from Dad's mouth. 'Because you're too young to have a child. Because it was a child forced on you . . .'

'I've already told you, Callum didn't . . .'

'You didn't set out to get pregnant either, did you?' Dad interrupted harshly.

'It's too late to get rid of it. I'm too far gone,' I pointed out.

'There are ways, drugs to take care of that.' Dad pointed to my stomach. 'Then they'd induce labour. It'd be relatively painless for you.'

And lethal for my child.

'If I say no, what will you do then?' I asked. 'Kidnap me like the noughts and force me to get rid of my baby?'

Dad stared at me. 'I know we're not close, Persephone, and I know that's my fault, but I would never, ever do a thing like that.' His voice held such incredible hurt that it got to me, in spite of myself.

'But what you're doing is no different,' I cried. 'You may not be using direct force but you're pressuring me into having an abortion. It's the same difference. Callum's life or my child's. You're trying to coerce me into making a decision. *Your* decision.'

'That boy's life is entirely in your hands.' Dad stood up. 'It's up to you. I know you'll make the right choice.'

And with that he left my room. I locked my diary and put it in its hiding place, moving around my bedroom on auto pilot. I wanted my brain to shut down so I wouldn't have to think, so I wouldn't have to decide. But it didn't work that way.

If I had an abortion I'd be saving Callum's life. He wouldn't spend the rest of his life in jail, either. I'd work every hour of every day for the rest of my life if I had to, to make sure that he was released from prison. And if he came out . . . *when* he came out, we could be together again. We could have more children. It was the chance of some kind of future together against no future at all. But if we were together would we be able to live with the fact that our first child died for us? Or would the ghost of our child eventually drive us apart?

Callum's life or our baby's? That was the choice.

Oh Callum, what should I do? What would *you* do?

And then just like that, there was no choice. I had my answer. I knew what I was going to tell my dad. God help me, I knew.

LOSING MY RELIGION . . .

one hundred and sixteen.
Callum

'Jack, your mind isn't on this game, is it?'

Jack throws down his cards. 'I don't want to play any more.'

'I thought I was the one who was meant to be temperamental and moody, not you?' I say dryly.

'Sorry.'

I gather up the cards. Poor Jack! This is almost as bad for him. Almost! Bless him! He's the one who's kept me up to date with what was going on in the outside world. He's the one who told me that since my farce of a trial, Sephy has spoken out publicly against the guilty verdict and has openly declared that I didn't rape her. She's told anyone prepared to listen that the authorities refused to let her testify on my behalf. And apparently even some of the national papers are beginning to question the death penalty being given in my case. I'm hoping that Kamal Hadley doesn't emerge from this one smelling of roses, the way he always does.

A prominent psychiatrist stated in one of the so-called quality papers that Sephy was suffering from Kidnapper Empathy Syndrome. Some psycho-babble about the captive taking on the ideals and beliefs of the captor, to the extent that he or she begins to empathize with them. In Sephy's case that's just so much nonsense. If I could've spoken to Sephy, I would've told her not to say anything on my behalf. Once I'd been found guilty nothing on earth could've made the judges overturn the verdict. The reason is simple. I'm a Nought who'd dared to fall in love with a Cross. And worse still I actually made love with her. And even worse than that, she's pregnant with my child and doesn't care who knows it.

Poor Sephy! She never could tell when she was fighting a losing battle. I knew I was going to hang before the jurors were even sworn in.

And now I've come to my last day on this earth.

And I don't want to die.

'What time is it, Jack?'

'Ten to six.'

'Ten more minutes then.' I shuffle the cards. 'Time for a quick game of rummy?'

'Callum . . .'

I throw down the cards. 'It must be catching. I don't feel like playing myself now.'

Silent moments tick by. I don't want to spend my last ten minutes in silence.

'D'you ever wonder what it would be like if our positions were reversed?' I ask. At Jack's puzzled look, I continue. 'If we whites were in charge instead of you Crosses?'

'Can't say it's ever crossed my mind,' Jack shrugs.

'I used to think about it a lot,' I sigh. 'Dreams of living in a world with no more discrimination, no more prejudice, a fair police force, an equal justice system, equality of education, equality of life, a level playing field . . .'

'Good grief! Is that a thesis or a fairy tale?' Jack asks dryly.

'Like I said, I used to think about it a lot.'

'I'm not sure I share your faith in a society ruled by noughts,' Jack tells me, thoughtfully. 'People are people. We'll always find a way to mess up, doesn't matter who's in charge.'

'You think so?'

Jack shrugs.

'You don't believe that things get better? That they have to, one day, some day?'

'When?'

'It takes a long time.'

'But they do?' asks Jack.

'They do.'

But not for me. A long silence fills the gap between us. Until at last, I open my mouth to speak but Jack gets in first.

'Your girl, Persephone Hadley, tried to get in here to see you – and more than once as well,' Jack tells me softly. 'But orders came from way above the governor's head that you were to have no visitors whatsoever under any circumstances.'

I digest this piece of news with regret. Kamal Hadley's influence no doubt.

'Jack, can I ask you for a favour?'

'Just name it.'

'It might get you into trouble.'

'My dull life could do with a bit of sprucing up.' Jack grins.

I smile gratefully. 'Could you find a way to deliver this letter to Sephy?'

'Persephone Hadley?'

'That's right.'

'Sure thing.' Jack takes the envelope from me.

I hold his wrist. 'You have to personally put it into her hand. Promise?'

'I promise,' Jack replies.

I let him go and watch him put the letter into his pocket. Sighing, I sit back on my bed, my back against the cool wall. There're still so many things I want to do, so many things I want to find out. I would've loved to see my mum again, just once more. Just to say . . . sorry. But it hasn't been allowed. Heaven only knows what she's going through now. Her husband is dead. Suicide or murder – take your pick. Her daughter is dead. An 'accident'. Her youngest son is going to die because of his own self-inflicted stupidity. And her eldest son is . . . missing? Wanted – dead or alive. Poor mum. What has she ever done to deserve all this? My thoughts are flitting around now. I wonder about Jude? I miss him so much. I'd love to know if he's OK. Is he safe or in prison? Has he linked up with Morgan? Has he come up with a way to deal directly with that traitor Andrew Dorn? A newspaper article is all very well, but how can he be sure Dorn won't weasel his way out or just disappear? Dorn doesn't deserve to disappear after everything he's done. Will Jude catch up with him? I'll never know.

And Sephy, how does she feel about me now? Is she

still going to have our child? I'm sure her mum and dad are doing their best and then some to make her get rid of it. Maybe she has already. Our time together in the rose garden was so brief. All those things I'd wanted to say to her – and now they'll never be said. If I could just see her one more time then I could make sense of all this, I'm sure I could.

I hear the security door click at the end of the corridor. Jack jumps to his feet and heads out into the corridor to stand by my open cell door.

This is it then. I stand up and pull down my T-shirt. I can feel little prickles of heat break out all over my skin.

I don't want to die . . .

Governor Giustini stops in the corridor outside my cell. He looks at the cards scattered on the floor and the bed and then at me.

'Do you have a last request?' Governor Giustini asks sombrely.

'Just get it over with.' My voice trembles over the last couple of words. I'm going to break down.

Oh, please God – if you're up there, somewhere – don't let me break down . .

No more words. I can't risk it.

Don't show them how terrified you are, Callum. Don't show them how you want to clutch at them and beg them not to kill you. Don't show them . . .

'Put your hands behind your back, Callum,' Jack says quietly.

I look at him. Strange . . . His eyes are shimmering. I try to comfort him. No words, just the briefest of smiles in gratitude for his pity before I turn around, my hands behind my back as I wait to be handcuffed.

'D'you want a priest or some kind of spiritual counselling?' Giustini asks.

I shake my head. I never really believed in it when I was alive, so it would be hypocritical to call for it now.

When I was alive . . .

I'm not dead yet. Not yet. Every second counts. There's still time. I must have hope. Hope till the very end. Miracles have happened before. My cell door opens wider. Giustini leads the way, with two guards I've never seen before on either side of him. Jack walks next to me.

'You're doing fine, Cal,' Jack whispers. 'Be strong. Not long now.'

They lead me down the long corridor. I've never been this way before. Early evening sunlight streams in through the high windows and dances across the floor all around me. It's so bright I can see the dust motes swirling through the air. Who would've thought that dust could look so eerily beautiful. I try to walk as slowly as possible, to drink in every sight and sound. To make each moment last a lifetime.

'Good luck, Callum . . .'

'Spit in their eye, Cal . . .'

'Bye, Cal . . .'

Anonymous calls from the cells on one side of the corridor. I'm tempted to turn and study the faces behind the words but that would take too much time. And that's the one thing I don't have any more. I look straight ahead. The door opens at the end of the corridor. More blazing sunshine. Such a perfect day. We step out. I stop abruptly.

Faces. A sea of faces, even more than when my father was about to be hanged. Lots of Crosses, come to watch the show. But the sun is before me and dazzling my eyes. I can't see much. Besides, the scaffolding is in the way. And the noose up there, gently swaying in the evening breeze.

Don't look at it.

I want to cry.

Please God, don't let me cry . . .

Please God, don't let me die . . .

Giustini and his guards move to one side of the scaffold. Jack leads me to the stairs. I climb up them. He follows.

'Forgive me, Callum,' Jack whispers.

I turn my head. 'Don't be silly, Jack, you haven't done anything.'

'Neither have you,' says Jack.

I pause to smile at him. 'Thanks for that.'

We're at the top of the scaffold now. The noose is less than a metre away. And beneath it a closed trapdoor. I turn to look at the governor. He's standing beside another man, a nought with blond hair wearing a black suit. The nought stands behind a long lever. The lever for the trapdoor.

My life in your hands.

I don't want to die . . .

There's still time. There's still hope.

I look around, scanning the crowd, searching the audience for her. But I can't see her. If I could just see her one last time . . . Where is she? Is she even here? Sephy. And my child that I'll never see. Never hold. Never know.

Is she here?

Please, God . . .

'I've got to put your hood on now,' Jack says softly.

'I don't want it on.' How will I find her with a hood on?

'I'm afraid you have no choice. Those are the rules,' Jack apologizes.

He pulls the hood over my head. I try to pull back. I'm not trying to run away. I just want to see her . . . One last time . . . The hood is over my head and hangs down to my shoulders. The world is black as night. Jack pulls my arm to lead me to the rope.

Please God, I don't want to die . . .

Sephy . . .

Tears run down my face. Now I'm grateful for the hood.

'I LOVE YOU, CALLUM . . .'

Wait . . .

'I LOVE YOU, CALLUM. AND OUR CHILD WILL LOVE YOU TOO. I LOVE YOU, CALLUM, I'LL ALWAYS LOVE YOU . . .'

The noose is being pulled down over my head and around my neck. But I can hear her.

I can hear her. She's here.

'I LOVE YOU, CALLUM . . .'

Thank you, God. Thank you.

'I . . . I LOVE YOU TOO, SEPHY . . .' Can she hear me?

'I LOVE YOU, SEPHY. I LOVE YOU, SEPHY.'

Wait . . . Please wait . . . Just a moment longer . . .

'I LOVE YOU, CALLUM . . .'

'SEPHY, I LO . . .'

one hundred and seventeen.
Sephy

The trapdoor opens.

'I LOVE YOU, CALLUM,' I scream frantically.

He drops like a stone. My words die on my lips.

There's no sound except the rope creaking and groaning as Callum's body swings slowly to and fro.

Did he hear me? I don't know. He must have heard me. Did he say I love you '*too*'? Maybe I just imagined it. I can't be certain. I don't know.

Dear God, please let him have heard me. Please.

Please.

If you're up there.

Somewhere.

BIRTH ANNOUNCEMENTS

At midnight on 14th May
at Mercy Community Hospital,
to Persephone Hadley
and Callum McGregor (deceased),
a beautiful daughter, Callie Rose.

Persephone wishes it to be known that
her daughter Callie Rose will be taking
her father's name of McGregor.

AUTHOR'S NOTE

The African-American scientists, inventors and pioneers mentioned in chapter 30 are all real people and their achievements are very real. When I was at school, we didn't learn about any of them – except Robert Peary, the white European-American explorer. I wish we had done. But then, if we had, maybe I wouldn't have written this book...